ENVIRONMENTAL ETHICS IN BUDDHISM

This book contains a logical and thorough examination of some metaphysical and ethical dimensions of early Buddhist literature to determine their environmental significance and demonstrates that early Buddhism can be recognized as an environmental virtue ethics. The author explores the meaning of nature in the early Buddhist context through a survey of general Buddhist teachings on *dhamma*, *paṭiccasamuppāda*, *saṃsāra* and the cosmogony of the *Aggañña Sutta* concluding that an inherent sense of nature is integrated within these teachings. The ethics included in early Buddhist literature is essentially considered and arguments to show that aspects of this ethics correspond with an environmental virtue ethics are advanced. The book proposes that environmental ethics in early Buddhist thought stems predominantly from the inclusive ethical beliefs of the religion as grounded in a "cosmic" understanding of nature. The book also contains a chapter on the *Jātakas* – a collection of over five hundred folk tales – that have been of interest to environmental ethicists due to their so-called nature-related content. Overall, this work presents an innovative approach to the subject and puts forward a distinctly Buddhist environmental ethics that is in harmony with traditional teachings as well as being adaptable and flexible in addressing environmental problems.

Pragati Sahni is currently Lecturer in the Department of Philosophy, Delhi University. Her current research interests include Environmental Philosophy, Applied Ethics and Early Buddhist Philosophy. She has published some articles and has been a recipient of the Commonwealth Scholarship.

ROUTLEDGE CRITICAL STUDIES IN BUDDHISM

General Editors:
Charles S. Prebish and Damien Keown

Routledge Critical Studies in Buddhism is a comprehensive study of the Buddhist tradition. The series explores this complex and extensive tradition from a variety of perspectives, using a range of different methodologies.

The Series is diverse in its focus, including historical studies, textual translations and commentaries, sociological investigations, bibliographic studies, and considerations of religious practice as an expression of Buddhism's integral religiosity. It also presents materials on modern intellectual historical studies, including the role of Buddhist thought and scholarship in a contemporary, critical context and in the light of current social issues. The series is expansive and imaginative in scope, spanning more than two and a half millennia of Buddhist history. It is receptive to all research works that inform and advance our knowledge and understanding of the Buddhist tradition.

A SURVEY OF VINAYA LITERATURE
Charles S. Prebish

THE REFLEXIVE NATURE OF AWARENESS
Paul Williams

ALTRUISM AND REALITY
Paul Williams

BUDDHISM AND HUMAN RIGHTS
Edited by Damien Keown, Charles Prebish, Wayne Husted

WOMEN IN THE FOOTSTEPS OF THE BUDDHA
Kathryn R. Blackstone

THE RESONANCE OF EMPTINESS
Gay Watson

AMERICAN BUDDHISM
Edited by Duncan Ryuken Williams and Christopher Queen

IMAGING WISDOM
Jacob N. Kinnard

PAIN AND ITS ENDING
Carol S. Anderson

EMPTINESS APPRAISED
David F. Burton

THE SOUND OF LIBERATING TRUTH
Edited by Sallie B. King and Paul O. Ingram

BUDDHIST THEOLOGY
Edited by Roger R. Jackson and John J. Makransky

THE GLORIOUS DEEDS OF PURNA
Joel Tatelman

EARLY BUDDHISM – A NEW APPROACH
Sue Hamilton

CONTEMPORARY BUDDHIST ETHICS
Edited by Damien Keown

INNOVATIVE BUDDHIST WOMEN
Edited by Karma Lekshe Tsomo

TEACHING BUDDHISM IN THE WEST
Edited by V. S. Hori, R. P. Hayes and J. M. Shields

EMPTY VISION
David L. McMahan

SELF, REALITY AND REASON IN TIBETAN PHILOSOPHY
Thupten Jinpa

IN DEFENSE OF DHARMA
Tessa J. Bartholomeusz

BUDDHIST PHENOMENOLOGY
Dan Lusthaus

RELIGIOUS MOTIVATION AND THE ORIGINS OF BUDDHISM
Torkel Brekke

DEVELOPMENTS IN AUSTRALIAN BUDDHISM
Michelle Spuler

ZEN WAR STORIES
Brian Victoria

THE BUDDHIST UNCONSCIOUS
William S. Waldron

INDIAN BUDDHIST THEORIES OF PERSONS
James Duerlinger

ACTION DHARMA
Edited by Christopher Queen, Charles Prebish and Damien Keown

TIBETAN AND ZEN BUDDHISM IN BRITAIN
David N. Kay

THE CONCEPT OF THE BUDDHA
Guang Xing

THE PHILOSOPHY OF DESIRE IN THE BUDDHIST PALI CANON
David Webster

THE NOTION OF *DITTHI* IN THERAVADA BUDDHISM
Paul Fuller

THE BUDDHIST THEORY OF SELF-COGNITION
Zhihua Yao

MORAL THEORY IN ŚĀNTIDEVA'S ŚIKSĀṢAMUCCAYA
Barbra R. Clayton

BUDDHIST STUDIES FROM INDIA TO AMERICA
Edited by Damien Keown

DISCOURSE AND IDEOLOGY IN MEDIEVAL JAPANESE BUDDHISM
Edited by Richard K. Payne and Taigen Dan Leighton

BUDDHIST THOUGHT AND APPLIED PSYCHOLOGICAL RESEARCH
Edited by D. K. Nauriyal, Michael S. Drummond and Y. B. Lal

BUDDHISM IN CANADA
Edited by Bruce Matthews

BUDDHISM, CONFLICT AND VIOLENCE IN MODERN SRI LANKA
Edited by Mahinda Deegalle

THERAVĀDA BUDDHISM AND THE BRITISH ENCOUNTER
Religious, missionary and colonial experience in nineteenth century Sri Lanka
Elizabeth Harris

BEYOND ENLIGHTENMENT
Buddhism, religion, modernity
Richard Cohen

BUDDHISM IN THE PUBLIC SPHERE
Reorienting global interdependence
Peter D. Hershock

BRITISH BUDDHISM
Teachings, practice and development
Robert Bluck

BUDDHIST NUNS IN TAIWAN AND SRI LANKA
A critique of the feminist perspective
Wei-Yi Cheng

NEW BUDDHIST MOVEMENTS IN THAILAND
Toward an understanding of Wat Phra Dhammakā and Santi Asoke
Rory Mackenzie

BUDDHIST RITUALS OF DEATH AND REBIRTH
Contemporary Sri Lankan practice and its origins
Rita Langer

BUDDHISM, POWER AND POLITICAL ORDER
Edited by Ian Harris

ENVIRONMENTAL ETHICS IN BUDDHISM
A Virtues Approach
Pragati Sahni

The following titles are published in association with the *Oxford Centre for Buddhist Studies*

Oxford Centre for Buddhist Studies

a project of The Society for the Wider Understanding of the Buddhist Tradition

The *Oxford Centre for Buddhist Studies* conducts and promotes rigorous teaching and research into all forms of the Buddhist tradition.

EARLY BUDDHIST METAPHYSICS
Noa Ronkin

MIPHAM'S DIALECTICS AND THE DEBATES ON EMPTINESS
Karma Phuntsho

HOW BUDDHISM BEGAN
The conditioned genesis of the early teachings
Richard F. Gombrich

BUDDHIST MEDITATION
An Anthology of Texts from the Pāli Canon
Sarah Shaw

REMAKING BUDDHISM FOR MEDIEVAL NEPAL
The fifteenth-century reformation of Newar Buddhism
Will Tuladhar-Douglas

METAPHOR AND LITERALISM IN BUDDHISM
The Doctrinal History of Nirvana
Soonil Hwang

THE BIOGRAPHIES OF RECHUNGPA
The Evolution of a Tibetan Hagiography
Peter Alan Roberts

THE ORIGIN OF BUDDHIST MEDITATION
Alexander Wynne

ENVIRONMENTAL ETHICS IN BUDDHISM

A virtues approach

Pragati Sahni

Routledge
Taylor & Francis Group
LONDON AND NEW YORK

First published 2008
by Routledge
2 Park Square, Milton Park, Abingdon, Oxon OX14 4RN

Simultaneously published in the USA and Canada
by Routledge
711 Third Avenue, New York, NY 10017, USA

Routledge is an imprint of the Taylor & Francis Group, an informa business

First issued in paperback 2011

Typeset in Times New Roman by
RefineCatch Limited, Bungay, Suffolk

British Library Cataloguing in Publication Data
A catalogue record for this book is available from the British Library

Library of Congress Cataloging in Publication Data
Sahni, Pragati, 1968–
Environmental ethics in Buddhism: a virtues approach/Pragati Sahni.
p. cm. – (Routledge critical studies in Buddhism series)
Includes bibliographical references and index.
ISBN 978–0–415–39679–0 (hardback: alk. paper) 1. Human ecology – Religious aspects – Buddhism. 2. Nature – Religious aspects – Buddhism. 3. Environmental ethics. 4. Virtues (Buddhism) 5. Tipitaka. Suttapitaka – Criticism, interpretation, etc. I. Title.
BQ4570.E23S34 2007
294.3′5691 – dc22
2006039713

ISBN: 978–0–415–39679–0 (hbk)
ISBN: 978–0–415–54472–6 (pbk)

CONTENTS

	Acknowledgements	x
	Abbreviations and Conventions	xi
1	Towards an environmental ethics in Buddhism	1
2	Nature: A "conservationist" analysis	32
3	Nature: A "cosmological" approach	63
4	Environmental virtue ethics in early Buddhism	92
5	The environmental virtues of early Buddhism	123
6	Environmental virtue ethics in the *Jātakas*	144
	Conclusion	164
	Notes	167
	Bibliography	190
	Index	199

ACKNOWLEDGEMENTS

I would like to thank Damien Keown for his encouragement and his belief in my vision. I am grateful to Ian Harris and Kate Crosby for their timely advice on how I could make my ideas work better. I also owe thanks to Veena Sachdev and Mohini Mullick for their wise words and erudite comments when I most needed them. And, above all, I would like to thank my mother, father and the rest of my wonderful family for their patience, unconditional love and support throughout this undertaking.

ABBREVIATIONS

A	*Aṅguttara Nikāya*
D	*Dīgha Nikāya*
Dp	*Dhammapada*
J	*Jātaka*
M	*Majjhima Nikāya*
PTS	Pali Text Society
S	*Saṃyutta Nikāya*
Sn	*Sutta-Nipāta*
Th	*Theragāthā*
The	*Therīgāthā*
Vin	*Vinaya*

Conventions

In this book, references to the original texts of the *Dīgha, Majjhima, Saṃyutta* and *Aṅguttara Nikāyas*, the *Jātaka* and *Vinaya* will include the abbreviated title (see Abbreviations) and the volume and generic page number of the PTS edition. References to the *Dhammapada, Sutta Nipāta, Theragāthā and Therīgāthā* however will comprise the abbreviated title and the verse number. Though this book is primarily concerned with the Pali language, Sanskrit terms in the quotations of other writers remain unchanged. The use of Sanskrit terms also remains unchanged in places where such terms have been analysed and explained by others in their Sanskrit rendering.

1

TOWARDS AN ENVIRONMENTAL ETHICS IN BUDDHISM

I entrust myself to earth,
Earth entrusts herself to me.
I entrust myself to Buddha,
Buddha entrusts herself to me.
Thich Nhat Hanh, *Being Peace*

Introduction

Dealing with questions concerning the nature and description of an environmental ethics in early Buddhism is a complicated task. Early Buddhism does not contain a defined environmental ethics.[1] Its central concern was suffering or *dukkha* that penetrated every aspect of life and the ultimate culmination of Buddhist teachings was in the attainment of liberation or *nibbāna* which spelt the end of suffering. Direct concerns related to the natural world and environmental devastation got little mention in early Buddhist texts. This can be attributed to the cultural context and mood of early Buddhism. Environmental ethics, on the other hand, is a relatively new area of study that became popular approximately four or so decades ago with the awareness that environmental resources were rapidly diminishing due to unsustainable overuse by human beings. There was a dire need to address issues related to environmental devastation and to understand in depth their implications for the fate of present and future generations of organisms and objects on this planet. Thus environmental ethics as well as other areas of environmental studies gained much attention. Not faced with such issues it is hardly surprising that Buddhist scriptures contain scant or no ideas that even faintly resemble a contemporary environmental ethics.

At the same time, and despite the above, it is often believed that the seed of environmental ethics is contained in Buddhist literature and nurturing this can lead to a philosophy of nature which is bound to have a profound effect on the protection of natural resources and of nature as a whole including animals. The relation between human beings and nature in Buddhism being contemplated as intimate and constant due to arguments in Buddhist texts that support human-animal continuity in the experiential world, trees acquiring respect due to their fruit and shade-giving qualities, the imperative of non-violence and many other factors support this belief. It has been remarked that "... there is much within traditional Buddhist ethics that does indeed speak to the ethical aspects of the environmental crisis confronting us today ..."[2] Based on these factors, scholars have attempted to form a notion of environmental ethics in Buddhism. But most such notions somehow fall short, for these scholars are not always able to defend themselves against the criticisms of those who hold the view that a firm adherence to Buddhist soteriology makes any form of environmental ethics impossible. It is believed predominantly that nearly all Buddhist teachings in their application to the environment remain unclear and ambiguous. Thus scholars at both ends of the spectrum have legitimate reason to trust their own interpretation and doubt others. Emerging from this it is no surprise then that much uncertainty and mystification in this area of study continues to exist.

Thus delineating the Buddhist response to nature remains a palpable challenge that must be enquired into in all seriousness. An investigation must be conducted to determine whether a favourable reaction to environmental matters can be discovered on the basis of which an environmental ethics can be developed that overcomes the above concerns. The indisputable objective of the ethical and metaphysical framework of Buddhist philosophy is enlightenment. The central aim of this book is to determine whether this framework contains, in addition, a compelling enough environmental dimension that warrants the development of a meaningful and satisfying relationship with the environment.

Method

In keeping with this endeavour an examination of a portion of early Buddhist literature with the objective of finding out whether an environmental ethics exists within its parameters is taken on in this book. Those ideas and principles that actively imply and partake of such an ethics shall be identified and discussed to bring to light the possibility of a genuine environmental ethics in early Buddhism. But before this can be done the stage, so to speak, must be set. It is extremely important to seek clarifications in the field of environmental ethics itself, particularly in the non-Buddhist context. The reason for choosing to bring in non-Buddhist ideas (even to a very limited extent) is to recognize the contemporary nature of environmental ethics and to acknowledge the relevance of these ideas to environmental theory especially if the latter is to be developed in Buddhism to be of significance in the modern world. The other reason for bringing in some non-Buddhist ideas is the presence of recurrent occasions in the past where Buddhist counterparts to environmental terms have been projected without any explication of the latter's true meaning or scope of reference. The inappropriate and loose use of environmental concepts has caused many serious problems and misunderstandings in the area of Buddhism and ecology. By seeking clarifications such instances can be avoided.

However, at the outset, I admit to being aware that in doing the above I run the risk of added confusions which are connected with speculating whether certain attitudes and ideas belonging to a particular time and mood can be integrated suitably or successfully into the ethos and outlook of diametrically opposed traditions. I may be open to the charge of trying to attribute contemporary ideas to the Buddhist way of thinking that do not belong there. I do not allow such views to undermine my enquiry for I have a deeper motive at heart: to uncover the many ideas that reveal foundational formulations on which environmental principles can be based in Buddhism. And this happens largely through a very basic understanding, and application of non-Buddhist concepts. However, always aware of the above charges, even while I use non-Buddhist ideas to begin with because I find them indispensable, I do so with the knowledge that the utmost care is required in their use. David Little has rightly argued that when we use terms in comparative studies, we must be careful to limit their meanings and must be "more, rather than less attentive to the various jobs those terms do for us."[3] I believe that once such caution is adopted the proper scope of an environmental ethics within Buddhism itself will be known. It can be added here that despite this exercise, in ultimate analysis the Buddhist position comes to hold its own and stands uniquely established in its own right.

This is a philosophical study that aims to analyse select Buddhist literature in detail to determine the shape and scope of environmental ethics within its annals. As mentioned earlier, Buddhist literature presents a perplexing picture. On the one hand it is indeed challenging to ascertain contemporary environmental features such as those, for instance, that address value, justice, conservation and sustainability. On the other hand there are ideas and beliefs in this ancient religion that apply to the world and nature (such as dependent origination) in a unique way and these can be embraced by an environmental ethicist quite progressively. In all likelihood the former can limit the latter. However when viewed differently such limitations lose their force (as will be shown in due course) and so are not permanently debilitating. A change in view would help in addressing the ambiguity of literary sources also that has disturbed claims to a consistent notion of Buddhist ecology. For this the possibility of investigation must be expansive. Accordingly Buddhist literature is explored not only for its deeper soteriological issues but also for those additional factors concerning the world and nature that get exposed inadvertently. Buddhism moreover has a deep moral perspective regarding actions and their consequences. Monitoring actions (*vis-à-vis* choices) of human beings can have a significant bearing on the environment. Thus beliefs about morality and other related matters will be continuously focused upon in the course of this book in the hope that these will support the emerging outlines of an environmental ethics.

Furthermore, my study will presuppose certain significant features of the Buddhist world-view that must be acknowledged by any Buddhist environmental ethics claiming legitimacy. These features, that form the core of almost all other Buddhist studies and are often cited, are inexorably interlinked with one another. Though mentioned below in brief my subsequent deliberations will keep returning to some of them frequently. These features are as follows:

1 Buddhists do not respond to questions about the existence of God. The Buddha in general is believed to have maintained a silence when asked metaphysical questions of this nature. However, clearly, the concept of God as the omnipotent and omniscient creator of the world is rejected and He cannot be held responsible for the state of the world. The Buddha is not regarded as a God either but his experiences of the true reality of the Four Noble Truths and attainment of enlightenment have gained a sacred status.

2 A fundamental belief that underlies all Buddhist thinking is the doctrine of *kamma*, according to which all intentional actions have consequences. Actions freely and intentionally performed lead to certain consequences. There is no escape from consequences and if persons do not suffer or enjoy them in this lifetime these are bound to follow them into the next. Thus consequences are strictly determined (even though the Buddha admitted that certain factors could affect their intensity). In other words the individual must act out of free will and must then bear the burden of the determined consequences of such actions. The quality of *kamma* is subtle here and so encompassing that the whole notion of individual responsibility becomes illuminated. It is also made adequately clear that intentional actions can be conceived as good or bad, right or wrong. This forms the foundation of the moral essence of the religion.

3 *Kamma* is acted out within *saṃsāra,* which is metaphorically speaking a stage or platform where actions are performed as also the state of wandering beings. It is characterized as endless and cyclical. According to Buddhist literature *saṃsāra* is divided into levels or realms and beings are born into these according to the actions that they have performed in the past. *Saṃsāra* includes realms such as heaven for moral beings and hell for evil and immoral ones. The experience of good or bad realms depends solely on the nature of actions performed. Thus responsibility of birth in *saṃsāra* and its various realms rests on the individual himself.

4 Connected with *kamma* and *saṃsāra* is the early Buddhist theory of rebirth. Buddhists believe that individuals are born over and over to suffer the consequences of their deeds. In fact the present life is an outcome of the acts performed in previous lives and the acts of this life will be responsible for the quality of future lives. Consequences generate a power that propels rebirth and ensures that this life is not the only one.

Thus there is continuity between birth and death and then birth again and so on such that the thought of absolute annihilation at death (without enlightenment) is not considered.

5 And finally, early Buddhism believes that all the above features have at their centre the notion of *dukkha*. *Dukkha* forms the focal point of Buddhist philosophy and underlies all existence. Though difficult to explain, it includes all sorts of bodily pain and psychical anguish, sorrows, existential angst and unsatisfied needs and even joys, due to their impermanent nature. Life is marked by the constant strife to overcome *dukkha*. However Buddhists see an end to *dukkha* and therefore to constant rebirth in the *saṃsāric* universe in the attainment of *nibbāna* through the Eightfold Path. Nibbāna is eternal freedom from *dukkha, saṃsāra* and rebirth. It is not a state of heaven for in the Buddhist world-view this too is an intermittent state from which beings must eventually move on to their next existence. It is believed that *nibbāna* is acquired through knowing and realizing the Truth; and Buddhism lays down how its attainment becomes possible.

Keeping these features in view and after having discussed the foundational principles of Buddhist philosophy along with citing some significant early Buddhist references to the natural world carefully, my enquiry will make it adequately clear that an unconventional route must be tread. The task of a Buddhist environmental ethicist, if she is to succeed, has to be eclectic and must include the Buddhist world-view. Buddhist concepts such as the feature of uniform causality, the continuity of beings and commonality of beginnings and their bearing on nature must all be examined minutely to draw out the Buddhist impression of nature and environment. It will be seen then that the seed of a philosophy of nature was always buried in these unexpected quarters. A logical corollary to this investigation is the recognition that what truly sustains the presence of an environmental ethics in early Buddhism is its ethical doctrine embodying virtues. Of late many western environmental theories are admitting that virtues have a powerful bearing on the state of the environment and that the behaviour and attitude of human beings can, to a large extent, transform the environment. The ethics of Buddhism can be said to accept certain virtues and vices. Though these are not necessarily directed towards environmental betterment, the virtues approach is so foundational in Buddhism that it embraces every action performed in the world. Due to this the virtuous principles of non-violence, modesty and contentment can be believed to apply to the environment and have a resounding effect on the latter's quality. Most importantly this approach considerably reduces the possibility of negative interpretations within the area of Buddhism and ecology and enhances the prospect of identifying an unambiguous environmental ethics in Buddhism substantially. This could be called an *environmental virtue ethics* and considered the primary Buddhist environmental position.

. . . These make up the greater part of the *Sūtra* [Pali: *Sutta*] *Piṭaka* . . . it is the *sūtras* which are recognized as the primary source for the doctrine of Buddhism."[6] Thus supported by sections of the *Khuddaka Nikāya, Vinaya* and the *Abhidhamma*, a comprehensive theoretical account based on the first four *Nikāyas* of the *Sutta Piṭaka* is probably a good place to begin. It is my belief that an environmental ethics based on *Sutta* literature along with the remaining Canon would yield a fair picture bound to be of use to future study. In addition, as an exception, I will dedicate one chapter to the *Jātaka* texts of the *Khuddaka Nikāya* for purposes that will be revealed in the chapter itself. The *Jātakas* are referred to commonly as Buddhist folklore and their inclusion also corroborates the environmental beliefs found elsewhere in the Canon.

Historically each text mentioned above has its unique chronicles, style, approximate dates and peculiar inspirations. My study will not reflect on such history (except of the *Jātakas* briefly). However it is important to keep in mind that various scholars have established that portions of these texts were added at a much later stage than others for they are linguistically and stylistically different. There is also additional commentarial material added at times. This can cause many difficulties of interpretation. This study acknowledges these concerns (as most ancient historical and philosophical studies must) but will not dwell on questions that deal with linguistic and other anomalies. Potential concerns to do with authenticity and timing are too complex to be dealt with here. Nevertheless this approach does not rule out a faithful representation of these Buddhist texts. Neither does this approach rule out a more expansive understanding and interpretation. In this regard it has been stated that when dealing with the *Nikāyas*, scholars need to attend to "the spirit rather than letter of the teachings: and it follows from this that overall coherence was always meant to be of central importance," for the *Nikāyas* are cryptic to read and open to many interpretations.[7] My study aims to reflect this attitude. In the final analysis I hope to show that it is possible to envisage a genuine environmental ethics in Buddhism. I focus not only on creating an academically oriented theory but also on sharpening Buddhist literary insights to address real environmental issues that have a lasting impact.

Approaches to Buddhist environmentalism

At this juncture, it will be valuable to analyse how environmental ethics in Buddhism has been treated by scholars up to this time. I include a somewhat detailed review here as it leads up to my own position. Even though from the mid 1970's onwards a curiosity to understand environmental issues in Buddhism began to develop, it is in the last two decades or so that a considerable quantity of research dedicated to the subject has been undertaken and literary works supporting or disputing Buddhist environmentalism have appeared.[8] This research area has grown at a pace coinciding with dawning awareness of the negative impact of large scale environmental devastation and the need to address it. An evaluation of important approaches to Buddhism and ecology not only acknowledges this history but also recognizes the premises on which scholars have based their conclusions; the evaluation is also indispensable for recognizing both existing and potential problems.

As I go along, this study makes it possible for me not only to identify the plurality of views and lack of consensus among scholars working in the area of Buddhist environmental ethics, but also to identify possible strengths and areas of challenge systematically. I have limited myself to an examination of that literature which is based primarily on the earliest form of Buddhism in keeping with the theme of this book, and references to later Buddhism are minimal. I have also limited myself to trace the development of thought in the last two decades or so as far as possible. However I remain aware that despite my best efforts an exhaustive survey is impossible and I do not represent all the views that may exist in this particular field and within the time frame being considered. I now take a closer look at the literature.

The more significant research in this field includes works by Lambert Schmithausen. Schmithausen's focus has been primarily on ecological ethics in general as well as on determining the sentience of plants.[9] His research is based primarily on early Buddhist literature and he admits that it is hard to establish an indisputable environmentalism in early Buddhism due to the presence of opposing views regarding nature. But he remains optimistic and draws constant attention to the more positive examples as well. Alan Sponberg has made relevant contributions to the area too. He includes both early Buddhism and Mahāyāna and looks at Buddhist environmentalism mostly from the soteriological point of view. Armed with a more liberal approach Sponberg finds that the seed of environmentalism is contained in the Buddhist doctrine of no-self.[10] He understands that the Buddhist sense of self requires that "individual identity is perceived as a dynamic and developmental stream of karmic conditioning" that continues over many lifetimes and life forms.[11] Viewing the self in such a way, he believes, will lead to a "compassionate, environmental sustaining altruism."[12]

David Kalupahana also takes a strong stand on the issue of the presence of environmentalism in (primarily early) Buddhism in his essay "Towards a Middle Path of Survival."[13] Kalupahana claims that most interpretations of Buddhism in the modern world are based upon misunderstandings and so do not comprehend that the Buddha's was not an absolutistic theory of nature. Human beings were a part of nature; they were dependently arisen like everything else that existed. And according to Kalupahana, the dissolution of this distinction in understanding will reveal a significant relation between nature and humanity. In a later work he introduces the idea of a virtue approach to environmental ethics.[14] However, sadly, he does not elaborate on this. Peter Harvey in his book, *An Introduction to Buddhist Ethics*, devotes a chapter to the Buddhist attitude towards nature and animals.[15] The chapter is informative but general for it covers almost the entire history of eco-Buddhism as well as the state of environmental matters in Buddhist countries. Harvey writes that though Buddhist principles may not always be conducive to modern ecology (for instance, no mention is made of the protection of species in Buddhist literature) Buddhism can be seen as ecological in that human beings are not set against nature and have the potential to act in a compassionate manner towards all other beings. P. D. Ryan's book *Buddhism and the Natural World* is particularly positive in its portrayal and creates a vivid picture of Buddhist environmentalism especially through deconstructing the myth of the *Aggañña Sutta*. Ryan's writings are also inclusive of analyses on wilderness, animals and images of nature based on ideas of interdependence and compassion.[16]

On the other end of the spectrum are scholars who are somewhat sceptical about the presence of an environmental ethics in Buddhism on various grounds. Despite their somewhat pessimistic conclusions, it must be admitted that a majority of these writers have acknowledged some of the more positive ecological features that Buddhism may be seen to contain. Ian Harris questions the presence of environmentalism in Buddhism and has essentially adopted such a critical approach. He points out:

> . . . it is dysteleology deeply rooted within Buddhism that is the essential problem . . . It is not so much that Buddhism has a difficulty in deriving an ought from an is, it is that it faces the more fundamental difficulty of defining an "is" in the first place.[17]

Thus, Harris finds that methodologically Buddhism is unable to sustain an environmental ethics. Malcolm David Eckel too considers the issue from a critical perspective and questions the authenticity of an environmental ethics in Buddhism.[18] He believes that Buddhism does not contain a unified view about acting for the sake of nature, and the only sense in which the well-being of nature could be guaranteed is through developing human discipline, compassion and mindfulness.

Paul Waldau devotes his research to the Buddhist attitude to animals. He examines the concept of "animal rights" and finds that though Buddhism does offer some perspectives supporting such rights, this is not a consistent feature. In this regard Waldau's main contention is that the treatment of animals in Buddhism has two distinct features – one sympathetic and the other not so. He also finds that Buddhist texts lack a naturalistic content.[19] This conclusion is also supported in his thesis, where Waldau has examined references to key animals in the Pali Canon. He finds that an inadequate understanding of animals results from the Buddhist preoccupation with human beings.[20] On a similar note, Florin Deleanu also examines Buddhist references to animals. He draws the conclusion that unfair treatment was given to animals. However, he finds that this attitude was not universal and there are instances of sympathy towards animals. Unfair images, according to Deleanu, may have been a result of literary conventions.[21]

Apart from the above works, another prototype of literature on Buddhism and nature consists of edited collections that incorporate an extremely wide range of essays and articles. The articles base themselves from anywhere between the earliest forms of Buddhism to the more contemporary opinions of engaged Buddhists on the subject of nature. All the collections include more than one form of Buddhism. This approach is summarized in the introduction of one of these books as adopting:

> . . . various methodological perspectives, including anthropology, sociology, textual analysis, historical studies, and philosophical or theological approaches. The essays also share tensions between a descriptive and a critical perspective on the one hand and a more interpretive and engaged perspective on the other."[22]

Examples of some such books are *Buddhism and Ecology, Dharma Gaia, Dharma Rain* and *Buddhism and Ecology: The Interconnection of Dharma and Deeds.*[23] (Henceforth the latter book will be referred to as *Dharma and Deeds.*) It is beneficial to keep in mind the broad variety this literature embraces for it draws attention to the complexity that one is bound to encounter in such studies. It should also be noted that some of the articles are more discursive than others. Of the more academically oriented, the book *Dharma and Deeds* contains a section on "theoretical and methodological issues" that arise in such studies, and has contributors such as Harris and Sponberg, who have been mentioned above.

Other studies in the field have explored the practice, teaching and application of ecology in relation to Buddhism. In this context an important contributor is Joanna Macy's book, *World as Lover, World as Self*, which revolves around environmental spiritual practices.[24] A major portion of her work relies on Buddhist scriptures for inspiration and contains some very important insights drawn from them. She discusses the concept of dependent origination from where she moves on to the nature of the self: she understands a sense of self that is co-extensive with the world, so that acting for the sake of the one would mean acting for the sake of the other. She refers to this idea as the "greening of the self."[25] Padmasiri de Silva's *Environmental Philosophy and Ethics in Buddhism* contains, amongst other things, a valuable chapter on the role of Buddhist pedagogy and its implications on ecological sensibility.[26] He also constructs a theory of economics based on Buddhist principles he finds ecologically meaningful. Toni Page, like Waldau, has written on Buddhism and animals, though he approaches the issue more from the practical rather than philosophical angle.[27] His work principally explores Buddhist attitudes towards vegetarianism, vivisection and animal activism.

Though the above evaluation does not include all works that speak of early Buddhism and ecology (a task quite impossible), it attempts to represent broadly most views that have been propounded thus far. I now take a closer look at this literature. While reviewing the above literature I found that it could be classified into four approximate categories based on the conclusions that were drawn and the method that was used to reach these conclusions. This categorization corresponds to the one used by Ian Harris; however I have modified his account to accommodate my own views on the matter.[28] In addition I have limited myself to only a few works that are suitably representative of each position. The four categories are as follows:

1 Writings that unquestioningly believe Buddhism to be environmental (though the evidence they base this on may be inadequate) are all part of the first category. In this category I also briefly mention the writings of and about Buddhist nature activists who are working towards saving the environment as well as practising Buddhists who suggest Buddhist meditations and other practices as useful in promoting environmental consciousness. I have named this category "Partisan."
2 The view of those who believe Buddhism to be environmental, and use genuine Buddhist sources to validate their claims is the second category. Their use of such resources often appears as ambiguous or controversial thereby raising serious doubts about their validity. I refer to these writers as "Positivists."
3 The third category includes writers that have adopted an initially non-judgemental approach in order to determine to what extent Buddhism may be seen as ecological. This approach includes the questioning and analysis of various texts and their contexts and, in this, these writers have come up with results varying from the "fairly optimistic" to "inconclusive but still optimistic." I have called this category "Sanguine."
4 Finally, some scholars are sceptical about of the presence of environmental ethics in Buddhism and they belong to the last category. These scholars find other approaches flawed or inaccurate or plainly misleading and their writings are suggestive of areas that require further investigation. This position also has an extreme end, where environmental Buddhism is considered conceptually impossible.[29] I refer to this category as the "Sceptics."

The rest of this chapter contains four sections, each one devoted to one of the four categories. Some points of significance and others of contention have been included to represent each position. Each section includes a critical appraisal. No position is, as I will demonstrate, entirely satisfactory even though every position contributes something of value. My evaluation goes to show that proving early Buddhism as containing an environmental ethic is no easy task. In the overview I will take the opportunity to suggest some possible alternatives that may be adopted to ensure a more convincing and compelling outcome: alternatives that lay the foundation for the rest of this book.

The "Partisan" environmentalists: Environmental ethics in Buddhism as a given

This section examines essays and articles that can be seen as representative of the first category labelled the "Partisan" environmentalists. The supporters of this position take the notion of ecological protection seriously and have been involved in practices to raise awareness. To them Buddhism inherently promotes ecological living and illuminates the connection between everything. The assumption here is that Buddhism is undoubtedly environmental. I will draw attention to some setbacks this position faces. It must be remembered that this position is not particularly aimed at a scholarly audience; it seeks to address general readers.

The quantity of Partisan literature is overwhelming – contained in journals, books, magazines and newspapers. I have limited my selection, for the sake of practicability, to a few articles contained in three books: *Buddhism and Ecology, Dharma Gaia* and *Dharma and Deeds*, which, I find, give a sufficient indication of the true nature of Partisan thought. That the essays are not limited to early Buddhism alone, does not detract from their importance to my study, as, first, they do contain aspects of early Buddhism and, second, they contain useful ideas that are indicative of a philosophy of nature in early Buddhism. Additionally, I have selected essays on few Buddhist practitioners that have embraced environmental issues in a partisan sense as these contribute in presenting a more holistic picture.

A question that springs to mind while reading Partisan literature is their factual dependence on the sources under consideration – it is important to note that though conclusions drawn here can be found to be connected with the Buddhist literary tradition in a legitimate way, more often than not conclusions are based on reinterpreted Buddhist ideas. Instances of writings that reflect Buddhist ideas more faithfully are as follows. Martine Batchelor's essay is a compilation of passages from scriptures that contain an environmental message.[30] She follows each passage with an analysis of how it can be seen as promoting environmentalism from the point of view of the Buddha's teachings. In the same vein, Lily de Silva's essay analyses the evolution of the world discussed in the *Cakkavatisīhanāda Sutta* of the *Dīgha Nikāya*.[31] She understands the *Sutta* as making the important point that the moral deterioration of humanity harms nature. She sees change as an important part of nature but man's lack of morality hastens these changes bringing about consequences that are harmful to human beings themselves. De Silva stresses a close relationship between human morality and the natural environment. Thus, though limited in their analysis, effective ideas are essentially introduced and prove to be fairly valuable. But in their enthusiasm, it must be remembered, these authors neglect the negative readings that may be found within precisely the same set of passages.

Other essays however are not clear in their presentation. For instance, Stephen Batchelor's essay entitled "Buddhist Economics Reconsidered" suggests the adoption of new terms and values for a Buddhist economic theory.[32] He writes that Buddhist economics must be based on the concept of non-duality in such a way that the separation between agent, act and object becomes conceptual. For this to happen the foundation must be *śūnyatā*, which the author understands as things and minds as empty of separation. The resulting economics would also have to consider the Buddhist acceptance of reality as "acentric," i.e. that no one thing occupies a central place as compared to others. Rita Gross' essay deals with the issues of population, consumption and the environment.[33] The essay is radical in its approach, and as the author admits, relies on the values inherent in the tradition rather than on any textual evidence. Gross believes that a Buddhist's religious duty does not include reproduction. She declares the existence of large populations to be as unacceptable as slavery and child abuse and believes that since the Buddha had suggested the middle path, both population and consumption should be moderate. Ken Jones advances the notion of eco-social Buddhology, which is the application of *dharma* (Pali: *dhamma*) to social and ecological problems.[34] These inspiring, innovative essays consider common grounds and find parallels in a way that Buddhism become relevant to the environmental scenario today but their authors are unable to pertinently elucidate their radical ideas.

More essays exhibit similar flaws. Padmasiri de Silva speaks of exploring a viable environmental psychology based on scriptures that is concerned with understanding the relation between humankind and nature.[35] However the implications of his essay are unclear. In another essay by Stephen Batchelor, the focus is on the nature of craving and delusion.[36] The core of delusion is understood as separation. Practice that includes discipline and insight is cited as that which will reveal the true nature of the universe, a universe of interrelated processes, which are expressed as compassion and love. The author thus links concepts, such as delusion and separation, without actually stating how he came upon such links.

In all it is noticeable that most Partisan writings contain in them some reference to Buddhist doctrines and concepts such as *anattā*, *śūnyavāda*, *paṭiccasamuppāda*, *dhamma*, *kamma* and others. As seen above, the intent of these doctrines is essentially modified to be environment-related by many essays. Though such modification can serve the environment quite well, their adherence to and superimposition on genuine Buddhist goals can be seriously questioned. Another instance is Jeremy Hayward's article that deals with the widening sense of self.[37] This widening of the circle of identification would apparently bring genuine sacredness to all that there is. By overcoming the ego, the greater sense of identification follows automatically. This, according to Hayward, is what the Buddhists understand by *anātman* (Pali: *anattā*)![38] This example, as well as the ones given above, are instances of an inadequate method of deriving logical conclusions and of misplaced intentions.

Meditation is also drawn on as a resource that supports eco-Buddhism. There are many references to the environmental crisis as being a spiritual crisis and it is believed that in addressing the latter, Buddhism inevitably addresses the environmental crisis too. Martin Pitt's essay stresses the point that meditation is at the heart of true ecological awareness.[39] Suzzane Head, on the other hand, describes in a very moving manner her direct experience of wilderness when on a retreat to re-establish a healthy relationship with the earth.[40] The focus here is on different ways to reconnect with nature, such as different sorts of meditations, mindful verses or *gāthas, haiku* poetry, or simply an attitude of gratitude towards the earth. Importance is given to this angle of experience, and many believe that a lot can be gained through it. However that the aim of meditation exercises was never an environmental one must not be forgotten. Meditation was prescribed to calm the disturbed mind and lead it towards peace and enlightenment, its singular purpose was not gaining environmental awareness or reconnecting with the earth or establishing a healthy relation with nature. If meditation did have environmental overtones these were added effects. The above essayists do not throw enough light on the latter aspect. A very interesting point is made in one of the articles about an eager audience awaiting the Dalai Lama's lecture on "Spirit and Nature." The Dalai Lama, however, never did address nature or the environment; he spoke of the nature of mind.[41]

Apart from meditation, activism and the concern about how to translate the teachings into action occupy an important place. Buddhist nature activists and observers try to understand the issues involved and the success of the ventures undertaken. The works of many Thai monks have been assessed. Kerry Brown has compiled talks and interviews of Ajahn Pongsak, an Engaged Buddhist.[42] For the Ajahn *sīladhamma* is not only morality, but is also harmony. Brown writes that he believes, "Dharma, the Buddhist word for truth and teaching, is also the word for nature . . . ."[43] Once this is truly grasped personal action would follow to undo the damage to nature. No effort is made to explain how this is the case either on the part of the Ajahn or on the part of Brown, even though there is no doubt that much has been done by the Ajahn in terms of personal action and teaching people about how they can contribute. Donald K. Swearer's article studies the hermeneutics of two renowned Thai monks.[44] Buddhadāsa Bhikkhu's ecological hermeneutic identifies *dhamma* with nature; Phra Prayudh's is more scholarly and is grounded in reason. The latter focuses on the life of the Buddha and the *sangha* as exemplifications of the Buddhist attitude towards nature. Once again, the work done by these monks is commendable, but difficulties arise in understanding *dhamma* as nature. In terms of practice some essays draw attention to the custom of the ordination of trees by Thai monks. That this is a Buddhist practice at all is controversial and more traditional *sanghas* have expelled many monks who supported it. The reason for this is that *pabbajja* or the ordination ceremony of a novice contains rules that state that the being that is undergoing ordination must state that he is human. As it is not possible for a tree to respond and therefore be ordained in this way, the extension of such ordination to trees is questionable. The traditionalists thus have valid serious objections to tree ordination. However, even then the effectiveness of this ceremony has been defended and cannot be undermined in modern-day environmental practice as noted by Susan Darlington:

> It is important to note that in this ceremony as in all tree ordinations, the monks did not claim to be fully ordaining the tree, as that status is reserved for humans only. The ceremony was used symbolically to remind people that nature should be treated as equal with humans, deserving of respect and vital for human as well as for all life . . . .[45]

She adds that such ordination is used to make people aware of the value of conservation. However the aspect Darlington is unable to defend is the one that proves the custom to be a truly Buddhist one. This casts doubt in general on the authenticity of environmental practices as genuine Buddhist practices.

On the whole, Partisan thinkers appear to be deeply positive and inspiring environmentalists but ineffectual theoreticians. Those who promote (eco) meditation and environmental action as Buddhist practices in order to resolve the ecological crisis must re-assess their analysis. Many of the essays and articles reviewed above lack clarity because they have overlooked details and failed to thoroughly examine Buddhist issues. In many other writings, here un-reviewed, biases run strong and superimpositions are common. Concepts that do not belong together are lackadaisically combined leading to new implications and added confusions. Moreover the tone of many is sermonizing with little substance to back up suggestions. Goals of unrealistic magnitude are pictured and methods prescribed to reach them are either flawed or ineffective. In all, the writings of this genre can be seen to be open to various challenges. But at the same time it can be admitted that this literature contains within it an endless possibility of ideas that, when based on further study and detailed analysis, could produce very worthwhile discussions indeed. Thus their endeavour is praiseworthy but clearly not indubitable. And so the Partisans must not be dismissed lightly for their worth lies in their vision and their belief in the spirit of Buddhism.

The "Positivists": There is an environmental ethics in Buddhism

This category represents those writings that convey certainty about Buddhism being ecological. These writers reach this conclusion by understanding the implications present in various Buddhist doctrines. However their analyses, though more deeply thought and perceptive, are radical and so court controversy. In this section I undertake an examination of Joanna Macy's treatment of certain Buddhist doctrines and their environmental worth. *Paṭiccasamuppāda* (dependent co-arising or dependent origination) is a fundamental Buddhist concept that engages Macy's attention and through a close study of its implications she is able to arrive at the conclusion that it does indeed positively contribute to an environmental ethics. After having analysed the Buddhist theory of dependent co-arising, she relates it to the Buddhist approaches to *kamma*, self, perception, and ethics. She believes that it is through the changing of the individual that a conversion in attitudes to nature can happen. This view culminates in the arising of a new sense of self. It also suggests how individuals can contribute to ecological goals by altering the way they see themselves.

Macy finds that the Buddha's teachings of dependent co-arising, which she also refers to as the law of causality, applies to the objects and events of daily life. She explains that for the Buddha causality did not imply one thing causing another in turn (in a linear sense), rather it meant that things provided the appropriate conditions or occasions for others to arise, and by the arising of others these things themselves were affected. In this Macy saw "mutuality" or a "reciprocal dynamic" where it was not the things themselves but the relationship between them that became important. She finds that two baskets of the Pali Canon – the *Sutra* and the *Vinaya piṭaka* – support this meaning but in the third – the *Abhidharma* (Pali: *Abhidhamma*) – there is slight change and shift in meaning. Macy believes, "These shifts tend to weaken the moral thrust of dependent co-arising, and blur its distinctiveness from the causal views the Buddha contested."[46] According to Macy the Buddha's understanding of impermanence is central in the early baskets and to this impermanence the *Abhidharma* scholars added the notion of momentary phenomena. Due to momentariness becoming central in *Abhidharma* what became important was the nature and duration of the moments or *dharmas*. These began to be seen as significant entities, wherein each *dharma* replaced another in rapid succession. She observes that so much importance was given to the *dharmas* that the *Abhidharmikas* spent a long time enumerating and classifying them as independent entities. As a result, the relationship factor that had played so noteworthy a part earlier became less important.

According to her this shift was corrected in the Mahāyāna, where not only the self was considered *śūnya* (empty) of substantiality, but so also were the *dharmas*. And so in Mahāyāna the focus was once more on relationship. It is fairly obvious that this sense of dependent co-arising has made a deep impact on Macy. It proves to her Buddhism's support for the interconnectedness of all entities. She states, "This doctrine has provided me ways to understand the intricate web of co-arising that links one being with all other beings."[47] However, her entire discussion raises the question of whether there is actually a sense of "reciprocal dynamic" in early Buddhism at all. And I think that it is quite clear there is not in the sense and to the extent Macy assumes. In addition the method she has employed is questionable and has made her susceptible to criticism. She speaks of the mutual conditioning of all phenomena as based on the formula of *paṭiccasamuppāda*. This means to her that everything depends on everything else. However, the causal formula with its various aspects only seeks to locate the cause of suffering. At the same time the shorter formula is suggestive of a universal application of causation to all phenomena and nothing more.[48] Nowhere, especially in its early form, is *paṭiccasamuppāda* suggestive of the notion of mutual conditioning that Macy wants to prove it has had all along.[49]

Macy's discussion of the Buddhist understanding of perception is also problematic. As Macy sees it, the world according to early Buddhism is neither realist nor empirical but rather dependently originated. To this understanding she adds that consciousness conditions perception, and is in turn conditioned by the objects perceived. Due to this Macy finds a strong similarity between the Buddhist theory of perception and the organization of open systems. By open systems it is generally meant systems that self monitor. Macy gives the example of oceans and their regulation of salinity levels. Of them she writes, "they watch what they are doing and adjust. They do this by a process of matching – matching the observed results of behaviour with their inner pre-established goals."[50] She adds that open systems arrange, adapt and modify themselves on account of feedback they get based on the interaction with their environment. Of feedback Macy has said, "In feedback the output of a system, its behaviour, is monitored back to its receptors, thereby signalling the degree of performance or non-performance of an operation in relation to pre-established goals. This monitoring by means of feedback loops permits it to regulate its behaviour in terms of these goals."[51] Feedback appears as "circular" and "self-referential"; cause and effect interact and modify each other. Macy appears to have committed a serious faux pas by likening the Buddhist theory of perception to the causal circuit of the open systems theory. If it is Macy's intention to indicate that through the process of perception the environment will adjust and adapt itself or vice versa then a careful study of the Buddhist doctrine quite easily shows that this is not the case. The Buddhist theory of perception is nothing like the causal circuit seen in open systems; it is simply the description of a process, the way in which perception happens to take place. How Macy finds a similarity is difficult to fathom.

Karma (Pali: *kamma*) and the Buddhist theory of *anātman* are analysed by Macy in terms of dependent co-arising. She writes that although the Buddhists do not accept a continuing and abiding soul, this does not imply that there is no moral responsibility, but simply that "... distinctions between the pragmatic and the moral dissolve."[52] She understands the concept of *anātman* from the point of dependent co arising, wherein the docr and deed are reciprocally conditioned. This sort of conditioning ensures that a person is responsible for his deeds and these deeds, at the same time, shape the way he is and his subsequent behaviour. Even though there is no notion of a continuous self in Buddhism, Macy finds continuity to exist. She finds it in the actions of persons and these actions condition the person due to dependent co-arising. She writes, "... our actions co-determine what we become."[53] However Macy is quite clear that the Buddha's notion of *karma* is not determined.[54] Macy believes once again the *karma* doctrine is similar to the systems theory. In open systems she finds self-organization and no direction from the outside. She also finds that in such systems past actions influence present decisions in a way such that past and present work in mutual interaction, rather than being determined. She further writes that as the system grows more complex "self-reflexive consciousness" emerges which implies that the system "has evolved to the point that self-monitoring is required for evaluation and selecting between alternate courses of action."[55] Though Macy may be correct in pointing out the similarity between karma and the organization of open systems, in that both are free from determinism and make personal choice possible and both are influenced by past as well as present actions, the idea of a "self-reflexive consciousness" does not appear in Buddhism.

Macy speaks of the self in a chapter entitled "The Greening of the Self." She explains what she means by the greening of the self: it encompasses the mystical and the pragmatic, and it overcomes "separateness, alienation, and fragmentation."[56] Such an expansion of the sense of self, she finds, empowers environmental action. Macy then isolates a number of factors that contribute to such a sense of self. One of the factors is the systems view, according to which, as has been discussed above, life is made up of dynamic, self-organizing systems and these are sustained in and through their relationships. According to such systems, Macy explains, there is no basis for construing a "me" as opposed to the "other." Everything that is "me" arises in interaction with everything else in the world and therefore there can be no fragmented, isolated self.[57] She goes on to say that another factor that leads to the dismantling of the ego-self and creation of the eco-self is non-dualistic spiritualities, an example of which is Buddhism. Macy believes that Buddhism undermines the distinction between the self and the other in a way similar to the systems theory. Due to Buddhism's acceptance of the dependent co-arising of phenomena, the isolation of an individual, continuing self is just not possible and from this she believes arises a sense of interdependence in that "we are profoundly interconnected and therefore we are all able to recognize and act upon our deep, intricate and intimate inter-existence with each other and all beings."[58] Macy then suggests that the concern we have for ourselves must be extended to all others. To the eco-self she gives a metaphoric as well as a dynamic status.[59] Such a self leads to strength and endurance and to a sense of optimism and power to defend one's cause.

In the same chapter Macy also adds that "moral exhortation" is not effective where environmental action is concerned and appears to agree with the deep ecologist Arne Naess that "virtue is not required for the greening of the self, or the emergence of the ecological self."[60] Macy appears to have committed two major flaws in her account of the self. The first one lies in her comparison of the Buddhist doctrine of no-self with the systems theory and the greening of the self (eco-self). Though in early Buddhist literature it is admitted that the various factors of the self are dependently originated, it is not claimed that such origination confirms an interconnection with all other life or that a person arises in interaction with everything else. Macy draws these conclusions without any support from the texts. The second flaw is Macy's denial of the role of morality in the greening of the self. By her own admission morality in Buddhism is one of the factors that reveals the self as an "idea" only (the others being wisdom and meditation) and this leads to the dissolving of an isolated self. Though she seems to support this she goes on to deny the role of morality and virtue in the emerging ecological self in general. Thus her account appears somewhat confused and inconsistent.

Ian Harris is extremely critical of Macy and others who have a similar approach. He blames them for having superimposed the teleological principle from process theology on to eco-Buddhism.[61] He finds Macy "guilty of anachronism in her reading of early Indic sources."[62] On causality supporting an ethics of the environment Harris believes Buddhism to be dysteleologic rather than teleological and this according to him is a grave threat to environmental ethics within Buddhism.[63] By letting go of the obvious differences that exist between entities and promoting a mutually causative form of *paṭiccasamuppāda* (*vis-à-vis* interdependence) Harris appears concerned about the possibility of understanding the true meaning of the Buddhist doctrine of *anattā* given Macy's interpretation. He asks the question whether Macy's eco-self can be reconciled with the no-self doctrine.[64] He finds that even if Macy's position of "mutual causality" is accepted there remains a problem; the dependence and interpenetration of all entities cannot be the source of ecology, for then all things will depend, for example, on nuclear waste that is itself a part of the totality of interdependent entities.[65]

The value of Macy's work lies in her unfaltering conviction and her acknowledgement that "We are capable of suffering with the world . . . ." Her expression of this form of *dukkha* is stirring and deeply expressive. However her methodology does not quite work when she tries hard to find an equation between early Buddhism and open systems. Moreover a rendering of *paṭiccasamuppāda* based on the principles of early Buddhism can be seen to be supportive of nature without bringing in the concept of interconnection of all life based on the mutual conditioning of phenomena as depicted by Macy.

The "Sanguine" environmentalists: There may be an environmental ethics in Buddhism

Lambert Schmithausen and Alan Sponberg are two of the foremost exponents of this category. I devote this section to the examination of Schmithausen's work on Buddhism and nature, which has prepared the ground for the acceptance of environmentalism in Buddhism as a logical possibility. Ian Harris has understood him as "optimistic about the possibility of an authentic Buddhist response to environmental problems."[66] In Schmithausen one sees a very thorough investigation of particulars and an outright reliance on texts to support the claims he makes. He finds that in order to survive as a religion Buddhism must deal with the environmental crisis maybe even through reinterpretation or reorganization.[67] Schmithausen's methodology is quite different from Macy's. He tries to establish an ethics of the environment based on what he understands to be factual Buddhist ideas, and notwithstanding that a definitive conclusion evades him, he remains optimistic about finding an environmental ethics in Buddhism. After an analysis of his work, I will conclude the section with some comments on Schmithausen's position.

Schmithausen understands the meaning of nature as containing two aspects, nature in the sense of eco-systems (especially those that are not tampered with by human beings) and nature as natural entities (individual plants and animals). Corresponding to this, misdemeanours towards nature could take two forms, that of damage to eco-systems and that of abuse to individuals. He searches for both these aspects in Buddhism.[68] It is also important to note while comprehending his work on nature that Schmithausen believes Buddhist texts to be ambiguous.[69] According to him, Buddhism contains various strands, out of which only some can be seen as ecological. For instance the strand of "detachment and release" considered all creation as ultimately unsatisfactory and the only aim worth achieving as liberation and so is not supportive of ecology.[70] He goes on to say that this strand does not imply that nature, as part of creation, either can be destroyed or needs to be conserved; all it implies is that Buddhism did not place ultimate value on nature, or for that matter on the civilized world. Value lay only in the attainment of enlightenment, and not in the preservation of nature.[71] However Schmithausen's attention is focused more on the ecological strands. Considerable attention is also devoted to the treatment of animals and plants. Though Schmithausen concentrates on early Buddhism, he does bring in later Buddhism to a significant extent as well.

Schmithausen focuses on the precept of *ahiṃsā*, not following which was considered to lead to bad consequences. *Ahiṃsā* (generally taken as non-violence) was a universal requirement and respecting this value applied to monks and lay followers alike. He points out that *ahiṃsā* in lay communities was also encouraged by the fact that certain professions, such as hunting and fishing that involved killing and injury, were prohibited and looked upon with contempt. However, the consequences of *ahiṃsā* depended on how seriously the precept had been violated. Schmithausen comments that some lay followers did not follow professions that involved the killing of animals. However, for a majority, upholding this precept unfailingly was almost impossible, for even if they were involved in a profession like agriculture there was a distinct possibility that small animals may be killed in its activities (such as ploughing).[72] He summarizes the reaction of early society either as that of ignoring the violation, or learning to live with it, or of compensating the killing with actions of merit. It appears to Schmithausen that *ahiṃsā* was sacrificed to the rigours of following a practical life. He appears critical of this because such practical considerations can reduce inhibitions and undermine *ahiṃsā*; this also explains to him the gap between the standard set by the texts and the actual careless observance of these standards in traditional Buddhist countries.

In early Buddhism, Schmithausen finds that *ahiṃsā* was categorical, to be followed without exception. He draws this conclusion from the fact that a monk is not allowed to kill even in self-defence; the advice given to a sick person to commit suicide is an offence; and evidence for the killing of a sick person or animal even out of compassion is absent. But then he notes exceptions in later texts where it is indicated that the *Bodhisatta* kills beings that cause injury out of compassion to others.[73] This becomes problematic, for from it can be derived the permission to kill animals that may harm others. He gives the example of the Mahāyāna *Mahāparinirvāṇasūtra* that goes so far as to state that in cases of conflict it is right to kill the morally inferior.[74] Since man is on a higher moral level, killing an animal appears as a valid option. This view grants that man is superior and confirms anthropocentrism rather than cosmocentrism to him. He identifies other examples of *ahiṃsā*, such as the *Vinaya* rule that prohibits monks from injuring plants and polluting water inhabited by tiny animals, but claims that such occasional and random examples hardly give a strong foundation to an ethics of environment.[75] Schmithausen also expresses discomfort on extending virtuous action to whole species. The object of *ahiṃsā* and other virtues is the individual and not species or eco-systems. Being directed towards individuals rather than species reaffirms the motivation as non-ecological.[76]

One of Schmithausen's most important contributions is his identification of two "strands" in Buddhism. The first is the pro-civilization strand.[77] As the name suggests, this strand favours civilization and focuses on what is suitable for humanity; wild nature is seen as a threat. Not only does Schmithausen find this strand anthropocentric, he finds that it springs from Indian rather than Buddhist thought.[78] Supporting this strand are instances in the *Suttas* that speak about planting fruit trees, building parks and so on. The sense of natural beauty this strand adopts is one that is suitable to man. In this context Schmithausen gives the example of the Buddhist paradise, *Sukhāvatī*, which is crowded with people and contains only bejewelled artificial trees and birds.[79] The hermit strand, on the other hand, reflects the life of the forest dwelling monk who is happy in such surroundings and seeks to gain spiritually from the solitude and hardships that he faces.[80] Schmithausen admits that even this strand is anthropocentric, in that the protection of the forests is for human benefit. But this strand does indeed give more positive value to nature for it is the surroundings as a whole that are considered rather than individual plants and animals. Even though there is little chance of a quiet and undisturbed life in wild nature today, Schmithausen is optimistic that this strand could be developed to form the basis of environmental ethics, albeit a human-centred one.

Other than this, Schmithausen has also spent a considerable time investigating the question of sentiency of plants in his work *The Problem of the Sentience of Plants in Earliest Buddhism*. Schmithausen understands sentience as something that is generally possessed by a being when it is capable of perception and sensation. He finds that Vedic religion contains some evidence that plants and seeds were regarded as sentient and that the Jains believed that everything in the universe had some level of consciousness.[81] However, the Buddhist position appears unclear to him. Even though there is an explicit rejection of the sentience of plants in later texts, the earlier canonical texts do not either accept or reject such sentience. Schmithausen concludes that the matter must be decided by induction and so he examines passages that shed light on the issue.

Schmithausen analyses *Pācittiya* 11, from the *Pāṭimokkhasutta*, which says, *bhūtagāmapātavyatāya pācittiyam*, which he understands as "If [a monk or nun] is ruthless with regard to plants, this is an offence to be atoned."[82] He faces some philological problems, but eventually understands *gāma* to mean "multitude or mass" and *bhūta* to mean "green, fresh, living plants." *Pātavyatā* he understands as "ruthless," in the case of plants it could mean cutting, felling, etc. The *Suttapiṭaka* supports this; wherein it is seen that a monk's morality includes abstention from injuring seeds and plants (*bījagāma-bhūtagāma-samārambha*).[83] Schmithausen then looks into the underlying reason for this abstention. The reason may be anthropocentric in that an injury to cultivated plants might be damaging for the owner. Though this is mentioned in several places, he finds that in the above two cases no such restriction is mentioned and that some commentaries to the verses even include moss, which is uncultivated. He rules out the case of plants being protected as an abode of animals as a motive for it does not account for the prohibition to injure seeds. Further, dry plants may be the abode of insects as well, and these are never mentioned.[84]

In his search for a reasonable motive, Schmithausen examines the introductory stories to the *Pātimokkha* rules, given in their commentary. In one of the stories a monk hit the arm of the child of the deity inhabiting the tree while felling it and this is what prompted the rule.[85] But he rejects this motive too for, as in the above case, it does not explain non-injury to seeds. Schmithausen looks at another story that hints that the motive may be the disapproval of people who regard trees as living.[86] Though he finds the story is in keeping with the beliefs of the time, Schmithausen questions it as a historian, for the story is believed to belong to a later period and not really associated with early Buddhist thought. Moreover, even if the story is accepted it only reflects the beliefs of the time and not Buddhist attitudes.[87]

At various places in the *Suttapiṭaka* it is stated that left-over food should not be thrown where there are green plants or in water with living beings. In such instances Schmithausen sees the possibility of proving that plants are sentient by drawing a parallel between small animals and plants. But he finds that the situation becomes complicated by the fact that there is an example in the scriptures where it is said that evacuations of excrement, snot, phlegm, etc. are not to be dropped on vegetation and water.[88] Since early Buddhists are definitely not inclined to regard water as sentient, the parallel between plants and small animals can also be ruled out by the same extension. Schmithausen finds that the commentaries to the various texts do mention the protection of plants, but points out that such protection is mostly anthropocentric. The focus is primarily on plants that human beings use and water meant for human consumption. He notices that in Buddhism decorum and hygiene are associated with *ahiṃsā*.[89] On the basis of this mixed motivation Schmithausen identifies another two strands in Buddhism: one purely anthropocentric (for the sake of hygiene) and the other *ahiṃsā*-oriented (for the protection of small animals).

Even though Schmithausen acknowledges verses that include plants in the category of "animate beings" he warns that such passages are very few and matter of fact, and there is no passage expressly stating that plants are living.[90] But then, at the same time, he also acknowledges that there is no definite denial of their sentience either.[91] Schmithausen considers the various questions that may be faced in this debate. First, if the view of early Buddhism is taken as supportive of plant sentience, why and how did later Buddhism come to adopt an opposite stance? Second, was the sentience of plants adopted simply from beliefs that existed in society at the time? Third, if Buddhists believed plants to be non-sentient, why did they not explicitly say so?[92] In answer to these questions he sees several possibilities. It could be that certain canonical passages discussing plants merely expressed the views of their commentators or other non-Buddhists rather than reflecting Buddhist beliefs at large. Or then again, it could be that plants were seen as a borderline case, included and excluded from sentience as and when required.[93] In terms of wilful and careless destruction, plants could be included as sentient, but sentience could not be extended to vegetation needed for food due to pragmatic compulsions.[94] Schmithausen admits to being unable to prove conclusively that plants are sentient. However, he recognizes a general theme of respecting plant life in Buddhist texts. Seeds and plants are not to be injured, meditation is to be done in natural and aesthetically appealing areas and trees are often venerated, and so on. As an ecological requirement this appears to have some force.

With regard to animals, Schmithausen finds that Buddhism generally regards them as unhappy, and so their ecological protection appears to be unnecessarily prolonging their suffering. On the other hand he finds that an argument for animal protection could be that human beings are reborn as animals and so their protection would really mean that human beings are ensuring their own future or looking out for the interest of their ancestors. Another argument for animal protection, according to Schmithausen, may be derived from the anthropocentric angle – conservation of animals is important for the future of humanity. However, he rejects this argument if the idea of unhappiness in the animal realm is upheld. Another problem that arises from the anthropocentric angle is that it allows for grievous injury and suffering to animals for the sake of humanity. And Buddhism resists causing such suffering on principle.[95] Eventually, Schmithausen draws the conclusion that "unhappy animals" in the Buddhist context have to be seen within specific contexts where drawing attention to their suffering may be relevant. This should not be treated as *the* Buddhist stance on the matter. He also thinks that Buddhists have adopted such notions for didactic purposes, to express the workings of *kamma* and so they are not really a statement about animals.[96]

Finally, some attention must be drawn to Schmithausen's claim that the spiritual perfection of individuals, even though it may lead to sound ecology, inculcates a passive attitude to natural matters rather than an active one. To this is added that the environmental situation has reached such a critical stage that there is no time to wait for everyone's spiritual perfection. In this context Schmithausen speaks about finding resources that motivate the ordinary, non-liberated man.[97] I have some hesitation in using the term "passive" here, and accordingly will show in a later chapter, in attempting to establish a value-based environmental ethics, that this may not be the case. Schmithausen, himself, is not against the idea of establishing a value-based ethics of nature – he believes that it can be done by showing that nature has an intrinsic value "in spite of its *ultimate* valueness."[98] Even though he leaves this question unresolved, he appears hopeful of a positive outcome in this regard.

Summarized below are some of the more important points Schmithausen has made:

1 From the point of view of ultimate existence, the importance of nature is minimal.
2 *Ahiṃsā* and other virtues may be seen as having an ecological significance, even though this was not their primary motive. One major problem here is that these virtues are mostly pursued for anthropocentric reasons.

3 Two strands can clearly be identified – the pro-civilization strand and the hermit strand. It is the latter that to some extent, accords a positive value to nature.
4 Plants are seen as a borderline case, as neither their sentience nor their non-sentience in early Buddhism can be proved.
5 The belief that animals are unhappy is to be seen within specific contexts. It is recognized that animals hold on to life and recoil from pain and thus should be left alone to continue with their lives.
6 In their application to contemporary problems, Schmithausen speaks of the re-establishment of inhibitions such as the awareness that animals should not be harmed. He feels that the stress should be not on "killing as such but rather on needless and cruel killing and on destruction of eco-systems."[99] He also speaks of the chain of causes leading to the consumer, who should be aware of his role and responsibility.

Schmithausen's approach is one of cautious optimism. The main difficulties he faces in proving that Buddhism contains some sort of environmental ethics is the presence of inconsistent aspects and opposing strands as well as the unclear motivation of why certain actions were prescribed in the first place.

Some questions to do with his discussion must be raised at the level of definition. For instance, I find his definition of the word "nature" to be very limited. As mentioned earlier, nature for Schmithausen includes eco-systems, animals and plants, but not man. To understand nature in this sense in Buddhism would be self-defeating. A successful environmental ethics in Buddhism cannot escape including human beings as part of nature with the added qualification of moral accountability. I also disagree with his use of "anthropocentrism," a term that is taken as having negative connotations. Schmithausen works hard to bring out aspects where eco-friendly actions are seen to be done in the interests of human beings, and yet he shuns these for precisely that reason. However, anthropocentrism is not all bad; it is only defeating when seen in a limited sense. All this implies a significant change in thrust and a more careful analysis of the terms employed. Finally, I admire Schmithausen's approach and do agree with him that there is much to be done to determine Buddhism's final position. I understand this in terms of questioning the very foundations of environmental ethics itself.

The "Sceptics": Is there an ecological ethics in Buddhism?

Under this category are included critics of environmental Buddhism. This approach questions the basis of environmental Buddhism and includes the works of scholars such as Ian Harris and Malcolm David Eckel. In the section below I examine the views of Ian Harris who, as one of the most vociferous critics of eco-Buddhism, has made a definite impression in the field of Buddhism and ecology with his meticulous critical analysis. Harris' underlying premise is that the widespread belief about the conformity between nature and man in Buddhism has no doctrinal or historical basis. He finds that metaphysical assumptions concerned with contemporary ecology differ radically from the metaphysics of the Buddha's time making it impossible for an environmental ethics to form a significant part of the Buddhist world-view. During the course of this section, alongside examining his arguments based in early Buddhism, I shall give my reasons for disagreeing with some of his conclusions.

Harris examines Buddhist sources and probes methodological presuppositions that are often relied upon to make eco-Buddhism a valid possibility. In his analysis he encounters the added complication of defining the word "nature." In this context, he brings up Kalupahana's understanding of nature as *dharmatā*, which Kalupahana has treated as a synonym for *pratītyasamutpāda* (Pali: *paṭiccasamuppāda*).[100] Harris finds this rendering difficult to follow for it implies that all conditioned things are subject to *pratītyasamutpāda* and this would make human life part of the world process. From this discussion it is clear that Kalupahana's definition includes human beings whereas Harris obviously wants to keep human beings out of the definition of nature. Harris' reasoning, as can be inferred, is that he is unable to understand how conservation measures can be encouraged in Buddhism if the definition of nature would put human beings at the giving and receiving end. Other than that, he also points out that if nature were represented by *pratītyasamutpāda*, human actions would have unpredictable results. He writes:

> If nature is the realm of complex and mutually conditioning interconnectedness represented by the term *pratītyasamutpāda*, unilateral actions by human agents can have at best unpredictable results. It seems to me that under such conditions we shall be lead to the scepticism of David Hume.[101]

Harris claims that under such circumstances deciding which action is morally better would be virtually impossible. He criticizes Kalupahana as having strayed into deep ecology. Due to this and other methodological problems Harris appears to find more reasonable Karl Barth's definition of nature as ". . . the strange life of beasts and plants, that part of the world which is neither human nor artificial."[102] This definition, he finds, is not only adopted by environmentalist literature but also ensures that human beings are clearly left out of the definition of nature, so that it helps to stay clear of methodological problems such as those faced by Kalupahana.

Harris identifies another problem in equating *pratītyasamutpāda* with "nature."[103] This is to do with the Buddhist analysis being much more radical than any adopted in the West. Harris takes the example of methods adopted to save species from extinction. Environment here symbolizes a "fight against pollution and resource depletion." This is not how Buddhists would view the issue. He finds that though Buddhists may be sympathetic to this cause, their chief concern remains altogether different; to them all objects and entities are given more importance than is due because of ignorance. Life is really about conditioned existence, suffering and constant rebirth in *saṃsāra*, all of which draw attention to human impermanence. Harris believes that on this basis it becomes hard to find support for ecology.[104]

From the above it is clear that Harris is doubtful about finding an equivalent of the word "nature" in Buddhist philosophy. However, if one goes along with Karl Barth's definition and human beings are completely excluded from nature then it will be impossible to find a Buddhist equivalent. (This definition is, in fact, very problematic because of its vagueness on geological features such as rivers and mountains.) It is surely a mistake to assume that we can derive an ecological ethics in Buddhism free from human beings. Buddhism never really spoke of an explicit distinction or resemblance between nature and human beings and it treats them as subject to the same law of causation. An effort to understand nature separately is thus bound to be unsuccessful.

At the outset Harris also draws attention to the fact that since it is fairly obvious that environmental ethics is not an overt feature of Buddhism, finding the right way to approach the issue is important. However, this is difficult to do. He writes at one place that to be seen as having intrinsic worth, a Buddhist-based environmental ethics can adopt two approaches. First, implicit ideas in Buddhist literature could be used to define an explicit ethics. But for Harris this approach is problematic as Buddhist texts are set among "urbanized, educated, monastic elite," and rather unconcerned with the natural world. The second approach, he points out, could be elicited from other traditions that also exist within Buddhism, such as that of the forest-dwelling monk, towards which many have turned for eco-concerns. However, the problem he finds here is that there is no historical evidence that such traditions were ecological. For him both the textual and the anthropological approaches are problematic in their use. Therefore Harris concludes that the best position is confined to appraising the evidence in favour of and against Buddhism as ecological.[105]

In his survey of the material found in the Pali Canon and other literature, Harris proceeds with extreme caution. He scrutinizes examples and comes to the conclusion that they cannot really be construed as environmental at all or that the reasons for positing these cases were entirely different and sometimes even opposed to a respect for nature. The examples that support nature are a rare occurrence. Harris discusses some other examples from the Canon that are often given in support of ecology that he finds only superficially supportive. The ideal king in the *Cakkavatisīhanāda Sutta* is asked to give protection not only to human beings but also to animals and birds. Harris claims that this feature is also found in Kautilya's *Arthaśāstra*, and so is hardly a unique Buddhist feature.[106] In a similar vein, *ahiṃsā* is also seen not to provide much support to Buddhist ecology according to Harris, for rather than being directed outwards to improving the environment, its focus was inward-directed, purification for its practitioner. *Ahiṃsā* was to be followed because it led to a better rebirth for the individual.[107] Furthermore, it is added in the *Vinaya* that the killing of animals did not lead to serious punishment as compared to the killing of other human beings. All this makes Harris recognize that *ahiṃsā* hardly established the inherent worth of animals.

In the case of *mettā* (generally deemed as friendship or universal love) he finds that the advantages of universal love pertained to the practitioner once more and not to the being to which it was extended. He gives the example of the Buddha using *mettā* towards an animal, but it becomes clear that he is only doing so to calm down a dangerous animal (in this case the rampaging bull elephant Nālagiri).[108] Monks spent a lot of time in forests full of wild animals and *mettā* was seen as a way of calming these dangerous animals. The concern, he states, was never the welfare and good of animals. Harris says that *mettā* is often used to construct a Buddhist environmental ethics, but he questions this foundation for there are other examples that prove otherwise; environmental ethics is hardly supported by the fact that practitioners are deterred from giving *mettā* to specific animals and introspective *mettā* hardly goes hand in hand with activism. He adds that *mettā* is also directed towards individuals and not species and this may prove problematic as well.[109] Harris concludes that the Buddhist attitude towards animals is instrumental, suggesting that no intrinsic value is attached to them. Animals, rather, represent impermanence and decay and Buddhists are not really concerned with their preservation.[110] Harris notices that a similar attitude of instrumentality is extended to the treatment of plant life and vegetation. Partial injury to plants seems to be permitted to lay followers for the reason that they had to farm for the sake of food for themselves and the monks. Harris also says that one is unable to find much about the splendour of nature for the reason that the Buddhist world-view is mostly a sombre one where delight in nature only leads to suffering. Wilderness is praised only so far as it is spiritually uplifting.

However, the argument regarding the merit of *mettā* that Harris has framed can be viewed from another point of view as well. If Buddhists truly did not care for the welfare of animals, then the form of protection they suggested may have included the driving away of animals or plain indifference and the cultivation of *mettā* and universal love for inward spiritual growth could have been focused on other sources. But *mettā* is focused on animals and this draws attention to the fact that animals must have had some significance and value. As for the fact that practitioners were deterred from directing *mettā* to individual animals, this could simply be taken to mean that the Buddhists were ensuring non-attachment rather than establishing the worthlessness of animals.

Harris draws attention to the question of whether Buddhist causation can be seen as teleologically meaningful. He gives an example. To be teleologically meaningful, he suggests, would be to prove something like the world is better with black rhinos than without them.[111] He finds that this and similar views take for granted a teleological basis, as also the "predictability of cause/effect relations" which is extremely hard to prove on Buddhist principles. He states that there are two problems:

> In the first place, few of the Buddha's injunctions can be used unambiguously to support environmentalist ends and in the second, the dysteleological character of Buddhist thought militates against anything that could be construed as injecting an "end" or "purpose" in the world.[112]

He goes on to say that it is difficult to see how one can have a Buddhist position on "global warming or the diversity of species." This is a perfectly valid objection and difficult to overcome. However, it is worth contemplating that perhaps the success of an environmental ethic may not depend on the world having an end; it may be limited to refining attitudes. On a different note, Harris adds in a later paper that "since the practice [of *brahma-vihāras*] is directed towards beings within the world, the results are held to be basically mundane . . ."[113] His implication is that even though, through the practice of these activities, high principles of morality are expressed, the practices are limited to the mundane world. This implies that Buddhist principles of morality do not play a role in Buddhism's ultimate supra-mundane goal. That this is not necessarily the case will be illustrated in a later chapter.

Harris remains essentially critical of environmental Buddhism (even though some positive features are occasionally mentioned). His arguments are faultless but I have to admit to finding his position austere. An examination of canonical material, no doubt, proves that Buddhism is primarily concerned with its soteriology rather than worldly matters, but what exactly soteriology implies needs to be clarified. To base conclusions on just one aspect and ignore other positive elements is undoubtedly limiting.

Overview

An analysis of secondary literature to determine the nature of environmental discourse in early Buddhism shows that defining the latter is no easy task. The issues that govern both Buddhism and ecology are extremely complicated and those that have been debated on in the above enquiry are simply an indication of the immensity of the issue. Complicating matters further is that none of the four categories outlined above – Partisans, Positivists, Sanguines and Sceptics – in final analysis have reached entirely satisfactory conclusions. The discovery of one unified view or a view that is truer is an almost unattainable task. The differences and ambiguity that exist in the reading of texts leave their indelible mark on any outcome. Due to these factors a justification for environmentalism in Buddhism can become seriously restricted.

Having identified and examined some strengths and weaknesses of what has so far been accomplished in Buddhism and ecology, I propose a different approach. My approach intends to address two concerns. The first is to do with an impartial discussion of the implication of nature as employed in the history of philosophy. "Nature" is neither clear-cut nor unequivocal and its complexity must be acknowledged to avoid unnecessary problems. Only after analysing the term for what it is can nature's significance in Buddhism be comprehended. The second concern centres on how moral attitudes and ethical progress influence actions that then have the power to influence the state of the environment. Though both these spheres have been touched upon to some degree, they have not been given the attention they deserve or developed to a significant extent.[114] In what follows I wish to contribute something of value to both these areas in the hope that the discourse on Buddhism and ecology strengthens progressively.

These concerns are reflected thematically in the chapters that follow. Chapter 2 aims at a deeper understanding of the many facets of the term "nature" in order that general presuppositions about it stand questioned. A description of nature is sought that corresponds with Buddhism and is acceptable to general environmental theory. Many matters of concern discussed in environmental traditions in the West are employed to identify problems concerning the idea of nature in Buddhist environmental ethics. A part of the Buddhist position is then discussed. Chapter 3 continues the discussion on the theme of nature in Buddhism. The concept of anthropocentrism is focused on as well to uncover some fundamental foundations on the basis of which environmental discourse can be built ever more diligently within Buddhism. Chapter 4 examines the ethical structure of early Buddhism to verify whether Buddhist tenets can persuade a moral agent to act ecologically. It proposes that the early Buddhist approach to nature be looked upon as an environmental virtue ethics. In Chapter 5 Buddhist virtues and vices are examined in more detail to understand their nature clearly. Some difficulties in establishing general virtues as environmental virtues are discussed in the course of this chapter as well. Support for the thesis proposed is also gained from the *Jātakas*, a detailed study of which is included in Chapter 6.[115] My conclusion recapitulates briefly the sense of nature presented in the above chapters and states that an environmental ethics can be established in early Buddhist philosophy only once the true foundations of Buddhist thought and understanding are identified.

2

NATURE: A "CONSERVATIONIST" ANALYSIS

But it can also be put differently; and that is important.
L. Wittgenstein, *Philosophical Remarks*

Certain notions and concepts that are used in the theoretical discourse of environmental ethics are often found to be complicated and hard to characterize. Scholars writing on Buddhism and nature have also incorporated many such ideas and concepts (as was seen in the last chapter), but have failed to draw a clearer picture regarding their theoretical usage leading to many misinterpretations and obscurities. So while considering the presence of an environmental ethics in Buddhism, it becomes vitally important to know and understand what these concepts imply in theory. Since an exhaustive selection is not possible only two frequently occurring and very fundamental concepts that have added value in the Buddhist context will be discussed in the course of this chapter and the next; these are nature and anthropocentrism. Each of these concepts can be interpreted in several different ways leading to diverse outcomes such that can change the course and focus of environmental study entirely. Once at least some of these ways are identified, a detailed analysis of the occurrence of these concepts in Buddhism and their impact will be attempted. Related issues of value and future generations, constantly reiterated in environmental ethics, are also included in this analysis.

Through attempts to understand the way nature and anthropocentrism express themselves in Buddhism, a semblance of a Buddhist environmental theory begins to appear. And so this analysis is not purely about characterizing nature; it also plays an inevitable role in the construction of an environmental discourse in Buddhism that is able to express itself autonomously and articulately. Once again, as mentioned in Chapter 1, I am aware of the risk of of juxtaposing the notions and ideas of one world view (contemporary environmental ethics) onto another (ancient Buddhist philosophy) that do not clearly belong there. Yet I find that I cannot escape this avenue altogether if I am to arrive at a conclusion that is meaningful in the world today. I must however admit at the outset of this and the next chapter that in seeking to clarify these concepts I have tended to work through a Buddhist mind-set in that my understanding of nature and anthropocentrism is influenced unwittingly by Buddhist ideas. I have rethought and challenged some given categories because I find that early Buddhism proves to be quite elusive and hard to pin down in terms of standard environmental categories.

The meaning and scope of nature

Outlining the meaning and scope of nature is a requisite for most theories of environment that seek philosophical approval. As a result "nature" is the subject of much scrutiny and conjecture for modern day environmental philosophers. Etymologically, the word "nature" is a derivative of the Latin word *natura*. The word *physis* is its Greek equivalent. Both terms refer to origin, growth and development of some sort. Thus, nature initially implied the changing character of the physical world. Soon it came to suggest all physical entities. It ought to be added here that the *Oxford Latin Dictionary* defines *natura* in mainly two senses, first as the physical world and creation and secondly, as the characteristics of a person or a thing.[1] This twofold meaning is also highlighted in Greek dictionaries that define *physis* as either the world or a kind of disposition.[2] It is the former understanding of nature in both definitions that is of concern to an environmental philosopher. The idea of nature as the world or as a collection of entities that exist on this planet is what is going to be developed in this study.

Nature is often depicted as closely related to the concept of ecology. Ecology comes from the word "oekologie" and was employed to express the organization and existence of living beings in their environment. The word, used for the first time in 1869, is attributed to the German biologist Ernst Haeckel. Derived from the Greek word *oikos* meaning "house" and *logos* meaning "knowledge" ecology is now simply treated as a study focused on the different facets of the multitudinous organisms existing in the world. It has strong scientific leanings. However it does go beyond exclusive scientific usage and can be understood in several different ways. Yrjo Haila and Richard Levins point out some important variations.[3] Ecology as *nature* is the basis of all physical and organic existence and can be taken to represent all objects and organisms of the world. Ecology as *science* refers to a study of the natural systems of organisms – their interactions as well as their reactions to external factors. This is the most common use of the term. Ecology may also be taken as *idea*, and this pertains to ideas about human existence which come from human beliefs or knowledge of nature. Finally, ecology as *political activities* involves assessing ecological ideals (and in this can be included environmental activism) and getting society to consent to their practice. These writers imply that all meanings stand independent and incorporate different aspects, even though connections between them are not ruled out.

Ecology as nature is of importance in this work and I shall not be touching on ecology's scientific, ideological and political aspects.

An awareness of the word "environment" (an offshoot of "environ" or surrounding) is also required. The idea of environment generally refers to the natural world or specifically to the surrounding in which beings live, thrive and perish. All three conceptions – nature, ecology and environment – have their own individual peculiarities and traits and many intended senses but have also come to represent the physical/natural world in general. In this latter sense they share much common ground. Without going into any more detail in this work and at the risk of oversimplification I will consider only this common ground i.e. that sense that conveys the physical world. I use the ideas of nature, ecology and environment interchangeably to represent only the above. I hope to arrive in the following section at a broader understanding of the concept or idea of nature *et al.* whose description is for the most part applicable in nearly all given theories of environment.

Historical approach

A minimal definition of nature based on etymology as given above proves to be inadequate, as it does not shed light on the sense in which it is being used in environmental theories. Neither has meta-ethical enquiry provided "nature" with an exact sense or focus. In fact in the history of philosophy the concept of nature has developed in numerous ways, as has the attitude towards the so-called natural part of the world. This has led John Passmore to remark:

> The ambiguity of the word "nature" . . . is by no means a merely accidental product of etymological confusions or conflations: it faithfully reflects the hesitancies, the doubts and the uncertainties, with which men have confronted the world around them.[4]

Thus a wide diversity of ideas has existed in relation to nature that is more about beliefs about the world than "etymological confusions". By determining such beliefs in the writings of philosophers, whether or not they consciously included environmental concern, one can be led to the sense in which they comprehend or would comprehend nature. I follow the views of three philosophers – Angelica Krebs, René Descartes and Plato – for precisely this reason: to determine the sense of nature exuding from their belief system. My investigation in each case is deliberately brief as my aim remains to convey an idea rather than to provide a detailed exposition. I have selected these philosophers primarily because their understanding represents three different ways in which nature can be looked upon. It must also be especially noted that they belong to diametrically different periods of time.

NATURE: A "CONSERVATIONIST" ANALYSIS

Angelica Krebs

The recent phenomenal rise of environmental philosophy and ethics coincides with the realization that the environment is wearing away rapidly and that natural resources will not last forever. In keeping with this, most contemporary conceptions of nature and ecology have a fixed agenda. This agenda is well and succinctly expressed by the German philosopher Angelica Krebs in her book *Ethics of Nature* (1999) where in an introductory section she tries to determine the definition of "nature." Aware that countless definitions of nature exist she says ". . . we will search for a meaning of the concept which is relevant to the practical issues of nature conservation in which we are interested."[5] Thus nature must imply conservation unequivocally. Based on her aim, I call her approach to nature (and others similar to it) the "conservationist" one.

Krebs contrasts "nature" (as referring to something not made by man) with "artefact" (which refers to everything man made). Thus seas and mountains are nature whereas televisions and trains are artefacts. She claims that whereas pure nature (free of any human beings) can exist, a pure artefact (free of nature) is not possible at all, as everything human beings make depends on materials acquired from nature. She finds that in the present world the nature that is to be conserved cannot remain limited to pure nature only, but must also include things like forests and gardens that have been planted by man. However, things like automobiles and aeroplanes are artefacts, not included in nature at all and thus conservation does not apply to them. She also finds that the boundary between nature and artefact remains fuzzy due to unclear cases such as "how much genetic manipulation would turn tulips or mice into artefacts."[6]

Krebs goes on to exclude another two factors as a further qualification to nature as an object of environmental concern. These are the cosmos (due to the fact that it is out of human control) and the human body (which is studied under a separate discipline altogether). Environmental concern thus does not include the supernatural, human or artificial. She suggests calling nature "oikos" or "the environment" to exclude the above two aspects, but sees complications in replacing the term. Eventually, Krebs arrives at terminology that encompasses environmental concern: "ethics of nature." She defines the ethics of nature in two senses; in the wide sense it "addresses *all moral issues of our conduct toward that part of the world which has not been made by human beings* and is under human influence" and in a narrow sense concerns "the *nonhuman* part of the world which has not been created by human beings."[7] The second sense includes animal and environmental ethics. She also draws a contrast between the conservation of nature and its cultivation. The former implies not only leaving nature alone but actively contributing to its well-being. Cultivation, on the other hand, implies improving nature for the sake of human beings. Conservation aims at the good of nature and cultivation at the good of human beings.

Krebs' analysis is of significance here for it draws attention to some important ideas that define ecology and environmental ethics today. Conservation is a central concern. That most theories of the environment are overtly (or implicitly) focused on conservation is a fairly obvious feature that needs no further evidence. The discipline of environmental ethics has acquired prominence due to the attention it pays to safeguarding the environment. However, the Krebbian formula is not above reproach. Many questions arise about the nature of artefacts. Though Krebs admits that the line between "nature" and "artefacts" is "fuzzy," but that one can "fare quite well in many contexts with concepts that lack sharp boundaries" yet at another place she says that the definition of nature as "governed by causal laws is too wide" as it includes cars and atomic generators that do not fall within the bounds of nature conservation.[8] Krebs omits to consider boundaries in the latter case. Ian Harris also draws attention to Krebs' dichotomy appearing false as paintings and temples (i.e. artefacts) are willingly conserved even though they are not included in nature.[9]

Krebs' analysis raises another taxing issue of a slightly different nature. Krebs envisions conservation as the distinct rationale for her ethics of nature. However, if, hypothetically speaking, human beings lived in a perfect natural world, would her "ethics of nature" have any value or meaningful application at all? Can this implication be taken to mean that detrimental eco-activities that are powerless to disturb nature as a whole, however extreme, attract only moral indifference? Though this is a pure conjecture and Krebs' analysis may not allow for it, such a view would be difficult to sustain were it backed by the conservationist. In defence of Krebs and others who may fall within this category it seems reasonable to claim on their behalf that moral restrictions must apply indiscriminately no matter what the objective.

René Descartes

Going back to the end of the sixteenth century, this was a time when the popularity of mathematics had reached its peak and it was being absorbed by all disciplines of study. Philosophers were no exception and they made a liberal use of mathematical formulae and methods. In fact many mathematicians were accomplished philosophers and vice versa. As for the natural world, since mathematics extended an insidious hold over natural studies too, it came to be viewed as perfunctory. This approach was thus quite different from the conservationist one described above. Nature conservation had not developed into a serious concern at this time and there was no vision pertaining to a future consisting of depleting resources. However questions about the relation between man and the world were rife. And it is in such questions that an idea of nature can be sensed. This approach is somewhat well represented in the well-known French mathematician and philosopher René Descartes' philosophy and will become clear from the discussion below.

Descartes supported a dualism between mind and matter. Mind and body were the two constituents of the world and were wholly independent and separate of one another. Their characteristics were contrary to one another. Minds had no physical dimension, did not occupy physical space, were not extended and were considered immaterial. Minds were characterized as conscious, thinking entities. Descartes says in *Discourse on the Method* that ". . . I was a substance the whole essence or nature of which is to think, and that for its existence there is no need of any place, nor does it depend on any material thing. . . ."[10] The indication is that not only is consciousness bestowed with the nature of thinking but also that it can survive without the body, thereby making it wholly independent. On the other hand the bodies, whose properties were quite unlike those of the mind, occupied physical space, were extended and considered material. Bodies were without any thinking capacity and therefore, without consciousness. Though Descartes does not specifically say so entities such as mountains and seas to the more organic flora and fauna can be included under the category of body with extension and without mind. Mind, however, was clearly outside and above the bodily category. The general belief that follows from Cartesian philosophy of the division between mind and body is that only human beings with the gift of consciousness (even though made of mind and of body) were of supreme value.

Once again Descartes' philosophy has its share of difficulties. Descartes encountered many logical problems, the most urgent focused on the interaction of the mind and body. Descartes was unable to clearly explain how two things whose characteristics were so opposed to each other were able to interact effectively. Their influence on each other was palpable – mental exhaustion leading to physical fatigue and physical pampering leading to mental pleasure are common instances of interaction encountered by human beings. However, how one event could lead to the other could not be fathomed on Cartesian principles. Even during his lifetime Descartes struggled to find a solution and rather unconvincingly insisted that the union was an inexplicable phenomenon. He attempted to introduce God to dissolve the problem of interaction, but this introduction remains a controversial one. Another problem raised by a contemporary of Descartes, Antoine Arnauld, was that the mind as an independent entity, without body, was impossible unless it could be specifically seen and proved as complete and whole without being linked with a physical substrate.[11] Arnauld was most likely reacting to Descartes claim in the *Meditations* that ". . . it is certain that this I [that is to say, my soul by which I am what I am], is entirely and absolutely distinct from my body, and can exist without it."[12] Contemporary philosophers such as Gilbert Ryle have criticized Descartes' dualism vociferously saying that the conception of a spirit or mind in a mechanical body is confused and the result of a category mistake. Ryle's twentieth-century book *Concept of Mind* in fact gained much attention for its anti-Cartesian stand.

One of the extreme outcomes (mentioned by several supporters of animal welfare) of the Cartesian outlook that had a direct environmental effect was that animals could be reduced to non-conscious bodies. Speaking of animals in the *Discourse*, Descartes wrote ". . . they have no reason at all, and that it is nature which acts in them according to the disposition of their organs just as a clock, which is only composed of wheels and weights, is able to tell the hours . . . more correctly than we can do with all our wisdom."[13] Descartes appeared to be implying that animals were like unconscious objects that could not suffer pain; they only went through procedural crashes. The mindless disposition of animals vindicated the utmost violence towards them. Tom Regan elaborates this point and in his rather candid discussion is particularly critical of Descartes' account that animals had no consciousness whatsoever. He goes on to say that it was this understanding that led to the somewhat revolting treatment of animals by Descartes' followers that broke all bounds of commonsense. Regan quotes a passage by an unknown contemporary of Descartes:

> The (Cartesian) scientists administered beatings to dogs with perfect indifference and made fun of those who pitied the creatures as if they felt pain. They said the animals were clocks; that the cries they emitted when struck were only the noise of a little spring that had been touched, but that the whole body was without feeling. They nailed the poor animals up on boards by their four paws to vivisect them to see the circulation of blood which was a great subject of controversy.[14]

It is no surprise that animal liberationists such as Regan regard Descartes in an unfavourable light with regard to animals and believe that depraved attitudes followed quite logically from Cartesian thought.

Coming back to the principles of Cartesian philosophy there was constant focus on the importance and significance of the mind. Descartes' ideas imply the identification of nature with body and the inferiority of both to the mind. This has led nature philosopher John Passmore to remark that of the two leading traditions in modern Western thought, the one that is Cartesian in inspiration regards matter as inert and passive, "and that man's relation to it is that of an absolute despot, reshaping and reforming what has in it no inherent powers of resistance. . . ."[15] Mindless nature, since treated at par with the body in the Cartesian universe, is similarly of secondary importance and must be managed by the mind. The lesser importance of the body and nature, and the superiority of mind stand in stark contrast in this understanding such that the worth of the former falls by an alarming proportion. Herein are situated the roots of marginalization by which I simply imply a reduced value or worth of nature in any given world-view. Therefore this approach can be labelled the "marginalization of nature" or simply "marginal-ism" (to coin a phrase). Even though there is no doubt that Descartes, a product of his times, introduced pertinent arguments not only with regard to mind and body but also regarding the rational understanding of reality and the position of man, his understanding of the body left many disappointed. When Descartes' views are applied to environmental ethics in the sense described above, a view marginalizing nature is arrived at.[16]

Plato

Having discussed the conservationist and marginal-ist ideas about nature, a third idea is encountered that is marked by its rather unusual nature. Having labelled it cosmological, I take the example of the ancient Greek philosopher Plato's work *Timaeus* to showcase its features. Some may find the selection of Plato controversial as he displayed no obvious nature philosophy; in fact many claim that he is a precursor to Cartesian dualism and mathematical analysis, and so for that reason also to Cartesian marginal-ism.[17] However the *Timaeus* does give due regard to nature and other physiological aspects and allows for a perspective on nature to be developed. The possibility of isolating an idea of nature in the *Timaeus* cannot be ruled out. This view has been gathering support recently and it has been said that ". . . Platonic ecology provides a distinctive and fruitful approach to environmental thinking. . . ."[18]

Plato's own writings follow those of the pre-socratic philosophers who preceded him and whose most important contribution lay in their search for a primordial first factor or *arche* that, though itself unchanging, could explain the changes and modifications that beset the everyday world of experience. Several first factors were suggested. For instance of the pre-socratic Milesian philosophers, Thales pictured the notion of water as the ultimate real and Anaximenes imagined air as the primary substance. Plato posited his own understanding of an unchanging reality. He spoke of the theory of Forms and his account continues to fascinate scholars even today. Briefly this theory implied that the ever changing objects of the sensible world were an image or a copy of the unchanging; the unchanging had an independent transcendent reality. The latter were referred to as Forms or Ideas. Though Plato did not delve into the relation between the Forms and sensible objects he believed true reality to belong only to Forms; the reality of objects was established through their participation in Forms. The worry here is that in according full reality only to the Forms this theory begins to appear to reduce and reject the value of the experiential world (as Descartes' did) and thus is not as supportive of environment causes. But scholars beg to differ and it has been remarked by Gabriela Carone that Plato "is *not* denying the reality of the sensible realm. . . . The sensible realm . . . is not classed under non-being, but between being and non-being, and even then there is no agreement that this means between being existent and not being existent. . . ."[19] Thus caution must be exercised in denying the value of the world; the sensible world never lost its significance for Plato as is adequately endorsed in his accounts on politics and education.[20] And that he speaks of the world of Forms and the sensible world does not necessarily make him a dualist either. John Burnet writes:

> What we say of the world is not, indeed, the truth, but it may be more or less like the truth and it is our business to make it as like the truth as possible. The boundary-line between the intelligible and the merely sensible is not a fixed one, and the sensible may be made progressively intelligible. . . . Unfortunately, however, his followers were not able to rise to this point of view, and Plato has been generally credited with an absolute dualism.[21]

In all fairness the works of Plato have been analysed and understood in many, many different ways and so arriving at one final view is impossible. A study of Forms makes this clear. Moreover awareness about Plato's own changing views as he progresses in time from one work to the next is required. It is with the theory of Forms as background that the *Timaeus* must be considered.

In the *Timaeus* Plato veers towards natural science more than ever. The *Timaeus* best embodies Plato's cosmological speculations.[22] The account of creation is deliberated upon thoughtfully by Plato through empirical observation and mathematical calculation. The *Timaeus* accepts the world of Forms and a Demiurge as the creator of the universe (though not of matter) and then devotes itself to explaining the formation of the experiential world.[23] The world is modelled on a complex Form that is itself an amalgamation of other subordinate Forms. The latter Forms are of four species whose members live in the sensible world – these are heavenly bodies including earth, birds, fish and animals that move on land.[24] The created world is living, intelligent and self-sufficient. The universe has a cosmic soul with sacred value; it is complete, ageless and free of sickness.[25] Human beings are modelled on the universe, their soul on the cosmic soul (even though human beings are less perfect).[26] The soul is considered of higher value than body both in case of universe and of human beings. Sickness can happen in human beings when balance and proportion are disturbed and ways of re-attaining equilibrium are discussed. Other beings (such as animals) do exist as well to complement perfect creation but their value depends on how close their being is to the body and soul of the cosmos.[27] Plants are living, sentient entities with souls and without reason.[28] There is mention of the material elements in many sections, though no detailed accounts are given.

The true essence of Plato's philosophy lies in his focus on the universe and not man alone. In his approach he covers the entirety of creation and beyond. Carone believes ". . . for someone to appreciate the value of anything in the universe, particularly in cases of things which we call inanimate, one must come to appreciate it as part of a larger, dignified whole."[29] Even the presence of transcendental Forms does not have a damaging impact on a concern for nature. It has been remarked by a defender of environmentalism in Greek philosophy that:

> The question he [Plato] would want to ask, when confronted with the massive destruction of the environment that is a feature of the modern world would be: Is exposure to such destruction liable to make us morally better or worse? And there is little doubt that he would believe that it makes us worse, for he has, he thinks, an objective standard, the Form of the Good, by which he can measure correctly, and not in some fallible way depending on some fallible judgement of a man or a group of men picked at random, what makes the soul better and what makes it worse.[30]

So the theory of Forms does have its positive benefits. The focus of the sensible world too is on all aspects of creation to make it more complete, be it human beings, animals or plants.[31] Plato's thought thus suggests harmonious evolution with a hierarchy (of creatures) that is based on rationality as an underlying principle. Hierarchy is supported by scholars like Carone too. Individuals and creation as a whole are valuable objects. Another important outcome of Plato's philosophy is the recognition that human beings are not on the outside of nature but rather a part of it.

In a book entitled *Plato's Universe*, Gregory Vlastos writes "In English *cosmos* is a linguistic orphan, a noun without a parent verb. Not so in Greek, which has the active, transient verb, *kosmeō*: to set in order, to marshal, to arrange."[32] Plato's cosmos is *kosmeō* and it is on this basis alone that his approach to environmental ethics may be considered to be the "cosmological" one. Plato's sense of nature is one that is defined by its driven-ness. Creation implies a continuous striving for perfection in such a way that everything contributes to that perfection. Furthermore through his theory of creation he imparts an inclusive blueprint that extends to all in existence fulfilling their respective roles. This understanding suggests that the whole scene must be surveyed simultaneously rather than by observing portions of nature in a fragmented manner. The existence of a unifying factor or principle or process must be admitted. Madonna Adams can be seen to support this view to some degree when, while questioning the function of the Demiurge in Plato's philosophy, she writes:

> . . . Plato's interest lies, not in explaining the absolute origin of matter, but rather in explaining why the universe exists as we know it, namely as a beautiful and ordered whole or cosmos. By asserting that the Demiurge, the maker and shaper of the universe, is intelligent and

> good, Timaeus can assert that the world, his product, is ordered, intelligible, beautiful and good. This implies that the world has causes that function with some regularity and therefore we can understand it, since knowledge requires a grasp of causes of a process or change.[33]

The above description of the *Timaeus* is evocative (as also suggested by Carone) of the cosmos as a whole being Plato's central concern. It may be added here that were one to deliberate on Plato's rather limited explicit analysis of the means of protecting nature, a misinterpretation of his views concerning nature would follow quite naturally. However on the cosmological plane his position on nature becomes clear. Nature is acknowledged in the *Timaeus*, but only at the cosmological level. Nature and cosmos cannot be isolated as independent ideas within Plato's cosmological framework.

In accepting a cosmological understanding of nature however, an awareness of one major drawback is required. If cosmic nature, in general, includes shared processes, evolution and the inclusion of everything to which these apply, then those products that harm the cause of nature, but at the same time are subject to such laws, must be accepted as a legitimate part of the cosmos. This defeats the purpose of an environmental ethics for the simple reason that it provides a justification for the presence of environmental ills. I believe, hypothetically speaking of course, that Plato would address this problem, first, by asserting the existence of the Demiurge who ensures an ordered and beautiful cosmos without environmental evils at the stage of creation and secondly, through his ethical theory at the sensible stage of subsistence and striving, which is more developed in works other than the *Timaeus* (for instance, in *The Republic*). In addition it can be kept in mind that "Plato's argument is not that there is no ugliness or disorder in the world, but that they are local and insignificant compared with the marvellous organization of the cosmos as a whole."[34] I establish later that though early Buddhism is dominantly cosmological in its understanding of nature and faces a similar drawback, it deals with the problem through its inherent virtue ethics. In such an ethics the existence of certain values is challenged, hence also challenging their corresponding non-environmental physical effects.[35]

Overview

These then are three possible interpretations of nature in the history of philosophy. It is especially noteworthy that on a preliminary reading the first is very positive to the cause, the second apathetic and third obscure and yet focused on the natural process. The third does not ensure ethical action towards nature, but clearly neither does it disallow it. (However the overwhelming respect for the processes of nature makes it more inclined to the former than the latter.) The above analysis is important for it demonstrates the justifiable possibility of a third interpretation of nature which is neither positive nor negative; it just states the way the world is (with its processes and struggles) and the direction it takes or ought to take. Understanding nature and environment on this interpretation is unusual, to say the least, but immensely rewarding for in philosophies such as Plato's where though one might have a sense of nature it is always hard to lay claim to the latter's rather elusive character.

Awareness is also needed in extending these approaches to nature to other theories and systems. To look for one approach to nature in a theory where another is more fitting is problematic. For instance, were Descartes' philosophy examined for only its cosmological value surely no sensible solution would be found. Similarly were Plato's *Timaeus* studied for its principles pertaining to the conservation and protection of nature's resources the hope of finding much information would be small. On this understanding to suppose that the beliefs of Plato or Descartes have nothing to add to the environmental debate is unfair.

Apart from exercising caution with regard to the above problem some important conclusions can be drawn from each interpretation of nature. The recent conservationist view differs from the other two approaches in that its most important objective is the protection and conservation of nature. It seeks justifications and arguments that support conservation. It examines human behaviour to determine its compatibility with a concern for nature and suggests ways and means of establishing or increasing concern. This is the most obvious approach to nature philosophy; it is direct and focused on environment alone. The concepts it employs seek to clarify matters of environmental concern. Nature is an independent idea deserving of independent study. Human beings, in general, may be placed by such a view as beyond the realm of nature. Though the particulars of this approach may vary from thinker to thinker, the final focus remains the same – "the well-being, the well-functioning, the health, the "good" of non-human nature."[36]

The view that marginalizes and devalues nature, that treats mind and consciousness as all-important, nurtures tendencies that appear to allow the most damage to the environment. It encourages an attitude of duality. The lesser must serve the purpose of the higher. By granting a superior place to man therefore, those who hold this attitude would possess reasonable grounds for the exploitation of the natural world. No recognition of the contribution of nature is likely to find a place if environmental discourse is built along similar lines. Notwithstanding these comments, the approach of marginalization does have a positive angle. It draws attention to the relation between man and nature and is forthright enough to admit that man is somehow different. It does not undervalue this difference or deny it and, in this, its attitude is special and practical. From one point of view, understanding the relation and difference between human beings and non-human beings is central to environmental ethics and the position draws attention to this aspect.

From the cosmological perspective the importance of nature lies in its being a part of a whole or in sharing certain commonalities or aspects. The cosmological perspective includes human beings and other beings and non-beings in its fold. Of course the role of human beings would differ according to the cosmological theory under scrutiny. In Platonic terms human beings and non-human beings were a part of the universe and so ultimately unified within one cosmos but human beings are endowed with rationality and so have a special status. There is recognition of hierarchy, therefore, in Platonic thought. A cosmological interpretation may also be reminiscent of a greater transcendental objective. This may sometimes confuse the issue for an environmental ethicist for it conceals the importance of what other features may truly mean and how they contribute to the objective. However, at heart, Plato and many others who can be classified as cosmologists are simply searching for a deeper meaning of existence; their aim is not to denigrate phenomenal existence in any way. It only appears this way due to absorption in the former alone.

It is a possibility that a combination of two or three approaches may appear in one particular theory. The above discussion also clearly does not imply that the search for conservationist tendencies in Platonic and Cartesian thought can be neglected. Conservation is an important principle and ideal and any even remotely positive sign in its support must be considered. At the same time the unavailability of such a sign may not be necessarily debilitating to the quest of finding the meaning of nature. The three approaches – cosmological, marginal-ist and conservationist – together embody some important aspects of nature. However, these positions remain limited to representing only part of the debate on nature and are not necessarily inclusive of all that has been said on nature so far. Inevitably a slightly more detailed analysis would reveal the existence of countless other views and influences. Awareness that Plato, Descartes and Krebs do not embrace all facets of their respective position needs to be maintained as well. However, their importance remains crucial for indicating specific issues that define these approaches. Additionally caution must be exercised in classifying any position as more or less successful. Finally the three views are not just limited to categorizing nature within a certain framework: they contribute to a sustained environmental discourse as was mentioned in the introduction to this chapter. What remains important also is the possible power any and every of these approaches may possess to transform attitudes and eventually transform the state of the natural world. Having said this, I must confess that the following work relies heavily on the cosmological perspective for a number of reasons that will be explained in due course. Yet, marginalizing and conservationist tendencies cannot be excluded, their presence must be considered in the Buddhist conception of nature.

Nature in early Buddhism: The conservationist approach

In the light of the above discussion I will consider now which approach to nature exists within or can be best adapted to the Buddhist world-view. Accordingly, my objective is twofold. First, I will show that the conservationist view is hard to establish, even though some positive support for it can be garnered within the literature that is being considered. Secondly, I will demonstrate that understanding nature from the cosmological point of view is a much more logical and valid stance for the early Buddhists. The cosmological understanding in its turn creates a solid foothold for building on a genuine environmental ethics. Possible tendencies marginalizing nature will also be examined within Buddhist literature to determine their significance and bearing.

As for the conservationist approach, the literature of early Buddhism under consideration does not contain a definition of "nature" that coincides with, or is at least similar to, that proposed by Angelica Krebs. However, the *Nikāyas* and other texts contain references to natural entities that can be possibly considered conservation-oriented. Expanding on the earlier discussion, a conservationist approach to nature implies specific ways in which human beings can act for the sake of the different entities that make up the environment in order to safeguard and protect them from harm (in other words, conserve them). With this intention, this section will analyse some of the references from early Buddhism that specify how human beings ought to behave towards other species and objects of nature – namely animals, plants and material or geological entities such as rivers and mountains – to determine the Buddhist contribution to the spirit of conservation. Two additional factors will also be considered in support of the conservationist view. These are (1) the aesthetic descriptions of nature that can be found featuring in the texts and (2) the use of nature-based metaphors and analogies to present and elucidate their point of view more emphatically. These two factors – aesthetic descriptions and metaphorical inclusion of nature – can be seen as having an influence on conservation if it is assumed that they reflect and express a Buddhist image of nature that otherwise remains concealed.

Problems for the conservationist are encountered right from the start. This is because direct examples of specific human behaviour towards the non-human world are, unfortunately, described in no detail. Furthermore specifying environmental attitudes in existent examples also poses many problems. The matter is considerably complicated as the behaviour towards non-human beings is mostly qualified by some condition, such as the action being done for one's own benefit rather than for environmental reasons. Moreover, there are unavoidable interpretational complications as well for most examples can be interpreted in more than one way due to either use of language or an unexpressed intention in the light of which the example may be justifiably re-examined. The latter is a common problem in environmental philosophy and Allan Greenbaum has expressed this very effectively, when he speaks of oppositions found in ecological descriptions:

> . . . *On the one hand*, if humans are not above the rest of nature, then humans have no right to dominate and exploit the rest of nature (no special status); *on the other hand*, if humans are not above the rest of nature, then humans have no special obligations to sacrifice their interests to those of non-humans or natural systems (no double standard). *On the one hand*, nature is organic, hence nature is complex, ordered, or vulnerable; *on the other hand*, nature is organic, hence nature is monstrous, dirty, squalid, gooey, rank, bleeding, killing and dying. *On the one hand*, nature is sentient and alive, so nature can be creative, can be hurt, can be a victim or friend; *on the other hand*, nature is sentient and alive, so nature can be cruel or evil or an adversary. . . .[37]

In the Buddhist context too it is not easy to distinguish which sense is being referred to due to the many concerns that must be simultaneously addressed.

This confusion is immediately clear from the following example. The *Aṅguttara Nikāya* relates the story of a certain monk who was bitten by a snake and subsequently died. When this was told to the Buddha he justified the incident by saying that the man did not practice universal love (*mettā*) towards snakes.[38] He then advised the other monks to practice universal love towards snakes for their own protection. The *Sutta* contains the following verses:

> Let me have universal love for the footless; and for those with two feet; let me have universal love for those with four feet; and for those with many feet.
>
> Let not the footless harm me; nor those with two feet; let not the four-footed harm me; nor those with many feet.[39]

The verse goes on to say that the person who practices *mettā* towards these beings safeguards himself against being harmed by them. This verse can be taken as implying three things. First, that kindness is to be practised towards animals. Secondly, it is to be practised for one's own protection only for the verse does not specify that it should be practiced for the sake of animals. And thirdly, the *Sutta* includes other categories of animals besides snakes – in that it mentions the footless and many footed beings. The setting of the *Sutta* and the conclusions are compatible with the Buddhist world-view of practising compassion and kindness towards all beings regardless. The show of compassion and kindness towards animals may be considered an element of conservation, as this is one effective way in which animals could be safeguarded against potential harm. However, another interpretation of the same verse (also noted by other scholars) makes it appear detrimental to the environmental cause as it highlights the motive of kindness as a selfish one. This interpretation implies that kindness to animals is not required where there is no room for personal benefit, thereby making the example distinctly non-environmental. As for the unexpressed historical context, this verse has elicited the following remark from Schmithausen:

> It is tempting to *develop* this feature into an ecological interpretation of *mettā*, i.e. into a concept of *mettā* as entailing an appreciation and protection of species *as such*. But *historically* the transition from an alliance or . . . friendship contract with wild animals (or nature) to a concept of *mettā* explicitly excluding in its aim the protection of species . . . is . . . problematic. Alliances . . . are hardly made because of a positive evaluation of tribes and species . . . but rather because these tribes and species are composed of virtually dangerous individuals. . . .[40]

If one were to follow the motivation of selfish concern as explained earlier or Schmithausen's interpretation then this verse can hardly be used legitimately to convey the conservationist point of view.

Animals

The most compelling support for protection of animals undoubtedly comes from the Buddha's opposition to sacrifice. The Buddhist opposition in the *Suttas* is seemingly a reaction against the Brahmanical tradition that encouraged animal sacrifice at the time. Such sacrifice is severely disparaged in the *Kūṭadanta Sutta* of the *Dīgha Nikāya*. The description of a sacrifice is given here which contains no slaughter:

> In this sacrifice, Brahmin, no cows were killed, no goats were killed, no cocks and pigs were killed, nor were the diverse living creatures subjected to slaughter, trees were not cut down for sacrificial posts nor were grasses mown . . . The sacrifice was pursued with clarified butter, oil, fresh butter, curds, honey and molasses.[41]

Thus, it appears as if sacrifice was acceptable as long as no animals and plants were harmed. A similar theme is echoed in a discourse given to Brahmin Ujjaya. Here it is said that great seers do not attend sacrifices where goats, cows and pigs are killed; but they do attend ones that involve no such slaughter.[42] In another instance when Buddha learns that King Pasenadi has planned a grand sacrifice ceremony involving the slaughter of animals, he comments that such sacrifices bring no great result.[43] In fact it is categorically stated elsewhere that animal sacrifices rather lead to three diseases – longing (*icchā*), hunger (*anasaṇa*) and decrepitude (*jarā*) – that eventually multiply into ninety eight diseases.[44]

It may possibly follow from this, as cited above, that the condemnation of animal sacrifice was only a reaction to the elaborate rites and rituals of the Brahmanical culture. Buddhists may also have believed that no *kammic* good followed from such sacrifice. Undoubtedly, and as commonly acknowledged, these appear as the primary reasons for ending sacrifices (clearly highlighted in the example of King Pasenadi). But if these are taken to be the only reasons then the disapproval of sacrifice has no ecological bearing. However, in due course it becomes fairly certain that these are not the sole reasons. Suspicions about the presence of another reason for ending animal sacrifice are aroused when rites and rituals are not censured fully, only certain parts of them pertaining to plants and animals are suspended. This indicates that compassion for animals may indeed have been an additional reason for the censure. Evidently, all the above examples do not end with the description of what should not be done in a sacrifice but go on to give specifications on how a proper one is to be conducted; this is proof enough that the Buddhists were motivated by compassion for animals and not only by the *kammic* good that they could gain. It is also interesting to note that it is the latter sacrifice, free of animals, that brings great *kammic* fruit and pleases the deities.[45] In this way Buddhists seem to not only acknowledge but also actively encourage compassion *vis-à-vis* the protection of animals.

Another *Sutta* records a conversation between King Pasenadi and his queen Mallikā, whereby the King enquires whether the queen held dear anything more than her own self. The queen admits that her self is the dearest to her. On being asked a similar question by the queen, the King admits that his self is his dearest possession. When this conversation is brought to the attention of the Buddha, he agrees that this indeed was true to all and asks the King to refrain from the killing of other beings, as their self was dear to them too.[46] If it can be assumed that this *Sutta* is directed at animals too, i.e. that the "beings" mentioned in it include animals, it would strengthen the case for compassion towards them. However, questions are often raised about whether compassion towards animals is connected with conservation and there is doubt that the one necessarily leads to the other. Sometimes radical conservation could require the culling of some animals and this aspect clashes with the element of compassion. The Buddhists, great upholders of compassion, would be opposed to such measures. Thus an ecological presence is not inevitably indicated through compassion towards animals.[47] Moreover, many would (and do) consider kindness to, for instance, individual domestic animals a moot issue and not really connected with conservation focused on species.

However, compassion in Buddhism is not limited to individual domestic animals alone. That kindness and compassion towards animals on a wider scale is an inherent part of Buddhist literature can also be seen in another instance. The *Kandaraka Sutta* of the *Majjhima Nikāya* describes one certain sort of person as unappealing. It relates the Buddha's dialogue with Pessa, wherein Pessa says that a type of person does not appeal to him for he torments others who yearn for happiness and recoil from pain. Buddha agreeing with this explains that persons who are butchers, fowlers, deer-stalkers, hunters and fishermen, as well as those who are executioners and jailors are all a part of this category of persons.[48] This shows that wild animals and fish are also included for the reason that they undergo pain and so professions that cause such pain are unacceptable. At the same time Buddhist monks were also enjoined not to throw left-over food where there is greenery or into water that contains living beings.[49] These examples can be treated as supportive of a more wide-ranging conservation but nevertheless it must be accepted that there is no reference to species conservation as a whole.

This leads us to the question of the status of animals in Buddhism. It is pointed out often that two reactions to animals in Buddhist literature can be isolated. At one place in the *Suttas* the Buddha agrees that human beings are a tangle while animals are like an open clearing.[50] This is the more positive view and can be seen to have deeper psychological ramifications in that the minds of animals are seen as uncomplicated compared to human minds. However, on the other hand, in most descriptions animals appear ill-fated and birth as an animal is not one that is sought after. The Buddha described the animal realm as full of anguish. Animals are incapable of following the *dhamma* or ethical actions, a privilege reserved for human beings alone. Animal birth was characterized by survival based on devouring weaker beings thereby showcasing the violence and struggle that animals have to face.[51] However in all there appears to be little doubt that animals suffer. Paul Waldau categorically states that the Buddhist tradition considers *dukkha* to apply to human beings and animals.[52] Though there is little clarity on the issue the above observations offer a slight indication that animals could be regarded as moral beings in early Buddhist literature.[53]

Nonetheless, whether the early Buddhist tradition truly understood the nature of animals is fundamentally an even more obscure matter. Waldau has also examined references to key animals and to Pali terms (such as *sattā* and *bhūtā*) that represent animals in early Buddhist scriptures. Of the latter he says that they are used loosely and are not concepts that are definitely inclusive of animals or exclusive of other things.[54] Of animals themselves, Waldau concludes that though animals were noticed for their abilities they were considered to be "fundamentally inferior" to human beings. He also adds that their characterization was not accurate.[55] He writes:

> . . . the negative view of other animals results in systematic depreciation, and at times dismissal, of the diverse realities of the many different kinds of *other animals*. These views were adopted as a whole,

> and applied to all non-human animals. They have been maintained *regardless of the course of events* and without regard for careful investigations of the day to day lives of the more complicated of other animals such as members of the key species.[56]

Florin Deleanu has reached a somewhat similar conclusion with regard to animals. Deleanu observes that despite an overwhelming presence of animals in Buddhist texts, Buddhist authors are not primarily concerned with animals. He examines some tales in the Pali Canon where animals are seen in complex relations with the environment. However, he finds such examples rare and not entirely representative of the entire corpus of the literature under review. Deleanu also surveys certain conceptions and misconceptions regarding animal behaviour by focusing on the behaviour and image of five animals that are often mentioned in the Pali Canon: elephant, deer, monkey, lion and jackal. Such a characterization reveals to him that animals are often ascribed features unfairly. He views misconceptions about animal behaviour as a "potentially serious problem" even though not all characterizations are incorrect.[57] Deleanu finds that such misconceptions may be due to literary conventions to stress some doctrine or other and this may explain why Buddhism has inclined towards "abuse[ing] the image of animals."[58] In his conclusion he states that since animals are sentient, possess what may be seen as intelligence and are included in the cycle of rebirth, they have a right to live their lives and are most certainly deserving of universal love.[59] In final analysis, Waldau's and Deleanu's observations about animals in Buddhist scriptures on the one hand and animals being accepted as moral beings on the other, create more ambiguity and confusion for the conservationist approach. Thus no ideal solution elucidating the presence and extent of animal conservation is clearly available.

Plants

The above-mentioned *Kūṭadanta Sutta*, apart from censuring sacrifice, also restricted the cutting down of trees and grasses even though the *Sutta* itself does not specify the reason for objecting to such cutting of trees and mowing of grass. As previously noted, the *Brahmajāla Sutta* of the *Dīgha Nikāya* contains a discussion of major and minor ethical precepts where it is very clearly stated in one precept that seeds and crops are not to be injured.[60] This is commonly mentioned throughout the *Nikāyas* whenever there is a discussion of the precepts. The undertone of this precept and the forbidden act of cutting trees and grasses in the *Kūṭadanta Sutta* appears similar in that they both promote non-injury to vegetation. Supportive evidence can be gained from the *Vinaya* that contains many examples of the Buddha extolling his disciples not to harm plants. There are also injunctions specific to *Pātimokkha* disallowing injury to plants often described as "*eka indrīya jīva*" or beings that have just one sense.[61] What remains unclear, however, is why such actions were disapproved.

Scholars have repeatedly pointed out various instances and justifications (some given below) for why Buddhist precepts enjoined that vegetation was not to be harmed. An analysis of these reasons can reveal the support they provide to the conservation of trees, grasses and so on.[62] One of the more obvious reasons is that they were regarded as sentient. Sentience can be assumed as the reason for trees and grasses being excluded from sacrifice. However, there is no direct evidence to support this. In general, the sentience of trees in early Buddhist literature remains an obscure point and therefore weak support for conservation.[63] Another reason that has been cited for the protection of vegetation is that it is considered bad to cut or harm a tree or branch needlessly if one has received something of advantage from it such as fruit or shade.[64] This implies that since trees supply us with some benefits we should be grateful in return and not resort to cutting them down. But there is very little to support the view that trees should not be cut down out of gratitude in literature to act as a basis for conservation. One more motive for not harming vegetation can be traced to the *Snātaka* rules. According to these rules tearing of grass is viewed as a sign of lack of control over the emotions. Māra (the personification of evils and passion) is depicted as tearing grass when he is unable to tempt the Buddha and draw him away from his concentration at the time of liberation. From this it can be inferred that a motivation not to cut grass (for sacrifices and so forth) could be to imply that emotions are under control.[65] But if this accepted as a motive then it provides no support to conservation at all. Another rationale has been that it was a common belief that trees were the homes of deities. Since deities occupied a glorified position, their abode, the trees, were not to be destroyed. However, as often pointed out, this position attracts a number of related problems. The first problem is that it advocates the protection of only those trees and vegetation that are considered as homes of deities, and so remains selective. Secondly, nowhere is it said that seeds contain deities making non-injury to them acceptable. But if this is so then this is in direct contradiction to the precept that promotes the non-harming of seeds. The third problem is outlined in the *Vinaya* when it is stated that this was what people in general wanted, thereby pointing out that protecting the trees as the abode of deities was based on an appeal to popular belief rather than Buddhist beliefs.[66] The *Vinaya* also hints that it was the people who believed that trees were one-facultied life rather than the Buddhists.[67] So if not a Buddhist belief then it loses its rationale here. Fourth, in a slightly different tone, in application to modern day conservation measures one has to be aware also of the spirit removal ceremony, which implies that if the spirit is removed then it is permissible to cut the tree. This complicates the matter of conservation even more. And so it appears to be extremely difficult to establish the reason for the protection of vegetation suggested in the *Kūṭadanta Sutta* and in the precepts, and that the reason may have been ecological and conservation-oriented is even harder to prove.

The importance of vegetation may also be seen from another angle. The *Suttas* say much about how the forests lend themselves to a much-desired isolation and support meditation. Praise of forest dwelling is generous. Other literature also describes sitting under trees and meditating to reach higher spiritual states as extremely significant.[68] The *Suttas*, *Vinaya* and the *Theragāthā* uniformly support the pursuit of meditation in the deep recesses of nature – in forests and groves. These act as a sacred space for the meditating *bhikkhus*.[69] An example is the *Mahāgosiṅga Sutta* where it is proclaimed that a monk who is a forest-dweller and who additionally exalts forest dwelling is the one who illuminates a forest.[70] In numerous other places are mentioned forests and natural spaces where monks take refuge to pursue their spiritual practice.[71] The Buddha himself is said to have dwelt in forests for they provided seclusion conducive for spiritual development.[72] However forests are not always glorified. Living in wilderness is acknowledged as difficult and dangerous.[73] In the *Theragāthā* the fear of wild animals, snakes and scorpions, irritants such as mosquitoes and gnats was always conspicuous but the monk is asked to strive on.[74] Despite this, wild nature and forests were important from the Buddhist point of view. The practitioner could live here without the mundane disruptions of community life. Protecting forests from being cut down seems to be in the interest of the Buddhists for it supports their quest for enlightenment. Schmithausen, as mentioned earlier, refers to this as the hermit strand and finds that it could be validly developed within the Buddhist framework for the protection of forests. He states that wilderness is "regarded as the most favourable environment for spiritual progress and true happiness. This seems to imply . . . positive evaluation, and what is positively evaluated here is not so much individual animals and plants but rather the whole ambience."[75] Even though Schmithausen finds the motivation clearly anthropocentric, and forest dwelling not a homogenous feature among early Buddhists, he still concludes that it is supportive of nature in one sense. So conserving forests for the sake of a spiritual quest appears as a reasonable motive.

Artificiality versus the world of natural vegetation also appears as a highly debatable area. For instance it is said, "Planters of parks and groves . . . For them merit always increases, both by day and night . . . these persons will go to heaven."[76] Not only is this not ideal from the environmental point of view, for it is an instrumental argument (planting trees for the sake of the shade and fruit they provide), it can be taken as promoting the artificial rather than the natural order of nature. Other than this, certain sections of the *Nikāyas* applaud artificiality and opulence (even though the Buddha himself is never connected with these and so unwittingly supports conservation). For instance, in the *Mahāsudassana Sutta*, groves containing palm trees made of gold are praised.[77] To eulogize unnatural vegetation thus appears to undermine the beauty of natural trees and plants. In addition it appears usually as contraindicative to ecological conduct for it is conducive to the overuse of resources. Continuing the artificiality theme, attention must be drawn to a passage about visions of a future time from *Cakkavati-sīhanāda Sutta* that has attracted much attention:

> [When] humans have a life-time of eighty thousand years, Jambudīpa will be opulent and prosperous; villages, towns and cities will be close together (like a flock of poultry). This Jambudīpa, just like Avīci, will be overflowing with humans as a thicket of rushes or reeds.[78]

In this passage human beings are said to live until they are 80,000 years old due to good moral behaviour. They dwell in cities and villages that are extremely crowded and populous; they are as populous as a flock of poultry. Ian Harris sees this passage as glorifying the artificial and as accepting of no wilderness and so is critical of it and Harvey disagrees with his rendering.[79] Harvey writes:

> Harris sees this as a vision in which civilization is compatible with the "total destruction of wilderness." And yet, in the period of conflict, people are said to have retired to the jungles and mountains to avoid killing and being killed. The implication is, perhaps, that in a highly moral society there is no actual need of wilderness, not that it should be "conquered;" and in any case, an urban environment may still have nature interspersed in it in a semi-wild park etc.[80]

The entire rendering of this passage by both Harvey and Harris seems problematic. The passage does not imply, as Harris believes, that there is no wilderness remaining, but only that cities and villages are very populous and close to each other geographically. Secondly, Harvey's derived implication that "in a highly moral society there is no need of wilderness" defeats the very ecological theme that he is trying to establish and together with his comment on reaching a compromise situation of a "semi-wild park" trivializes the need for, and importance of, wilderness. In any case it is hard to believe in the first place that there will come a time when semi-wild parks can create enough "wilderness." Other than this, the passage also faces philological problems in making sense of the use of the term "Avīci." Avīci in later texts represents the lowest of hells and many find its use in this passage ambiguous and confusing, ". . . hell does not seem to be its meaning . . . though its exact sense is doubtful."[81]

The theme of conservation of trees, vegetation and wilderness are hard to establish on Buddhist principles. To every argument that can be cited in support of conservation a counter argument can be prepared with equal force.

But it does become clear with this analysis that all is not lost and were the positive outcomes to garner more support a niche for conservation could be legitimately created.

Material entities

Apart from the protection of animals and plants, the conservation of material entities is a central theme in conservationist ethics. The reference in *Pali Suttas* to material nature – seas, mountains, air and so on – is very limited. More is said on the elements of which they are composed, but these deliberations have an altogether different mood. Discussions on them are largely philosophical and there is little effort to draw out their environmental or natural significance. When a monk wants to know where the four great elements, earth (*paṭhavī*), water (*āpo*), fire (*tejo*) and air (*vāyo*) cease without residue, the Buddha's answer, not in material but spiritual terms, is, "Where consciousness is signless, boundless and in all respects luminous; Here earth, water, fire and air have no footing. . . ."[82] Thus, rather than being an exposé on the treatment of material entities, a part of Buddhist metaphysical theory is presented. Ideas of conservation become difficult to derive under these circumstances leading thus to little information on how material entities are to be treated and preserved.

Early Buddhism believes that there are five groups of things that are coveted, and the first of these is the desire for material shapes. Under material shapes are mentioned the four great elements and the material objects that are derived from these. The word for element is *mahābhūta* or *dhātu*. All the elements are seen as having an internal and an external character, the internal referring to the composition of the body and the external to objects outside the body. For instance, the earth element as the element of extension is seen as having an internal aspect that includes anything that is hard and solid in the human body such as the nails, teeth, skin, heart, liver, etc. The external aspect, though not exactly specified, can be taken to refer to mountains, land, etc. In the case of the liquid element, the internal aspect is the blood and other fluids that make up the body. Of the external aspect of this element it is said that when it is agitated it carries away villages and towns and districts, the obvious reference being rivers. The heat (fire) and motion (air) elements are similarly treated and their impermanence is also stressed.[83] At times, the fifth element, space, is also added to these discussions.[84] The impermanence of the internal and external aspects of all elements is mentioned constantly. Each section ends by saying that this element is to be treated as "this is not mine, this I am not, this is not my self. . . ."[85] *Phassa* or sensory impingement is seen as the reason for the delusion of ownership. Attention is thus directed towards metaphysics and epistemology rather than ecology.

The Buddha recaps often that the elements are one of the five factors (*khandhas*) of which the transitory individual is made. Once this knowledge is imbibed through the process of perfecting wisdom, passion is cleansed and craving faded out.[86] This is confirmed by the *Mūlapariyāya Sutta* which attacks the notion of element as personal possession. Once the sense of ownership is abandoned the element can be seen as what it truly is.[87] The above discussion represents most of what has been said of the elements in the first four *Nikāyas* and it is possible to see that Buddhists are making two points: that the elements are not a part of the self and that their nature is one of impermanence. That material elements like the other psychical *khandhas* are impermanent and not the self amounts to what is often reflected in the *Suttas* about the nature of everything in existence namely that "all conditioned things (*sabbe saṅkhārā*) are impermanent (*aniccā*), and that all things (*sabbe dhamma*) are not-self (*anattā*)."[88] What becomes clear from this account is that every material object we have ever been acquainted with is bound by its very nature to cease to exist at some point in time and therefore the individual's identity with his material body belies the nature of reality. It is hard to derive any ecological aspect affecting conservation from such discussions. In fact the external aspects of matter being believed to be impermanent may indeed cause other problems, a frequently raised one being why protect natural entities if they are impermanent and will eventually cease to exist? It may seem that these discussions are of no relevance to the material environments as such, i.e. to the protection of rivers, mountains, air and so on. However, some underlying positive ecological implications can also be drawn out once the issue is examined more carefully.

It can be inferred that early Buddhists do not deny the reality of the world, in the sense of the actual existence of material elements. It is interesting to note in the above discussion that elements are acknowledged as substantial things; they are understood as existing. This is further confirmed when they are treated as impermanent. The reason being that impermanence is possibly best understood as the passing away of an object that exists. Only that which is born and exists can be destroyed or cease to exist. In relation to this matter A. B. Keith writes, ". . . it is essential to note that early Buddhism in its admission of the four material elements was realistic. . . ."[89] Clearly, more definition can be given to an ecology based on realistic rather than idealistic principles. And the Buddhist discussion of elements serves to confirm this. But it must be admitted that this suggestion, however effective, forms a part of the conservationist approach ambiguously and has rather shaky ecological foundations.

As an exception there is a rare reference to the conservation of a geological feature. As mentioned earlier, monks are asked not to throw their waste into water and this could be construed as the protection of water.[90] However, the motive again is questionable as in the case of the protection of trees; such an act may have been enjoined for the sake of the living beings in water rather than as a prevention of water pollution! However even such examples are few and far between. (Schmithausen has done detailed work on the *Vinaya* with regard to such examples, and arrives at the conclusion that though the *Vinaya* contains material on the treatment of natural entities, the acts are questionable with regard to their motivation. Water was not to be polluted because it would be unhygienic for human beings. Thus not polluting water was more a matter of decorum and less of conservation.[91])

One last point that may be relevant to the discussion of elements is related to the treatment of the physical body of the individual himself. Nowhere in the Canon is the mistreatment of the body recommended even though in certain parts of the *Nikāyas* the Buddha suggested that the body be regarded as impermanent, as suffering, as a misfortune, as decay.[92] This is reflected in the *Therīgāthā* which also speaks of the vileness of the body, of a beauty and youth that is not going to last as also are not feminine vanities that often delight.[93] Elsewhere as well the body is seen as unclean, foul, emitting odours, made of blood, fluid and flesh and a repulsive carcass that will eventually be taken to the charnel field.[94] However contemplating the body this way was clearly encouraged for the benefit of meditation alone. The Buddha's objective was certainly not to devalue the body. In fact his intention was quite the opposite – he recognized the importance of the basic well-being of the body so that it would not impede his spiritual quest in any way.[95] Extreme emaciation, he grasped through his own practice, led not to knowledge and insight but acted as a hindrance to meditative practice.[96] Additionally the Buddha supports Pessa when he describes his dislike for self-tormentors.[97] The Buddha's view appears to be about balance without being overly affected by bodily pleasures or self-torment.[98] It can be assumed that the body was valued as a means to attaining enlightenment. If this attitude is extended to the other aspects of nature, it means that care must be bestowed upon material entities such as water and air for these contribute to the health of the body which is the vehicle through which *nibbāna* becomes possible. Respect, protection and conservation of the environment on this understanding become extremely important. This is a fairly sound reason for conservation (and somewhat similar to Schmithausen's hermit strand) even though once more it is an instrumental one.

Aesthetic appreciation

Another angle from where the Buddhist attitude towards nature could have a bearing on conservation is in its aesthetic descriptions of nature. Buddhist texts include evocative scenes of sermons and meditations under trees, in groves, deep forests, caves and on rocks. Nature is mentioned poetically (though sparingly) in the first four *Nikāyas*. A *Sutta* in the *Majjhima Nikāya* describes the beauty of the Gosiṅga Sāla-wood as delightful on a moonlit night with the trees in full bloom due to which a pleasant scent wafts through the grove.[99] Again in the *Majjhima Nikāya* it is said:

> This occurred to me monks: "delightful indeed is this part of land and pleasing is the jungle thicket and the river flows transparent with banks that are delightful and pleasant and nearby is a village for the supply of food. Indeed this place is suitable for the striving of a clansman set on striving."[100]

There is a faint suggestion here that the *Nikāyas* appreciated the beauty of nature for otherwise they would not have felt the need to mention this beauty. Gokhale says "the emergence of these archetypes in the imagery of early Buddhism indicated an attitude of acceptance and appreciation of beauty in nature and the animal world in the evolving Buddhist thought."[101]

However nature descriptions develop fully especially in the *Theragāthā*. The austereness of the *Nikāyas* is lost in these texts. Passion for the spiritual path is expressed but more so there is an unguarded acknowledgement of the beauty of nature and an articulated delight in its different aspects – the trees with spreading branches, the dark blue clouds, the crystal cool waters, rain refreshed lands, cries of creatures whose home this is such as black faced apes and timid deer, dancing peacocks, crags covered with insects described as "*Indagopaka*" or legions of *Indra*, away from crowds – these aspects charm and delight the monks vision and help them in their spiritual quest.[102] This is the perfect place to pursue spiritual practice and to arrive at perfect insight. Mrs. Rhys Davids, in the introduction of her translation of the *Theragāthā* says:

> . . . monachistic Theras sought out Nature as much because they were poets and children of Nature as because they were arahants. They present a unique blend of religious maturity, primeval shyness, and aesthetic sensitiveness. And very probably, given an efficient state of organization in the Order, to such exceptionally gifted men exceptional leisure was accorded as a necessity for their proper development, and not in any way a concession to ethical slackness or pagan and atavistic instincts.[103]

An appreciation of natural beauty was accepted and at the same time it was believed not to take away from the life of morality and detachment. A reading of the *Theragāthā* ensures that there is no mistaking the balance between delight in forest life and a life of detachment. The two aspects co-exist quite favourably in this text and following one does not imply neglecting the other.

However the appreciation of nature within Buddhist thought raises some pertinent questions. Some of these are more general questions and are concerned with whether an ethics of nature seeking conservation can be based on aesthetic appreciation at all. Others are more specific to Buddhism and ask how instances that extol natural beauty can be accepted when the decisive mood of detachment from self-gratifying pleasures pervades texts (even despite there being the semblance of such balance in the *Theragāthā*). Undue reflection on beauty must be avoided, argue some sections of the literature, for it gives rise to lust. In the *Nikāyas* it is often said that *subha nimitta*, translated as the "sign of the beautiful," is the reason for the birth and intensification of sensual desire.[104] The Buddha is believed to have stated:

> Monks, I do not perceive any principle of conduct that causes the arising of sensual pleasure if not arisen, or if arisen, that leads to the increase and expansion of sensual pleasure as the sign of the beautiful (*subha nimitta*).[105]

In fact, Buddhists suggest quite the contrary contemplation of the unattractive. Colin Edwards in a short essay entitled "The Buddha: Friendship and Beauty" says of Buddha's caution about beauty in the *Aṅguttara Nikāya* "In this context the beauty is bodily – the previous references are to a 'woman's' form . . . and attractive physical attributes –, for a man the beauty of a woman. Bodily beauty creates and increases lust."[106] He later adds "It does not occur to him [Buddha] that aesthetic experience might be a factor in the development of the state of mind conducive to entering the Path, just as moral integrity or friendship may."[107] Though this is one opinion that follows from the passage above, it appears to consider all aesthetic experiences as of one sort. No attention is given to the references to nature made above. These suggest that aesthetic appreciation as far as delight in the beauty of physical nature (*ramanīya*) was concerned is significant and could have been unlike the lust-generating beauty cautioned against. This hunch gathers force when contemplation of physical body as unattractive is advised in the texts but no similar contemplation of nature as unsightly can be found (even though nature is neither overvalued nor romanticized). Therefore the appreciation of beauty may be considered in two broad senses. A conclusion that can be drawn is that nature appreciation was acceptable and not comparable to lustful aesthetic experiences connected with womanly beauty. Yet doubts remain as this conclusion is not always consistent.[108]

As to the first question about whether aesthetic appreciation is at all a sufficient basis for environmental ethics and conservation, there is some doubt. In general for environmental theories, more often than not, this idea is seen as not carrying enough credence to be the groundwork of an environmental ethics and therefore of conservation. Notwithstanding I believe that aesthetic appreciation of nature does have some significance in environmental thought. Acknowledging the beauty that exists within nature would be tantamount to extending at least some value to nature and this could give an impetus to conservation. Nevertheless it is difficult to adduce weighty arguments to convince someone who is doubtful of the direct relation between aesthetic appreciation and nature conservation.

Metaphorical references

There is one other way in which nature is alluded to. Animals, plants and material entities are often used in analogies and metaphors by early Buddhist literary sources to expound moral and spiritual behaviour. These metaphors act as iconic expressions of foundational Buddhist beliefs. One cannot, of course, directly base conservation on metaphors using nature. However, the question arises whether metaphors can be considered as indicating the first signs of emerging ideas and attitudes towards nature in Buddhism and so as ultimately supportive of ecology and conservation. It has been said that "What makes things clear in the distinctly Eastern mode of thinking . . . is often an effectively focused image, not a theory; an inexpressible and immutable experience, not an argument; an evocative metaphor, not a logically demonstrated truth;"[109] and again, "Indeed, there is a very long tradition, in both West and East, of discerning metaphors, symbols and so meanings in nature."[110] If metaphors are treated as environmental paradigms they could point to affirmative nature consciousness and be conducive to conservation. However, first the question if such references embrace genuine attitudes and ideas of nature must be resolved.

Trees (*rukkha*), creepers (*latā, sansappaka*), water (*udaka, jala*), animals (*satta*), birds (*sakuṇa*) are just some of the examples of how nature is used as a metaphor to represent good and bad desire, virtue, wholesome and unwholesome states, Māra's actions, and so on. However the hypothesis that metaphors reveal attitudes is not quite straightforward and leads to a multitude of problems for an ethics of environment. The main reason for this is that nature is not always portrayed in a flattering manner in them and so can also be used to represent quite the opposite position. For instance, in the *Kesi Sutta*, Kesi, the horse trainer visits Buddha. On being asked how he trains his horses the reply is that he trains some gently, others by force and some by both. And if the horse proves to be unyielding, he is destroyed. The Buddha says that is exactly how he trains men – some by good, others by harshness and others by both. However, he adds that he does not destroy an unyielding man in the sense that the horse is destroyed; he simply destroys by not considering it worthwhile to admonish the man.[111] If an attempt is made to draw conclusions from this about the Buddhist environmental spirit then difficulties appear. A number of implications here are contrary to conservation. First, it is casually suggested that the trainer uses violence to train horses and even resorts to killing them. Secondly, some rather unflattering light is thrown on the distinct value of human beings and animals: unyielding human beings may not be killed but an animal displaying similar qualities may be. Thirdly, the Buddha does not react to the use of violence and simply responds with his own point. The latter criticism is diluted if it be believed that the Buddha accepted some societal norms to do with the training of domestic animals and this example is not indicative of his attitude. But it may still seem that non-violence is not as universal as it ought to be.

That this may not necessarily be the case can be seen from another example. While discussing the foundations of mindfulness the constant reviewing of the body by the monk is mentioned. A monk is asked to be aware of the different elements that make up his body and it is added:

> Just as, monks, a skilled butcher or his assistant, having slaughtered a cow, were to sit at a corner of a crossroad having divided [the carcass] bit by bit, so monks, a monk looks upon the body as it is, in terms of elements. . . .[112]

It seems here that the Buddha accepts the profession of a cow-butcher, which is just not the case. This profession was completely denounced by the Buddha on a number of occasions, to say the least, but it did exist in the society of the time. By the same logic then, the arguments drawn from the first case become weak.[113]

Rather than looking for naturalistic content, another way in which analogies can be analysed is by considering their object of reference. By deciding whether the reference is really negative or positive, the analogy can then be seen as negative or positive. If a particular analogy or metaphor refers to aspects of liberation, morality, or any other Buddhist theory with a positive connotation it can be categorized as a positive symbol. If an analogy refers to impediments to liberation, immorality or any such theme, it can then be categorized as a negative symbol.[114] By doing so one may hope that the analogy can then be seen without ambiguity but also as mostly positive.

Yet there is danger in this position too. If the analogy is relatively clear-cut then this method may work. For instance, in the *Majjhima Nikāya*, the Buddha whilst explaining the Eightfold Path used the analogy of kindness towards deer:

> But monks, if some man came to that great herd of deer, desiring its benefit, desiring its welfare, desiring its uttermost safety, and if there were a road calm and safe, he might open up that road, he might cover up the bad road, disturb the decoy, destroy the decoy; thus, indeed, monks, in future time this great herd of deer would meet with prosperity, growth and unity.[115]

The Buddha then compares himself to this man and the way leading to security as the Eightfold Path. The bad man, not desiring the welfare of the deer, is compared with Māra. Not only is the analogy positive by way of reference, for it alludes to the Eightfold Path, it also promotes the welfare of animals. Since Buddha is compared with the good man his position becomes one of compassion and protection towards the animals, a position that is very environmentally viable. Another example is of a skilled teacher who increases the happiness of his disciples for a long time; this teacher is compared with a cowherd who leads his cattle safely across the river during the rainy season.[116] Similarly the cleanness and stillness of a deep lake are compared with the peacefulness of the wise when they have absorbed the teachings of the Buddha.[117]

However, not all metaphors are so easily understood and all examples are not as straightforward as the above. In many cases the analogy is clearly environmental and the reference may be negative. For instance it is said that when seeds are well looked after they sprout; similarly an act done with lust or malice is bound to have a corresponding effect.[118] Thus the nurturing of seeds (an ecological action) is compared with the growth of lust and delusion (actions not conducive to spirituality). In other cases, the reference may be positive and the analogy clearly non-environmental. The training of the mind during meditation is compared to the skill with which an elephant trainer employs a hook to restrain a savage elephant.[119] Though the training of the mind is a positive spiritual practice, the latter is non-ecological as it interferes with the life of wild animals and that too in a rather inhumane and violent way. In some cases both the analogy and the reference are negative. For instance, in the *Dhammapada* the easy life of a shameless person is compared to an insolent crow that is full of pride, dishonesty and viciousness.[120] Finally, the conclusions drawn from the analogy may be ambiguous in application to the environment or just indifferent. In describing how one is to abandon unwholesome states and devote themselves to wholesome states to increase *dhamma* and discipline, the analogy of a sāla-tree grove is given. Weeds are choking the grove. A man that desires the well-being of the grove comes along and he cuts and throws away the crooked saplings, tends to the straight-formed ones so that the grove would grow well and prosper.[121] One message this conveys is care and concern for nature (ecological action), with the reference of increasing *dhamma* being positive as well. But this analogy can also be seen as negative, for if the grove is taken to be a natural one then the weeds are a part of its natural state and best left alone. If looked at in this way, the *Sutta* essentially encourages interference in the ways of nature and has a negative connotation. Thus, the use of analogies as a basis for an environmental ethics can be seen as fraught with various difficulties.

Additional concerns arise in the above analysis. The nurturing of seeds by farmers may not indicate an ecological action. It can be said, however, that when such nurturing is extended to a nearly extinct species of vegetation then it could be considered ecological. But since the ecological angle arises here by way of extension, many scholars would disagree with its effectiveness in conservation. Nevertheless nurturing seeds per se may also act as a symbol for ecology. But problems don't end here. For all the above examples in their proper context are about process and are suggested with a particular purpose in mind. Due to this they can be easily dismissed as not being about conservation at all. It must always be kept in mind, as Deleanu writes, that Buddhist authors were mainly interested in exploring metaphors due to their potential as "literary devices" for expounding "doctrinal practices."[122] Thus the purpose of these expressions appears limited to imparting the Buddhist doctrine more effectively. However, on a more positive note, Ryan says "the imagery of the discourses [referring to the use of nature symbols in Buddhism] – detailed, vivid, full of warmth and friendliness towards the world and nature – enables us to get some sense of this [ecologically enlightened] attitude on the imaginative level."[123] In all, however, analogies as a reflection of attitudes are to be used very cautiously.

Overview

Examples that support conservation in Buddhism, either directly or indirectly are hard to come by. Moreover, one invariably stumbles upon instances that are damaging to conservation, such as the indefinite status of animals; apparent indifference to the fate of rivers and mountains; metaphors that liken calming of the mind with the taming of a savage elephant with a hook and so on. Despite this constant ambiguity, there is no denying that there is contained within Buddhist literature a sense of conservation that comes from respect towards animals, plants and the aesthetic appreciation of the beauty of nature. In one way or another we come upon this sense again and again – either through the condemnation of sacrifice of animals or through the need to be in the wilderness for meditation or in reference to metaphors that speak of kindness to animals. From this it can be inferred that the conservationist view in early Buddhism is not strong or foundational but neither is it non-existent. It therefore needs support from other aspects of Buddhist thought to develop more fully and in order that its negativities may be contextualized. This support can be derived from the Buddhist embodiment of the cosmological approach to nature and from Buddhism's ethical character (both demonstrated in the following chapters) possibly revealing the religion's true ecological intentions.

3

NATURE: A "COSMOLOGICAL" APPROACH

The attitude we think it appropriate to take towards living things depends on how we conceive of them and of our relationship to them.
Paul Taylor, *Respect for Nature*

Previously Plato's approach to nature was seen as a cosmological one. In this chapter I shall consider the possibility of the early Buddhist approach being cosmological as well. An examination of the conservationist approach to nature earlier revealed that Buddhist literature contains an idea of conservation that is not only underdeveloped but also faces the constant fear of condemnation from aspects that are contradictory in nature to it. As for marginalization of nature, many may find that it exists in the fact that *Nibbāna* in early Buddhism is recognized as the only worthwhile goal. Thus everything else is reduced to insignificance and this includes nature and the environment. The worry here is that devaluing environment may provide the justification needed for exploiting the resources of nature. However this view in Buddhism can be questioned as will be demonstrated in due course.[1] It now remains to be seen if the Buddhist approach to nature is a cosmological one. References to nature in the cosmological sense can be identified in Buddhist literature especially in relation to *dhamma, paṭiccasamuppāda, saṃsāra* and the early Buddhist story of the origin of the world. A cosmological vision implies that entities, plants, animals and man and everything else are a part of the specified universal order. It also suggests implicitly that any definition of nature must not consider aspects in isolation as this would obscure their true value. A cosmological approach implies most importantly shared laws or a shared progress among the different aspects of the cosmos. I believe that it is this cosmological sense of nature that exists in Buddhism, even though, admittedly, the latter's main interest was never the determination of the meaning of nature but the understanding of suffering and its removal. This portrayal also throws up some interesting questions related to value that will be looked at in due course. Contrary opinions that speak only of human supremacy and value in early Buddhist thought will be addressed in the last section of this chapter.

The cosmological approach

Dhamma and *Paṭiccasamuppāda*

The term *dhamma* plays a very significant role in Buddhist philosophy and has multiple meanings that have perplexed scholars for a long time. John Ross Carter, who has worked extensively on the meaning of the term notes, "The scope of meaning that the term had was baffling. The depth of meaning was intriguing."[2] Damien Keown's *A Dictionary of Buddhism* defines the term as having three important senses.[3] First, *dhamma* refers to the natural order or universal law that forms the basis of all events in both the physical and moral dimensions of the universe. Secondly, it represents Buddhist teachings and in this sense forms one part of the Buddhist *triratna* (three jewels), the other two being Buddha and *Sangha*.[4] It is believed that Buddhist teachings explain the "universal law" and seek to ensure that the individual is in harmony with it, therefore the name *dhamma* is given to the teachings. Thirdly, *dhamma* also refers to individual phenomena or entities that form part of the experiential world. This meaning is limited to the *Abhidhammikas* who classified *dhammas* as not only external but also internal (such as psychological processes). *Dhamma* can be used in other contexts as well. For instance, *Dhamma* frequently occurs in reference to the political sphere. The king is referred to as *dhammiko dhammarājā* or the upholder of *dhamma*.[5]

My main attempt will be to examine the conception of *dhamma* with reference to Keown's first sense only – as a universal or cosmic law that applies to the physical and moral spheres. The *Nikāyas* contain many examples of *dhamma* as cosmic law. For instance, in the *Saṃyutta Nikāya* the monk Channa requests that he be given a *dhamma* talk so that he may see the *dhamma*. The latter *dhamma* is obviously in reference to the universal law.[6] Even though scholars mention this sense quite often, not much attention is given to its full significance. Among those who have considered this aspect of *dhamma* are Mrs Rhy Davids and I. B. Horner. Rhys Davids writes:

> And indeed this is never lost sight of in the Pāli books: – that the Buddha is expressing not only his own convictions, the fruit of intense effort and self-communing but also something that was, and had in the infinite past been, and would ever be, objectively and constantly valid and true for any and every human society, nay something that was cosmic law, eternal, necessary, omnipresent, whether discerned or not.[7]

Horner states that "the term dhamma meant the natural state or condition of beings and things, what supports them, the law of their being, what it was right for them to be, the very stuff of their being, *evam-dhammo*."[8] However, nothing was said about "nature" in connection with this cosmic law.

Dhamma as universal or cosmic law has certain important implications for nature. This becomes clear if we trace the origins of the word. The term is believed to have come from the Brahmanical term *ṛta*. M. Hiriyanna while speaking of the term in Vedic literature says, "It [*ṛta*] has ceased to be used in Sanskrit; but we shall see that under the name of *dharma*, the very same idea occupies a very important place in the later Indian views of life also."[9] Many others support this view.[10] A. L. Basham writes "The origins of *dharma* lie in the Ṛg-Vedic concept of *ṛta*, the course of things or the cosmic order, the maintenance of which was entrusted to the God Varuna. . . ."[11] The relation between *ṛta* and *dhamma* becomes important because *ṛta* itself is looked upon as intrinsically associated with the natural world. A. T. Embree, writing on the *Vedic* period and its response to nature says of *ṛta* that it was:

> . . . the sense of a cosmic order or law pervading the universe. This cosmic law was not made by the gods, although they are the guardians of it. It is reflected not only in the physical regularity of the night and day and of the seasons but also in the moral order that binds men to each other and to the gods . . .[12]

His words summarize the *Vedic* use of the word *ṛta*. What also becomes clear from Embree's understanding is the deep relationship between *ṛta* and the natural order.

Ṛta represented the continuously ordered world where day followed night and seasons changed discernibly. Of Varuna, the custodian god of *ṛta*, it has been said in the *Atharva Veda* "this earth is his, to him belong those vast and boundless skies; both seas within him rest. . . ."[13] This passage then goes on to suggest how highly cherished Varuna is for simply being a guardian of the cosmic law. The gradual development of the term, first in application to nature and then to the moral order can be traced in Vedic literature. As one commentator notes:

> According to the thought of the Indians of those days, the Rita manifests itself equally in nature and in human society; the river constantly flows, the dawn comes after the night, the sun traverses the sky, the moon and the stars keep their courses, and everything in human society goes on as it ought to, when it is in accordance with the Rita. Thus, the order of nature is identified with that of human society or the moral life of mankind through the ideas of the Rita.[14]

In this way a connection is established between the cosmic law that governs both nature and human beings in the concept of *ṛta*.

The *Vedic* term *ṛta*, however, never figures in Buddhist texts and the term *dhamma* appears constantly in keeping with the prevailing trend. Importantly here too it remains the universal cosmic law (as becomes clear from various *dhamma* references in the *Nikāyas*)[15] even though the Buddhists had given it a more distinctive identity of its own. By implication it may be said that for the Buddhists human beings and non-human beings were equally subject to the same law. In the light of this, if asked the question whether the environment can be looked on as part of the totality of *dhamma*, the answer must be positive. But the above account also makes it clear that *dhamma* functions not only in the context of nature, but has a much wider application.

Closely related to *dhamma* as universal cosmic law is the doctrine of dependent origination.[16] *Paṭiccasamuppāda* is often cited by environmental scholars as a foundation for environmental ethics in early Buddhism. Invariably their search has led them to cite mutual inter-dependence based on *paṭiccasamuppāda* as a sound basis for environmentalism in Buddhism. However this does not naturally follow from *paṭiccasamuppāda*.[17] The argument in support of an environmental ethics is located elsewhere in the doctrine. But first clarification regarding what the Buddha meant by *paṭiccasamuppāda* is needed. Early Buddhism made it amply clear that in seeking liberation the individual would have to strive for awareness of the cause of *dukkha* (best understood as universal existential suffering). So indispensable to the Buddha was the recognition of *dukkha* that he declared it as the First Noble Truth. He claimed to have found the underlying cause of it through his insight. The Buddha's reflections revealed that the existence of everything, including *dukkha* and rebirth, was dependent on certain causal conditions (that had to be removed in the quest for liberation). This is what the Buddha understood by the dependent origination of things. In *paṭiccasamuppāda* he drew attention to the process through which things actually came into existence – through necessary dependence on certain conditions.

Buddhist texts generally express *paṭiccasamuppāda* through two formulas. A shorter formula is often given to describe dependent origination such as when it is said that a monk is skilled in dependent origination when he knows that: ". . . when this is, that comes to be; with the arising of this, that arises; if this is not, that does not come to be; from the stopping of this, that is stopped."[18] The fascination with the formula lies in the fact that not only does it draw attention to vital linkages indicating that nothing exists unless it is conditioned by something but in that it hints at the connection and quiescent power of purpose present in the universe. A lengthier formula is also described in Buddhist texts, which mostly follows the shorter one. This lengthier formula has various chronological orders, which predominantly but not always begin with ignorance (*avijjā*).[19] It is believed by many scholars that the order was not important to the Buddhists as their sole intention was to identify not a first cause but a sequence of events where one factor caused another in proper order. Thus the first link of the chain, whatever it happened to be, was indelibly linked with the last and so the process went on indefinitely. There was also a difference in the number of links, ranging from eight to twelve.[20] Later a classical formulation was arrived at. Given below is one such formula:

> On birth (*jāti*) depends old age and death, grief, sorrow and suffering (*jaramaraṇā* etc)
> On becoming depends birth (*jāti*)
> On grasping depends becoming (*bhava*)
> On craving depends grasping (*upādāna*)
> On feeling depends craving (*taṇhā*)
> On contact depends feeling (*vedanā*)
> On the field of six senses depends contact (*phassa*)
> On name and shape depend the field of six senses (*saḷāyatana*)
> On consciousness depend name and shape (*nāmarūpa*)
> On *kamma* formations depends consciousness (*viññāṇa*)
> On ignorance (*avijjā*) depend *kamma* formations (*saṅkhāra*)[21]

In this manner arises the cycle of suffering (*saṃsāra*) and the stopping of each is the stopping of suffering. From this latter formula it becomes clear that though *paṭiccasamuppāda* was seen as a predominantly psychological doctrine, it has both physical and psychological applications. *Avijjā* or ignorance is of the Four Noble Truths and is caused by internalizing wrong beliefs of reality or the way things are; arising impressions are conditioned by such beliefs. These impressions lead to a consciousness (*viññāna*), which is also automatically conditioned by past deeds. This consciousness refers to the experiences undergone and not to a self (as this entity does not exist in the Buddhist scheme of things). The embodied individual comes next, and is a combination of five physical (*rūpa*) and psychical factors (*nāma*), namely, the *khandhas*. The relationship between the last two links is a reciprocal one.[22] Conditioned by *nāmarūpa* are the six senses or *saḷāyatana* (i.e. the five senses and the mind) that are responsible for perception. The six senses make contact (*phassa*) with their objects and this contact gives rise to feelings (*vedanā*) that are pleasant, painful or neutral. Craving (*taṇhā*) for pleasure and for the avoidance of pain is the result of these feeling. And from craving comes attachment (*upādāna*). From this attachment ensues a corresponding becoming (*bhava*) or being. This becoming leads to birth (*jāti*) which eventually leads to old age, grief, sorrow and death.

In this way the factors or links explain how suffering arises as caused by wrong beliefs and the ignorance of reality. *Paṭiccasamuppāda* defines every stage of life and also the passage from this life to the next. It also supports that accountability of actions rests solely on individuals. The above analysis of the longer formula proves that *paṭiccasamuppāda* has an application to human beings only. This becomes clear from the various sequences or stages that are contained in the formula. Finding an application to non-human beings in this instance is rare. (I say rare and not impossible because it is clear that though plants and vegetation appear not to be subject to the longer formula, application to animals cannot be ruled out immediately. The latter is a fairly complicated issue in itself but it may be said that if animals are accepted as moral beings and are taken as subject to *dukkha* then they could be part and parcel of the longer formula.)[23]

However, it is the shorter formula that is of interest to this study. The shorter formula does not specify an application to human beings alone. It remains to be seen what the "this" (*imasmiṃ*) in this formula refers to. Ramakrishna Puligandla refers to the "this" as phenomena and proceeds to give its definition:

> . . . . a phenomenon is anything that is or can, in principle, be an object of consciousness. Let it be immediately noted that all phenomena exist in time, although some phenomena also exist in space. Thus tables, chairs, trees, stars, galaxies, animals, people, etc – the so-called "external phenomena" – can be assigned both spacial and temporal co-ordinates; whereas thoughts, feelings, dreams, mental images, etc – the so-called "internal phenomena" can be assigned only the so-called temporal co-ordinate. The hallmark of a phenomenon, then is existence in time; that is, all phenomena are time bound existents. . . .[24]

Thus, according to this definition all of nature, since subject to temporal laws, is included within the bounds of *paṭiccasamuppāda*. That this is the case becomes clear from some examples from the *Nikāyas*. Even though these examples do not directly state that causation exists in nature, they appear to take it as given. Nature is used in these examples as an analogy, to explain how the process of causation works. It is hard to believe that the early Buddhists used such analogies without believing that causation existed in the plant world. In the *Saṃyutta Nikāya*, immediately after it has been stated that an individual comes into existence owing to certain causes, it is said that a seed sown in a field sprouts owing to specific factors – soil nutrients and moisture.[25] Then again in the *Aṅguttara Nikāya*, Ānanda states that if there were no worlds of sense desires and no actions to ripen, there wouldn't be any becoming or rebirth. He then likens action to the field, consciousness to the seed, and craving to moisture, in that if there is no contact between the three the plant does not arise.[26] Then, again, in another context, it is said that if healthy, unbroken and unharmed seeds are burned by a man and reduced to ashes, which he throws into a strong wind and allows to be carried off by a swift stream, those seeds would not sprout in future. The analogy this time is with actions; if actions are not performed out of malice, lust or delusion they will not arise in future time.[27] Numerous similar examples can be found in the *Nikāyas* and other texts. What becomes clear from these examples is that the way the process works in nature is how it works in the psychological context of *paṭiccasamuppāda*, with the difference that the process in the case of nature (though unexplained) is physical and that in the case of human beings is psycho-physical.

What I wish to propose here is that the shorter formula be focused on as the basic statement of the causal formula and as one that has an application to all objects and entities of the world. In other words, it applies universally to all phenomena. It therefore includes non-human nature too. Additionally, owing to the nature of the Buddha's doctrine (with its final aim of enlightenment) a longer formula was also proposed for the sake of the individual seeking liberation. It was one personalized to a purely human quest and one that appealed to human psychology. The basis of the two formulas, however, remains the same – the universal causal law.

The implications of this suggestion are important. The most important is that it imparts a certain uniformity to the world of human beings and non-human nature alike. No one can escape the functioning of the causal law. Nature is defined by causation, and human beings are somehow all parts of its reality; human beings are not disconnected or separate from the world. D. J. Kalupahana has also noted the nature-related similes and has remarked of the Buddha's theory that it was:

> . . . not an absolutistic explanation or theory of nature in which the lines are drawn sharply and distinctly so as to make the human being either a hapless object or the epicentre of the universe. A human being is a part of nature. Like everything in the teeming and dramatic richness of nature, he is dependently arisen or causally conditioned. He comes into being depending upon various conditions, contributes his share to the drama, and makes his exit. He is part of nature, that is, in a constant process of becoming (*bhava*), evolution (*parināma*) and dissolution.[28]

At the same time Kalupahana does admit that man is also accorded a special value, for it is he alone that can work towards liberation. Kalupahana has also claimed that "*Dependent arising* is often referred to as *dharmatā*, which is the Buddhist term for *nature*."[29] Obviously, Kalupahana, too has come to this conclusion based on the grounds that dependent co-arising is a universal doctrine.[30]

Paṭiccasamuppāda brings out the "rational, coherent structure of the world."[31] In addition *dhamma* as *paṭiccasamuppāda* brings out the basic connection with the order of nature. This is where *paṭiccasamuppāda's* importance lies. It unifies the world under one formula. The Buddhist rendering of this concept simply reveals the world as "cause based" where every entity is the result of a cause and this is a universal and categorical certainty. *Paṭiccasamuppāda* is seen as a law that extends to everything in existence or potentially so. An awareness of *paṭiccasamuppāda* is the awareness that nature, be it human or non-human, is governed by the same law. In this uniformity and universality lies cosmic connection.

However the above analysis of *paṭiccasamuppāda* raises an important question. As was mentioned in the discussion on Plato in the previous chapter, a universal formula for all things also includes environmental evils such as the generation of nuclear waste or the dumping of toxic chemicals in rivers: these incidents are effects of some causes and thus a very legitimate part of the "cosmos." Does it mean that we can then logically accept their existence due to their causal nature? In one sense each aspect of nature – good or bad – must be accepted on a causal understanding. However such an interpretation would be a gross misrepresentation of what the theory of causality actually stands for. Buddhism does not condone certain realities because they exist as the effects of some causes but simply draws attention to how they have come to be and operate. The causal law is a natural law that is not and does not pretend to be regulatory in nature. However regulations are introduced at a different level – the ethical – and Buddhist environmental ethics must be looked upon as an amalgamation of both doctrines. The implication is that with realization of the true meaning of *paṭiccasamuppāda* consideration for nature may follow as a corollary; the latter is not a direct outcome. So though *paṭiccasamuppāda* lends itself to the cosmological approach to nature, it also points out the glaring need for an ethical component. A more detailed discussion on ethics is presented in the next chapter.

Saṃsāra

"*Saṃsāra*" is generally treated in the manner of a "circulation" or "moving on."[32] However the word in the *Nikāyas* is more often used to express the various realms of existence in which a being may wander. It may also represent the *dukkha* that accompanies this process. Some important aspects of *saṃsāra* can be enumerated in early Buddhist thought. These are:

1 The process of *saṃsāra* has no known beginnings.[33]
2 *Kammic* actions are the basis of the birth of all beings into different realms.[34]
3 Both *dukkkha* and the quest for liberation happen within this *saṃsāric* interplay.
4 No realm of *saṃsāra* is permanent. There is constant movement from one to another realm.
5 Wandering in *saṃsāra* comes to an end only once enlightenment (*nibbāna*) is attained.[35]

Thus movement from realm to realm of beings is due to their *kamma*. Incited by a lack of knowledge and the presence of ignorance (*avijjā*) about the true nature of reality such *kamma* exerts an even stronger hold over the being trapped in *saṃsāra*. To *saṃsāra* is attributed much anguished dissatisfaction and the only way to disassociate from this seemingly never-ending cycle is spiritual practice (*vis-à-vis* the Eightfold Path). It is such practice that unveils true reality leading to ultimate liberation (*nibbāna*).

The various realms of existence (*gati*) vary between five or six in number.[36] These are hell (*niraya*), the animal realm (*tiracchānayoni*), the ghostly world (*petā*), the titans (*asurās*), the world of human beings (*manussa*) and heavenly existence as a god (*deva*). Birth in the first four realms is a consequence of evil action and these are unhappy rebirths. The last two are considered good realms and are a consequence of righteous acts. Buddhist hells are full of intense pain and grief (and vivid descriptions of these are rife in Buddhist texts) and therefore they are not desirable places to be.[37] However these are impermanent and so the being continues to wander even after the consequences of bad deeds are fully undergone in this realm. Animal birth is also associated with much suffering.[38] The *petā* and the *asurā* worlds are not looked upon very favourably either.[39] Human rebirth has a somewhat distinctive significance. Though like the above realms it is defined by *dukkha*, unlike the above it allows for the possibility of *nibbāna*. Therefore this birth is regarded as an extremely important one. The most fortunate birth is that of a *deva*; their abode, heaven (*sagga*), is described as full of happiness.[40] The *Nikāyas* describe stages of heavenly existence, the uppermost being reserved for the most ethical agent. Mostly heaven too is temporary and in time one returns to *saṃsāra*.[41] Clearly the value of birth in each level varies and thus a sense of hierarchy is tenaciously implied in the doctrine of *saṃsāra*. There is also a strong sense that human birth is most valuable as human beings have the capacity for the pursuit of liberation. The concept of *saṃsāra* also implies constant inherent movement – birth in one realm follows another and then another. Beings, therefore, do not have an enduring identification. Often the superimposition of identification on the way things exist nurtures egoism and discrimination. Clearly the *saṃsāric* continuity does not allow these attitudes to strengthen.

The movement and connection that the doctrine brings out is indispensable to a cosmological outlook. The concept of *saṃsāra* is an important link in establishing the cosmological approach to nature in early Buddhism for various other reasons as well. First, it clearly conveys information that the realm of human beings is only one among many and therefore isolating it from the others would not really be in keeping with Buddhist beliefs. Secondly, even though birth in the human realm is an opportunity for the attainment of *nibbāna*, its place in the ladder of *saṃsāra* is not the highest. Interestingly enough, despite all the importance given to it, there is humble acceptance that human birth is intermediate. Had the value of human beings been superior they would not have occupied this position. Thirdly, one realm is composed of animals and in this Buddhism acknowledges their presence in the existential and metaphysical sense. The *saṃsāric* picture points to a sense of undeniable continuity between human beings and animals as well.

Finally, keeping in mind the Buddhist understanding of *saṃsāra*, concerns about "future generations" are addressed and mitigated. Interests of future generations are generally regarded as important and are a common theme in environmental literature. Avner De-Shalit, writes that ". . . we have not considered *all* aspects of environmental policies if we do not address the question of the distribution between generations and our obligations to future generations. . . ."[42] Buddhists include generations of the future within their world-view in an interesting and unique way. It is implied, on *saṃsāric* terms, that there exists a clear connection between past, present and future beings. Within Buddhist philosophy no life is completely independent of another. Connection is palpable and each life emanates from another. There is no single beginning or final end as the present carves the future and their link through *saṃsāra* and *kamma* is inevitable. In this way the continuity of *saṃsāra* encompasses future generations. On the other hand, when environmentalists in general talk of future human beings they only see a genetic connection with present beings and do not recognize continuity and connection in this wider sense. The latter rather limited rendering is impossible in Buddhist *saṃsāra* where the same beings return again and again until liberation. Thus future beings are a part of the cosmological universe exemplified by *saṃsāra*. There are no new beings. In this sense the *saṃsāra* based cosmological approach is inclusive of future beings as well.

It is important to address one other issue in relation to *saṃsāra*. An argument that can be used by those who are doubtful of the presence of environmental ethics in Buddhism is as follows: though there is no doubt that it is in *saṃsāra* that *nibbāna* is attained, it is ultimately escape from *saṃsāric* continuity (and *kamma*) that is the final goal of early Buddhism. If this is the case, then they can claim that it defeats the purpose of an environmental ethics, which is located very much within the realm of *kamma* and *saṃsāra*. This stance apparently encourages the marginalization of nature in that it gives rise to a dualistic perspective where one aspect (*saṃsāra*) is regarded as insignificant and instrumental in comparison with the other – in this case the ultimate goal of *nibbāna*. Consequently nature is devalued as part of *saṃsāra* and human beings are glorified due to their innate capacity for liberation.

The understanding of a categorical distinction between *saṃsāra* (as the realm of *kamma*) and *nibbāna* is generally attributed to the writings of Winston King and Melford Spiro who speak of the ethics of *nibbāna* or *nibbanic* Buddhism and the ethics of *kamma* or *kammatic* Buddhism.[43] According to them one excludes the other and combining them leads to all sorts of confusion. They have given vigorous supporting expositions and collated much evidence for their belief. However, and without going into detail, their reading of a bifurcation between the *kammatic* and *nibbanic* forms has been severely criticized by many.[44] Harvey Aronson finds such a division unfounded and writes:

> While it is true that the teachings on liberation from rebirth are considered more profound than those on achieving high rebirth, the former are not totally distinct from the latter. Practitioners of insight, the so-called nibbanic Buddhists, are still very much working within the laws of cause (*kamma*) and effect. The cultivation of virtuous activities (*kamma*) insures good rebirth, but more importantly creates the nexus within which a practitioner can cultivate concentration and insight in the present.[45]

Aronson, in a sense, is talking of a balance between the two forms, and does not believe that Buddhism considers one form to the exclusion of the other.

In his paper "The Theravāda View of Saṃsāra," James Boyd also finds that the concept of *saṃsāra* is misunderstood. Scholars often treat *nibbāna* alone as significant. He concentrates on showing that this is not the case. Among others, he cites a passage in support of his views from the *Nikāyas* where the Buddha is quoted as saying that it is within the fathom long body (*kaḷebare*), with its thoughts and perceptions, that the world exists, along with its origin, its cessation and the means leading to its cessation.[46] Boyd then goes on to say that it is clarified elsewhere that the end of the world is not the world's end.[47] In a description of the "world" yet again it is said that that world is that by which one has perception (*lokasaññī*) and conceit (*lokamānī*) of the world.[48] It is clear here that by giving these examples Boyd wants to show that it is the mind that must be freed and it is in this that the end of *saṃsāra* lies. The end of the world has nothing to do with the ending of "the external material world of saṃsāric process." Boyd also draws attention to the definition of *nibbāna*, which is not about the end of *saṃsāra*, but rather the end of desire (*rāga*), hate (*dosa*) and delusion (*moha*).[49] Once this is attained the *arahant* "lives the freedom of *paññā* (wisdom), *mettā* (universal love) and *karuṇā* (compassion)."[50]

These opposing renderings of the same doctrine are possibly enough to doubt the interpretation of the *saṃsāra-nibbāna* dichotomy. Both Aronson and Boyd are of the view that the gulf between subsisting in the *saṃsāric* world and final deliverance is not as evident in early Buddhism as it is made out to be. According to many other thinkers too the two concepts have to be known in sync for an impartial interpretation to become a possibility. By implication, the divide between the supreme value of human beings and the devalue of nature stands questioned. This also calls into question the view that marginalizes nature in Buddhism.

Buddhist cosmogony in the *Aggañña Sutta*

The meaning of cosmogony is generally taken to be "an account of the creation or generation of the world."[51] Early Buddhist texts expound no exceptional or dedicated account of creation. However, a brief version of the Buddhist cosmogonic myth is introduced in the *Aggañña Sutta*. This account explains the formation of the world – of sun and moon, plants and human beings in their physical and social landscape.[52] The cosmogonic myth has implications that can be seen to have a bearing on environmental ethics in a number of ways as will be shown below. But first more on the wider meaning of cosmogony in Buddhism ought to be noted.

Frank E. Reynolds in his study of the cosmogony of Theravāda Buddhism has identified more than one cosmogony in this Buddhism.[53] He considers Buddhist cosmogony expressed first through *paṭiccasamuppāda*. The second form of cosmogony he refers to is the myth of the *Aggañña Sutta*. The third is the cosmogony that speaks of the Buddha's formation of a world order in accordance with *dhamma*. This is the world in which Buddhists live, act and seek liberation.[54] The author finds that this form is brought into being from within *saṃsāra* but it eventually transcends it. Finally, he mentions the cosmogony that will be consummated by the future Buddha, *Metteya*. Thus, Reynolds portrays cosmogony in the widest sense possible: as not only a portrayal of how the world came to be but also of how it continues to exist and evolve. He considers the relations between the different types of cosmogonies and their place in the Buddhist system. Though his thesis is very interesting, in this section my focus remains on the story of creation of the *Aggañña Sutta* and the idea of nature it may contain.

At the outset of this discussion it is important to remember that no first cause was acknowledged by the Buddha. While speaking of the beginning of the experiential world or *saṃsāra* he says: "Monks, the starting point of *saṃsāra* is not known. Beings transmigrate and move continuously, hindered by ignorance and bonded by craving."[55] There are numerous other instances as well where the Buddha recognized that no decisive beginning could accrue to *saṃsāra*. He strongly hinted that it was a waste of time to search for an unknowable first cause. The description of the myth reflects this aspect and begins with the conventional description of the world formation from the potential to the actual. Clearly, a discussion of the first beginning is of no consequence here either.

It is possible to study the above myth in two parts. This is made clear by Fabel, who while speaking of cosmological purpose, distinguishes between two stages:

> The overt steps from an original singularity through the formation of stars, planets, complex molecules, the origin of life, and its ramification over time are sufficiently filled in. The obvious first phase of finding the material parts has been largely completed. The next stage of investigation . . . seeks to discern universal motifs, dynamics, and interconnections between the parts that might illuminate an inherent order and direction.[56]

I too will look at the myth in these two stages, first stating exactly how the myth is portrayed in the *Dīgha Nikāya* and secondly establishing its internal dynamics and leitmotifs that may throw light on the Buddhist understanding of nature.

The following is an overt description of the cosmogony. According to the *Aggañña Sutta* there comes a time, after a long period, when the world contracts (*loko saṃvaṭṭati*). At the time of contraction beings (*sattā*) are mostly born in a *Brahma* world (*ābhassara*). They dwell there and are self-luminous (*sayam-pabhā*), moving through the air (*antalikkha-carā*). After a long time the world begins to expand (*loko vivaṭṭati*). These beings are then born in the expanding world, with the same properties that they had in the *Brahma* world. At this time the earth is dark (*andha-kāro*) and covered with a mass of water (*ekodakī-bhūtaṃ*). There is no moon and sun (*candima-suriyā*), day and night (*rattin-divā*), stars (*tāraka*), years and seasons (*utu-saṃvaccharā*), male and female (*itthi-pumā*). Beings (*sattā*) are just beings. Then over time earth in great fineness (*rasa-paṭhavī*) spreads itself over the water. Some beings of a greedy nature (*lola-jātiko*) taste it and as a result of this there is a craving (*taṇhā*) in them for more. Other beings follow, and as a result of the craving and greed they eat more and more and lose their self-luminosity (*sayam-pabhā antaradhāyi*). Due to this sun, moon, day, night and seasons appear and to this extent the world re-evolves (*loko puna vivaṭṭo hoti*). As beings progressively eat, their bodies become coarser (*kharattañ*), some become good-looking (*vaṇṇavanto*) and despise the ones that become ugly (*dubbaṇṇā*). The good-looking beings become arrogant and conceited (*mānātimāna*) about their looks. As a result of conceit, the fine earth disappears (*rasa-paṭhavī antaradhāyi*) and a fungus like substance (*bhūmi-pappaṭako*) crops up instead, also of a good smell and taste. The beings feed on it and their bodies become even coarser. The good looking grow even more arrogant due to which even the fungus disappears and is replaced by creepers (*badālatā*), also of fine quality. The same process repeats itself, until finally the creepers also disappear. So the beings lament. Then rice appears – free from powder and husk – which renews itself everyday (*akaṭṭhapāko sāli pātur ahosi, akaṇo athuso*). This goes on for long, as beings become even coarser. Different sexes appear, and men and women become differentiated and are preoccupied (*upanijjhāyati*) with each other. They build dwellings (*agāraka*), are lazy (*alasa-jātiko*) and so start collecting rice to store (*sannidhi-kārakaṃ sāliṃ*). Once the concept of hoarding sets in, husk appears on the rice and it does not renew itself anymore. So now the beings lament and decide to divide fields with boundaries (*vibhajiṃsu*). Then one being takes over another's plot wrongly (*pāpakā*), and though rebuked for his action, he carries on regardless. And so the beings decide to employ one certain being who would punish such a wrong-doer. And they choose the handsomest and most capable amongst themselves – he is called "lord of the fields" (*khattiya*) among other things. And this is seen as the origin of the *khattiyas* or the ruling class. The *Sutta* goes on to describe the four-branched caste distinction on the basis of what the beings do; in this they break away from the Brahmanical understanding of caste as based on birth. Eventually, some being realizes that evil and unwholesome things (*pāpakā akusalā dhammā*) have crept up amongst them. Then some *khattiya* dissatisfied with this unwholesomeness goes into homelessness and becomes an ascetic (*samaṇa*). Beings from the other castes follow as well. The *Sutta* ends by saying that beings from all four classes, if they perform good deeds will have a heavenly rebirth; if they perform bad deeds they will go to hell.

The above account thus illustrates how the world came into existence the way it did. In addition it also brings up some issues that evoke curiosity as their meaning and intention is not explicitly stated. These require investigation and this is the second step, according to Fabel, for discerning myths and what they truly represent. What the *Aggañña Sutta* truly represents has in the past been understood in various ways. Michael Carrithers believes that the myth illustrates "metamorphosis and creativity in human life," and shows "how people use stories to create new social forms."[57] However, the most common belief about the myth is that it is a satire on the *brahmanical* caste system, for the *Sutta* not only starts with a discussion of the caste system but seems especially preoccupied with it. This view is possibly most vociferously articulated and advocated by Richard Gombrich. He has claimed that most Buddhists have taken the *Aggañña Sutta* to be an account of the origin of the universe and of society. However, his own research has revealed that the intent of the text is satirical. The text is a parody directed towards Vedic beliefs such as the ones outlined in the cosmogonies of *Bṛhad-āraṇyaka Upaniṣad.* He also finds that this *Sutta* has considerable incoherencies if it is taken as an account of creation.[58] He claims further that "strictly speaking, the *Aggañña Sutta*, is not a cosmogony, since for Buddhists an absolute beginning is inconceivable."[59] I am not disputing claims that have been put forward by Professor Gombrich, but I would like to make two additional points: First, that despite containing scope for such criticism, other aspects are also put forth in a more subtle way that also represent authentic Buddhist beliefs. If Buddhist ideas are faithfully reflected then other information contained in the *Sutta* can be used for collating further facts as well quite legitimately. For instance, the *Sutta* seems to be attuned to the Buddhist doctrine of *kamma*. It is said:

> And, Vaseṭṭha, as for a *Khattiya* who has behaved wrongly in body, speech and thought, who has wrong views, will, as a result of such wrong views and actions, at the breaking up of the body after death, arise in loss, downfall, a state of suffering, hell. And so for a *Brahmin* . . . and so for a *Vessa* . . . and so for a *Sudda* . . .[60]

The pattern of *kamma* that has been adopted in the *Nikāyas* in general is replicated here as are expressions of morality. There is an elaborate discussion of vices that also commonly occur in other portions of the Canon such as greed (*lola*) and arrogance (*māna*). Thus genuine aspects of Buddhist thinking can be derived from the *Sutta* even if its main intention is a parodist one. Secondly, even though the *Aggañña Sutta* may not necessarily be treated as a perfect cosmogony (which would pretty much be an impossibility in Buddhism) it does provide a description of secondary evolution from several perspectives such as the moral or political. It illustrates each aspect in a remarkable manner, and though this does not make up for the absence of an "absolute beginning," it does indicate the meticulous effort and interest of the early Buddhists in matters of cosmological concern that was also in unity with the rest of the scripture.

The environmental perspective ought to be explored as well. Some important implicit features of the cosmogony that contribute to a cosmological understanding of nature can be drawn out and emphasized. They are as follows. First it ought to be noted in the gradually expanding depiction of creation that the role of human beings is principal. It has been said of cosmic myths in general that "The object of the whole exercise is to conceive of the way in which man as subject fits into the whole of things. For man to fit in he has to find the sense of things; hence the fulfilment of the myth is in the disclosure of a cosmic meaning within which each individual can find his own. Man is seen as playing a part in a cosmic drama to which his role is essential."[61] This holds quite true of Buddhist cosmogony as well. Focusing on the role of humanity is not an unusual thing and is reflected in other Buddhist doctrines such as *paṭiccasamuppāda*. The description of the status and situation of human beings is an accepted feature of the cosmological approach. A second important aspect is that the four material elements get a mention and point directly to the co-evolution of physical nature and man. During the contraction, beings are seen as self-luminous and moving through the air. So the two elements of fire and air are already present. With expansion, the same beings are born in the expanding world, which is composed of water. Thus is introduced the third element. Finally, earth appears as subtle and fine. Gradually it becomes less ethereal and more like we see it today. P. D. Ryan and others have pointed this out in addition to saying that it is the moral nature of beings that affects the quality of these elements.[62] A third notable feature is that the *Sutta* only mentions foods that are vegetarian. Though this may also be construed as an argument in favour of vegetarianism from the cosmological point of view, it also points to the conspicuous absence of animals. And finally, in connection with the last point, the implications of the absence of (or ambiguity about) animals must be further investigated. The word "*sattā*" is used for beings that were born originally in *Brahma* world and there is some doubt about whether the term includes animals. Waldau has tried to determine the exact meaning of the term in a more general sense and concludes that "*sattaa* can also mean just human beings, but generally, the sense is much more generic."[63] Thus there appears to be general vagueness about the exact meaning of the term. If, on the one hand, animals are taken to be included in the term, they become an important part of the cosmogony of the *Aggañña Sutta.* If, on the other hand *sattā* is taken as not including animals in this particular *Sutta*, then this may point to an incomplete cosmogony. But this problem can be sorted once the myth is combined with the doctrine of *saṃsāra*, which shows that animals are recognized but at a different level (for they are really the same beings in circulation).

What becomes essential to the cosmological theme is that this *Sutta* for the first time presents the natural progression of living entities and material elements at a physical level. The *Sutta* is not advocating a law and it does not have a metaphysical import. It contains a purely physical description. It speaks of the formation of the world and how differentiation developed gradually. The beings (*sattā*) and the natural world (the elements and plants) are essential parts of this progressing reality. Its earthiness connects it more closely to notions of the environment. It may be added that the *Aggañña Sutta's* significance lies in its mythological status and in the ingenuity of its creators. But it is also indispensable because it displays a unique likeness to the scriptures by mirroring other Buddhist attitudes (inclusive of the environmental) perfectly. This reaffirms the Buddhist cosmological approach to nature, and of the *Sutta* it may be said that because it "sees the evolution of life as continuous with the evolution of matter [it] challenges us to formulate ways of living in a vast universe that seems largely indifferent to our existence."[64]

Overview

Dhamma, paṭiccasamuppāda, saṃsāra and the *Aggañña Sutta*, each in their own way express the notion of nature as cosmological. The presence of physical nature and plants is acknowledged in one sense. Animals are identified in another sense as they appear in *saṃsāra* and this characterizes their position. Man occupies a position in relation to all of these – he is clearly *central* but not *superior*. It is problematical to locate descriptions of non-human nature – natural entities, plants and animals – that relate to modern notions of environmental ethics, even if they are more than just conservation oriented. But this does not imply a negligence of nature, which on the above understanding is an intrinsic part of reality. As for questions of value, Buddhism does not seem to differentiate between intrinsic and instrumental values in any obvious way. Intrinsic value signifies that a thing must be valued for itself and not for the use others may get out of it. On the other hand, a thing has instrumental value when it is valued not for itself but for the benefit it may provide to others. Instrumental value, as such, has acquired a fairly negative association and many environmentalists think that only when it is proved that things have intrinsic value that respect for nature and conservation can become possible. Some thinkers however have questioned the very legitimacy of the idea of instrumental value. Yrjo Haila and Richard Levins claim that a purely instrumental view of nature is self-contradictory. They ask how one can differentiate between the "I" and the "nature" that is used as an instrument. Human beings are a part of nature and they depend on nature for their survival, and due to this connection it becomes impossible to treat nature as an instrument. Nature as mere instrument is then reduced to a cultural construct by these authors, which has only arisen due to the successful exploitation of nature.[65] Though nothing specific is said on value in early Buddhism the fact that every aspect of nature including human beings described in the sections above is a part of the cosmological continuum appears to support the position of Haila and Levins. The gap between human beings and nature is non-existent in early Buddhism too; everything has its unique position and role – under such circumstances according instrumental value to nature is ludicrous. However, in the final analysis, even though the above comparison attempts to bring out the Buddhist stance on value, such questions are difficult to address and rest uneasily within the Buddhist understanding of the universe. All things considered it can be judiciously accepted that the unconventionality of the Buddhist approach to nature may not find it necessary to establish intrinsic value in everything. There is a probability that it may just consider it as already existing.

The deeper quest of finding a motivation in all these doctrines (*dhamma, paṭiccasamuppāda, saṃsāra* and the *Aggañña Sutta*) that promotes environmental attitudes and responsibility must be attempted. Their analysis implies that though they describe how the world is, they do not describe the process through which it could be valued. They simply explain the way the world exists. But, I believe, such a description provides a firm impetus for the practice of morality. Additionally Allan Greenbaum, while writing on cosmological issues in environmental thought, has pointed out that descriptions of reality remain important:

> . . . not because of its considerable scientific and metaphysical merits as description of what *is* (and what will be whatever we do), but because of its even greater power as a symbol of what *is not*, of that desired connection with organic cycles which is felt to be lacking in modern life.[66]

This is precisely what is also aimed at in the early Buddhist cosmological approach to nature.

Environment, anthropocentrism and early Buddhism

The cosmological approach to nature in Buddhism draws attention to another difficulty that an environmental ethicist may face within this framework: this difficulty pertains to the superior value of man. The problem may be stated as follows:

Premise 1: Buddhist philosophy constantly focuses on human birth as this is the only realm in which the highest goal of life is attainable. This can be taken to imply that the life of humans is most valuable.

Premise 2: Anthropocentrism is a position where humans are considered central and only humans are said to have value or are believed to have the highest value.

Conclusion: Owing to this similarity the conclusion is that Buddhism is anthropocentric.

Since anthropocentrism is generally considered to be a detrimental moral position in environmental ethics as it implies an exploitation of nature, any likeness to it is bound to have negative repercussions for Buddhism and ecology. However the issue is not as simple as presented in the above argument for a number of reasons both within Buddhism and within environmental literature when it deals with the notion of anthropocentrism. Before turning to Buddhism an understanding of anthropocentrism would be useful.

Anthropocentrism in its dimensions

Anthropocentrism is a much mentioned term in environmental literature. Anthropocentrism comes from the Greek words *anthropos* meaning man or human being and *kentron* meaning center. A common perception of anthropocentrism maintains that human beings are the only entities that have value or the highest value and so their interests must be served irrespective of other interests Anthropocentrism can be said to imply the centrality of the interests of human beings so that all else comes to have instrumental value. Thus anthropocentrism is deeply related to questions of value. The logical culmination of this position may lead to an allowance of the use of natural resources in an unsustainable way and to cruelty towards animals. Though not condoning the cruel treatment of animals Tibor R. Machan takes the anthropocentric argument to its extreme whilst speaking of animals when he says "one reason for the propriety of our use of animals is that we are more important or valuable than other animals. . . ."[67] Some scholars have also essentially compared the idea of anthropocentrism with egoism (or egocentrism). Egoism, as the word implies, says that we ought to further our interests alone; nothing else is required of us. The pursuit of interests becomes a central moral concern – the motivation for every action is personal gain and little else. In fact, psychological egoists claim that human beings defend their interests as a matter of course and are capable of nothing other than this. In the case of anthropocentrism, it has been noted once again, the egoism represents the entire human species. Due to this and the above reasons anthropocentrism is frequently condemned by environmental scholars as discriminatory and narrow-minded. Often this position is also referred to as strong anthropocentrism in deference to the existence of other positions. Thus anthropocentrism in its strong form is generally adjudicated as inequitable because it refuses to value anything other than human beings.

As hinted, the above is a rather one-dimensional understanding of anthropocentrism and its complexity. There are two other anthropocentric claims that ought to be considered: that of weak anthropocentrism and of human perspective. I deal with the latter first. Some environmentalists claim that anthropocentrism is really about knowing and understanding the world from a human perspective and through human-based values and so it cannot be ignored. As Eugene Hargrove understands it "anthropocentrism . . . simply means 'human-centred,' and refers to a human oriented perspective – seeing from the standpoint of a human being."[68] Tim Hayward claims that anthropocentrism is about interpreting the world in terms of human values. To him there is an ineliminable element of anthropocentrism in all ethics and anti-anthropocentric rhetoric is counterproductive in practice.[69] Also most ethicists do not deny anthropocentrism in this form; but many hesitate to call this stand anthropocentrism at all due to the other connotations the term has come to have. For instance, calling the human perspective a "human epistemic locatedness" rather than anthropocentrism, Val Plumwood concurs that ". . . if we eliminated all knowledge of our experience of suffering not only would we be unable to consider ourselves properly, we would have no basis for sympathy with another's suffering."[70] An environmental ethics thus must be grounded in this interpretation of anthropocentrism since no human beings can be or act in any other way. Even those who attack anthropocentrism in its strong sense cannot disagree that it is only through a human perspective that the world becomes known. Since this is perspective-based anthropocentrism and there is little disagreement among ethicists about it, no more will be said about this position.

In addition to these two understandings some environmentalists endorse wholeheartedly the position that we can adopt a more moderate expression of anthropocentrism: namely, weak anthropocentrism.[71] According to them weak anthropocentrism as opposed to strong suggests that even though moral choices are made with human beings in mind, non-human beings are deserving of moral concern too; the difference being that the intensity of morality in the latter case is diluted in comparison. This makes sense of the fact that to human beings their interests are important but it also makes altruism more real. Weak anthropocentrism, it has been noted, is not compatible with strong anthropocentrism precisely for the reason that the latter contains no proviso for altruistic actions. Thus weak anthropocentrism is a position that says that human beings do not need to neglect their wider interests and at the same time human beings can encourage and reflect respect for others in their moral choices. Since questions of value are so important it must be added that anthropocentrism does not always imply that all but human beings have instrumental value. Hargrove claims that ". . . *anthropocentric* is not and has never been a synonym for *instrumental*."[72]

Bryan Norton explains one measure through which weak anthropocentrism can be recognized. He distinguishes between two definitions of human interests – as a felt preference and as a considered preference. He writes that a *felt* preference is a desire that can be satiated by some experience of the individual and cites the economic approach to decision making as an example – i.e., the decision makers ask people what they want, correct and compute these preferences and make a decision. On the other hand *considered* preference is the desire of an individual that has been deliberated upon and is consistent with a rationally adopted world-view – scientific, metaphysical, aesthetic, moral. It implies that desires can be dropped or modified if they do not fit the world-view. So then a theory is strongly anthropocentric when all value is explained by reference to the satisfaction of felt preferences alone and it is weakly anthropocentric when it is explained by the satisfaction of some felt preference or considered preferences – that is by taking recourse to some ideal or world-view. This implies that there is no check on felt preferences and an individual acting out of such interests would quite easily exploit nature. But there is a system of checks and balances in considered preferences and appeals can be made to the adopted ideals or world-view. So, Norton concludes "within weak anthropocentrism there exists a framework for developing powerful reasons for protecting nature that do not resemble exploitative reasons used by strong anthropocentrism."[73] As an illustration, consider that a cultural world-view speaks of sacredness in all aspects of nature (including animals, plants, water, etc.) as a way of acknowledging gratitude to them for making human life possible. Even those aspects that have no direct use but a possible one become worthy of veneration. That everything is sacred is a view that would influence human behaviour and inspire a concern for others. Thus by embracing this or a similar world-view the exploitation of nature as a "felt preference" becomes hard to justify.

A further development of weak anthropocentrism must also throw some light on how a fair balance can be sought between the self and other. A balance between self and the other can be sought for instance by believing that "Human beings like other entities have goods constitutive of their flourishing, and correspondingly other goods instrumental to that flourishing. The flourishing of many other living things ought to be promoted because they are constitutive of our own flourishing."[74] By adopting this world-view the perceived distinction between human welfare and that of others dissolves and promoting the well-being of all makes sense as they are a vital constituent of each other's welfare and not a channel to that welfare alone. Though the above world-view does not refer to weak anthropocentrism per se, the arguments fit well with the general ethos of considered preference that is being established here. Attaining a balance between the self and other thus can be sought within a "considered" world- view. This view questions pure egoism and makes way for universal regard for nature. Clearly a search for considered preferences can be quite an effective principle for environmentalists.

Weak anthropocentrism also reinforces a trust in human beings and a belief in their widening capacity of concern for others. Though not discussing weak anthropocentrism specifically. W. H. Murdy writes:

> An anthropocentric faith in mankind affirms that we are not isolated monads acting out absurd roles within a meaningless context, but that we are essential elements of a meaningful whole and that our individual acts are vitally significant to the self realization of the process of human evolution itself and to the enhancement of value in the world.[75]

A necessary part of human prosperity on Murdy's account is the recognition of the steadfast bond between human beings and the universe. Additionally within the boundaries of weak anthropocentrism there is space for the realization that each human action has an effect on the world – acts based on pure selfishness would lead to the devaluing of resources and acts from concern and other higher objectives would have quite the opposite result. It would endorse the belief that man has the innate capacity to increase beauty and value in the world by cultivating equanimity, compassion, sympathetic joy and loving kindness.[76] If these were employed in dealings with nature then the possibility of conservation and protection of environment would be very achievable goals.

However, it is not only strong anthropocentrism that is open to challenges and condemnations; weak anthropocentrism comes with its share of problems. The latter has some way to go before a satisfactory form is arrived at. It has been commonly noted by scholars that weak anthropocentrism has to deal with awkward questions that arise when the vital interests of human beings clash with those of non-human beings. Though it admits including interests other than those of human beings, it is mostly unable to clarify the extent of such concern and so is of little use in the practical sphere. There is theoretical discussion of a balance between various aspects of the natural world but in concrete terms questions of balance remain ambiguous. However balancing interests is not only awkward for weak anthropocentrism, it is similarly hard for other positions like biocentrism. As a theory biocentrism considers the interests of all living biotic entities. But most supporters of biocentrism admit to facing severe difficulties in deciding the grounds for acting in favour of one or the other member of the biotic community when choices are to be made.[77] In the case of weak anthropocentrism it has also been pointed out in addition that when faced with a choice between interests, selection of human life over any other would imply a swerve towards strong anthropocentrism such that in such instances "weak anthropocentrism" can be labelled an ineffectual theory unable to stand its ground. Tipping the balance in such a way can distort the fine line between strong and weak anthropocentrism, so that the notion of altruism stands compromised.[78] However efforts to resolve the issue of balance are underway – one example being Norton's thesis on felt and considered preferences.

The following are the conclusions I have drawn from the above discussion: First, that strong anthropocentrism in its egoistic and restrictive mode is unacceptable. Second, the anthropocentrism that implies that the world only be valued through a human perspective, a point of view that has been referred to by a scholar as "human epistemic locatedness" is almost universally accepted. And, third, that weak anthropocentrism, though as unsatisfactory as the other positions, appears as a more astute perspective to position a pragmatic environmental ethics on. This is because it addresses human beings and non-human beings. It responds to the needs of human beings and acknowledges their interests and goals. At the same time it considers the needs of the voiceless non-human world. Additionally weak anthropocentrism shows a relative optimism about the capacity of human beings to care for entities other than themselves. In this it is unlike strong anthropocentrism that portrays human beings as egocentric and narrow-minded. And this is where rests its resemblance to Buddhism. In all, even though not free from faults weak anthropocentrism is compelling due to its response to both human and non-human needs. Since this is a very real issue in the world today the value of weak anthropocentrism is important from the practical point of view.

Buddhism and weak anthropocentrism

The case of early Buddhism is very extraordinary. Buddhism is complex and has a world-view that grows progressively subtle as the understanding of Buddhism deepens and successive layers of thought get revealed. The first premise of the earlier given argument that claims Buddhism as anthropocentric can thus be ruled out immediately at one level. The major reason why Buddhism defies being anthropocentric is because it defies the very notion of a substantial person. A human being is a consequence of certain causes and conditions (*khandhas*) and he or she ceases to exist when these get dissolved. Thus to call Buddhism anthropocentric or human-centred when there is no "human" as such appears unreasonable from this point of view. However this absolute truth does not rule out a quite different conclusion at the experiential and worldly level where the separate identity of each individual is recognized and the individual lives out his or her life.

At the experiential level there is one apparent sense in which Buddhism could be regarded as making man (humanity) central. The teachings of the Buddha are focused on man and his escape from the mundane world of suffering. Buddhism does not deny that human birth is of central importance. Buddha's entire philosophy is based around the human being's quest for liberation which must come through the efforts made during a human existence. The training prescribed by early Buddhism for the attainment of enlightenment is morality, contemplation and insight (the Eightfold Path) – all only within the reach of human beings. As discussed earlier, birth in any of the other spheres of existence (*saṃsāra*), good or bad, is necessary for exhausting the consequences of *kamma*, but clearly not sympathetic to the pursuit for liberation. There is not even the simplest of suggestion that moral action can be performed in the other lower spheres (except perhaps animals). All one grasps is descriptions of torture. The life of a god is also considered a not good enough goal in early Buddhism even though happy, for it is not permanent; one eventually goes back into the ever-revolving circle of existence. The human condition, though it is a condition of *dukkha*, is the only one in which *nibbāna* can be attained. Therefore, understandably there is great stress on the importance of human life.

The Buddha had understood the meaning of *dukkha* and mastered its permanent destruction. He taught others like himself how to overcome it, i.e., he understood *dukkha* from his own (human) experience of the world and then shared this knowledge with other human beings. He was motivated by a concern for human beings. From all of the above it may follow quite reasonably that moral decisions may be taken such that the quest for human liberation is not impeded in any sense or precious human life threatened anyhow. Thus from this point of view Buddhism can easily be classified as anthropocentric or human-centred.[79] If this argument is taken a step further then it can be additionally inferred that the value given to human beings must be supreme.[80] The texts prima facie appear to corroborate this by mentioning that one's own welfare must not be neglected for the sake of another's, however great the latter may be.[81] This could then be taken to mean that the environment may be used to support human ends in any undignified or selfish way.

To say on the basis of the above discussion that early Buddhism is egoistic and strongly anthropocentric in that it encourages man to strive for his life and liberation makes sense but also raises many problems. To clarify, the roots of anthropocentrism in Buddhism lie at least partly, in its reading as a purely egoistic practice of pursuing liberation. Egoism, as mentioned earlier, is often likened to anthropocentrism because the latter too is concerned self-interestedly with the good of one entity alone i.e. the human species. This reading is further confirmed by the fact that later forms of Buddhism often criticized early Buddhist principles as selfish and concerned with personal liberation rather than the welfare of other suffering beings. But at the same time to obscure the broader context of Buddhism with these rather limiting categorizations would be a gross injustice and not true to its spirit.

Establishing strong anthropocentrism (and egoism) on Buddhist principles is absurd once the nature of human-centeredness it endorses becomes revealed through its theory. I anticipate here that though early Buddhism is anthropocentric, this does not transform into a strong anthropocentrism.

Buddhism is not egoistic in that the means laid down for attaining liberation, and indeed liberation itself must intrinsically accept some amount of altruist practices. The Buddhist path to liberation includes a strong element of morality whose practice has a beneficial effect on others and confirms that Buddhism is not egoistic. I will demonstrate that the early Buddhist position does eventually come close to "weak anthropocentrism" when it is used in application to nature. It supports weak anthropocentrism in two imperative ways. First, early Buddhism confirms through many instances that the most valued action is one where not only the agent but others are actively considered. Though non-human nature is not directly mentioned in these instances, the disposition of acting ethically, in the interest of others, is strongly recommended. Second, early Buddhism is a strong paradigm for the practice of considered preferences as opposed to felt preferences. Early Buddhists have a world-view dominated by the notions of continuity and retribution and the merit of actions must be calculated keeping these in mind and not just immediate desires. In addition Buddhism encourages a process of self-realization that is tied up with other ethical and altruistic processes in so significant a way that isolating one from the other would defeat the very purpose of human life.

Extending care to ourselves and others is a constant theme in the *Nikāyas*. Whilst discussing mindfulness in the *Sedaka Sutta* of the *Saṃyutta Nikāya*, the Buddha recounts the story of a bamboo acrobat and his assistant who are about to perform some feats on a pole. The acrobat instructs the pupil that they must watch out for each other during the performance. But the pupil disagrees and says they must watch out for themselves. The Buddha then tells his disciples that they should observe mindfulness and in so doing they will protect themselves and protect others too. And by protecting others they will protect themselves. The *Sutta* states:

> And how is it, monks, that by protecting oneself others are protected?
> By the continuous practice and cultivation of meditation . . . .
> And how is it, monks, that by protecting others oneself is protected?
> By forbearance, non-violence, universal love and sympathy. . . .[82]

This example makes two important points. First, that a person must cultivate Buddhist discipline and mindfulness to protect himself (so as to attain enlightenment). In this he also helps others (by making an example of himself). Second, he must practice patience (*khanti*), harmlessness (*avihiṃsā*), loving-kindness (*mettā*) and sympathy (*anudāya*) through which he can protect others. By protecting others he protects himself (for these qualities are essential for liberation). What comes across from this example is that for Buddhism the practitioner's spiritual advancement was a central concern. However the disdaining of others is not implied in the passage, for in advancing one's self others gain too. Gotama's attends to personal interests and other interests at the same time. He specifically says that in one the other lies and vice versa. Other scholars have noted as well that deeply spiritual practices that appear of no consequence to anyone but the practitioner can be of advantage to others. Steven Collins writes "The rationale for action which acceptance of Buddhism furnishes provides neither for simple self-interest nor for self-denying altruism."[83] Even though Collins reaches this conclusion by means of a different argument, this way of thinking is much in evidence in early Buddhist teachings.

Again, in the *Sallekha Sutta* the Buddha, while speaking to the monk Cunda says that it is not possible for one who is stuck in the mud to pull out another who is stuck in the mud; but it is possible for one who is himself not stuck in the mud to pull out another who is stuck in the mud.[84] Though once again this *Sutta* is framed in a monastic context, it gives a sense of general Buddhist beliefs. It implies that only after serving personal interests can the agent contribute to another's welfare. Piyadassi Thera has commented:

> To protect oneself is not egoism, not selfish security, but self discipline, self training, both moral and mental training. To the extent we are mentally strong and confident, so can we help others. If we are weak and diffident we can help neither our selves nor others. Altruism, as a principle of action, is based on our character and mental development.[85]

This statement sums up not only the above reference, but also clarifies the Buddhist position to a great degree.

The Buddha has also stated in the *Aṅguttara Nikāya* that there are four persons found existing in the world. There are those who do not work for their own advantage or for the advantage of others; those who work for the advantage of others but not their own; those who work for their own advantage and not of others; and those who work for the advantage of both themselves and others.[86] He goes on to state that the person who is bent on his own advantage as well as on the advantage of another was the foremost (*uttariṃ*) and best and most supreme of all of them. Thus the most coveted position in this example exemplifies pursuing personal advantage and that of others simultaneously. This again is a reflection of what is repeated in the *Suttas* often. In a later book of the *Aṅguttara Nikāya* the Buddha states three types of inspirations. He says that it is fitting and indeed worthwhile to make effort and strive earnestly where one sees some advantage for oneself, or for others or for both.[87] Thus, from this and the above examples once more the importance of welfare of both the self and others (in that order) comes across clearly. Other examples such as those that state that after the fulfilment of a personal quest it is time to consider others can also be evinced in support of the above thesis. Buddha instructs his learned disciples to impart teachings to others from compassion and for the latter's happiness.[88] Even in the case of monks that live in seclusion, many scholars cite, a concern for others can be a possibility: such monks can motivate and encourage future monks and their spiritual aspirations.[89] This point of view is also supported by Jayatilleke, who is of the opinion that Buddhist ethics is "a form of enlightened egoism or enlightened altruism, which could best be characterized as an ethical universalism" and that "the egoist must develop altruistic virtues for his own good."[90] Though his position is rather extreme, Jayatilleke seems to be implying that in Buddhism egoism and altruism become deeply intertwined such that the good of the self and others merge.[91] Most of the above examples have been used by scholars to show that early Buddhism is not egoistic; I additionally use them to show that early Buddhism though not strongly anthropocentric, is nevertheless weakly anthropocentric.

I reiterate that the above examples in Buddhist literature are not specifically related to the environment or posed in defence of the charge of strong anthropocentrism or egoism. But they are an important part of Buddhist beliefs that encourage a disposition that extends beyond personal concern. It is by embracing these aspects that life must be lived in the world and environmental actions enacted. As for the second reason why early Buddhism can be considered weakly anthropocentric, Buddhism's inadvertent support to the notion of considered preferences must be analysed. Norton's view of considered preferences, as mentioned earlier, signifies that human desires must be met against a substantial world-view that may be based in ethics, aesthetics and so on. The action ought to be done only once it gains acceptance within this world-view. In the case of early Buddhism the world-view against which actions must be conducted coincides with the cosmological conception of the world, the practice of moral values and the attainment of liberation. This metaphysical-physical-ethical world-view acts as a system of checks and balances for the functioning of considered preferences rather than felt ones. The earlier appraisal of the notions of *paṭiccasamuppāda* and *saṃsāra* prove an indelible uniformity of causality and continuity to exist between entities on the cosmological plane. On the other hand the theory of morality and retribution (that actions will have corresponding consequences) makes certain that actions are done in a way that ensures the best consequences. The understanding of cosmological realities and the practice of ethics are also indelibly tied up with the attainment of self-realization such that isolation from these would not allow the aspirant success in spiritual activities. Buddhism does not support an insubstantial theory of liberation; it is grounded firmly in certain ideals. Attainment of liberation though a personal quest is never a selfish one as it is made out to be. None of the above three signify that one's own interest ought to be fulfilled only or neglected for the sake of others. They simply suggest a "considered" framework within which life can be lived to the fullest advantage of one's self and others.

I am aware of the many protestations that can be lodged against classifying

Buddhism as (weakly) anthropocentric. The most important one is that to call Buddhism anthropocentric is to invite severe charges of anachronism. Objections may be raised that Buddhism has been set up in a category that is quite far apart from its ideology. I anticipate many Buddhist scholars saying that there in fact is no centre at all in Buddhism. However, avoiding anthropocentrism, according to some scholars, has its disadvantages and a sense of this comes through from the early Buddhist texts themselves. Often enticements of material or spiritual gain are given in these texts for the performance of action. Full scale descriptions of punishment are employed for ensuring good behaviour. This can be borne out by various examples quoted in the *Nikāyas* and other texts where persons are willing to change themselves for fear of bad consequences befalling them. By avoiding anthropocentrism then not only does one ecologically benefit by displacing human beings as a centre of all decisions but also stands to lose for all personal motivation and enthusiasm to act is gone and so is the possibility of acting in the true spirit of altruism by rising above singular selfish pursuits. Human centeredness may in fact be supportive if "being human centred means having a well balanced conception of what it means to be human, and how humans take their place in the world, then it may exemplify the sorts of virtues associated with normative ideas of 'humanity' and 'humaneness'."[92]

As another alternative to anthropocentrism it may be supposed that Buddhism, in its quest for the liberation of the individual, be called *nibbāna*-centric more legitimately. However, being *nibbāna*-centric leads to worries too. If it implies attention to only one aspect of life disvaluing all else it translates into a form of marginalization which is not the Buddhist stand.[93] Again if *nibbāna*-centric suggests simultaneous self improvement and involvement in the world then it is no different from weak anthropocentrism. If on the other hand *nibbāna*-centric implies that Buddhism does not give all human beings supreme value but only those who are capable of attaining liberation then many problems arise. For in each lifetime human beings contribute something to their pool of deeds and consequences that may eventually lead them to liberation or so one may hope. So to pick out certain human beings who are capable of attaining liberation in the here and now and filtering out the rest is simply not possible. If the life of each human being therefore be regarded as special, whether it is focused on *nibbāna* right now or not, it makes this position quite similar to strong anthropocentrism. So this alternative has distinct disadvantages.

The view that Buddhism is anthropocentric is not such a marked digression from its basic philosophy. However care must be taken in understanding its essence. Buddhist texts have never claimed that the world was created for human beings as may be often claimed by strong anthropocentrism. The mood is completely different in Buddhism. Buddhism is at best a weak anthropocentrism that does not collapse into narrow-minded egoism. The world was not created for man but remains pivotal in his quest for liberation.

Thus man must act in his own interest without neglecting others. Weak anthropocentrism implies striving for a balance between the two goals of personal concern and selfless action. In all, human beings are not expected to lose their identity; and neither are they expected to be preoccupied with themselves alone. The position has its problems, for it is never clearly stated in the Buddhist context how this balance is to be reached in practical application. But its possibilities in general and in Buddhism in particular and the many benefits of adopting it have been amply demonstrated. Thus, for now the focus can be that support for weak anthropocentrism is found in early Buddhism even though more remains to be said.

Conclusion

Nature is a principal theme in any ethics of environment. It is rare to find environmental literature that has not commented upon it, briefly or substantially, in one sense or another. In the last two chapters I have attempted to understand nature in the light of Buddhist ideas and how it plays an influential role in developing environmental undercurrents which make an impact. I have claimed that though in Buddhism one struggles to establish a conservationist view of nature, it effortlessly contains a cosmological one. I have also claimed that though notions of marginalizing the value of nature and world renunciation keep appearing, the cosmological view is consuming. My proposal then is that though conservationist and marginal-ist strands undeniably exist in Buddhism these do not define its position on the matter: early Buddhism is defined by its cosmological approach alone. I also arrived at the conclusion both through the cosmological approach and the discussion on anthropocentrism that the place of man is significant in early Buddhism but not superior. However my purpose was always to do much more than the above. I examined Buddhist ideas to find new ways for establishing an environmental discourse of significance. Though my method was unusual and unconventional it was exciting to discover a religion with a world-view that includes human beings and non-human beings in some senses "equally;" that focuses on causality and process; and speaks of concern and compassion for the self and for the other as inadvertently related.[94]

The cosmological view however does stand questioned on one count. Though it successfully provides a picture of the world, it does not provide the process through which the world could be actively considered. The latter support comes from the Buddhist doctrine of morality. Notions of conservation benefit from morality and marginalizing tendencies are quelled through it. Further, each section under the cosmological approach – be it *paṭiccasamuppāda* or *saṃsāra* or the cosmogony in the *Aggañña Sutta* – faces incompleteness in the Buddhist schemata without morality. Weak anthropocentrism also keeps returning to morality in order to be vindicated. Morality and the virtues have a critical presence in the early Buddhist doctrine as they were not limited to the upliftment of the practitioner through gaining higher spiritual states but also about dealing with all aspects of life. Thus morality not only contributes to true insight of reality but also to participation in the world defined by its cosmological character. On these grounds alone can a seeker realize the true nature of an environmental ethics in early Buddhism.

In conclusion it must be said that an environmental investigation in early Buddhism must paint a picture of the way the world is. Though environmental ethics cannot be based on such a picture alone, a culmination can come through morality which is expressed and endorsed within its parameters. After all, ". . . nothing can be moral that is in conflict with the physical realities of our existence or cannot be seen to fit within the natural laws of our environment. . . ."[95] The place of morality and the virtues in early Buddhism in relation to the environment will be examined in the following chapters. Buddhist ethics will be shown to be a virtue ethics, and correspondingly an environmental virtue ethics; and this will establish that early Buddhism not only presents a picture of the world as it is, it also seeks to make it a better place through a vibrant moral theory. Its morality, unsurprisingly, is also necessarily tied in with the final goal of transcending the phenomenal world. My objective in these chapters has been to actively attend to implicit beliefs about nature in early Buddhism but I hope to have achieved more than just this in my ruminations.

4

ENVIRONMENTAL VIRTUE ETHICS IN EARLY BUDDHISM

Destroy the forests (of desires) and not trees, from the forest is fear born, by removing forest and thicket, Nibbāna is attained, monks.

Dhammapada

An endeavour to create a picture of the Buddhist world-view that included non-human entities and human beings and at the same time agreed with Buddhist tenets was undertaken previously to truly understand how Buddhist literature provides a sense of nature. Termed as "cosmological," this picture was drawn out of early Buddhism's various doctrines. All these doctrines, which though not about the natural world in their original form, act as cryptic resources that subsequently reveal the status of nature in Buddhist thought. However the cosmological description simply paints a picture of how the world is and how it operates. Additional reasons are therefore needed for ensuring that human actions respond in a positive manner to the environment. The question why an individual ought to act for the sake of nature is not a new one and is often faced by moral theories trying to justify and encourage non-discriminatory and constructive action towards the natural world. Buddhist literary insights are able to respond to this challenge through their virtue-based moral theory which is woven into the very structure of its world-view and without which the cosmological picture discussed earlier remains incomplete. This and the next chapter will address the question of morality and virtue and how these extend to nature.

At the onset I propose that the Buddhist position on nature be understood as an *environmental virtue ethics*. I believe that Buddhist ethics shares many similarities and is closely allied with a virtue ethical approach such that considering nature ethics in Buddhism as a form of virtue ethics is an appropriate endeavour. By developing certain reasoning I shall demonstrate that not only is virtue ethics the most appropriate way of viewing the general structure of Buddhist moral philosophy, it is also the best way to understand responses to environmental problems in Buddhism. I clarify that the virtue approach is predominant here even though consequential or deontological strands can be seen. In this chapter I have undertaken to accomplish three objectives. These are, first, to illustrate briefly the nature and important characteristics of a virtue ethics and then explain how Buddhist morality can be seen as a form of such ethics. I have aimed to express clearly the character of an environmental virtue ethics and this is the second undertaking. Thirdly, following from this, I have demonstrated that environmental ethics in Buddhism can be legitimately considered as a form of such ethics. This step-wise procedure though gradual leads to a more convincing conclusion: that the early Buddhist moral doctrine can indeed be classified as an environmental virtue ethics.

The discussion of the various approaches to environmental ethics in Buddhism in the first chapter led to the conclusion that though meaningful and good work has been done in this discipline the true Buddhist position on the matter was yet elusive. Lambert Schmithausen's thorough investigation of references to nature in the Buddhist scriptures and Ian Harris's attention to teleology raised many important issues. At the same time they showed how such approaches were either inconclusive or negating to the cause of nature. None of the approaches seemed compelling enough to entail the thesis that Buddhism induces the agent to act for the sake of the environment. It was clear that a further enquiry along this route was not going to yield any positive results. Thus, with the ascertaining of the setting of nature within Buddhism, a change in direction incorporating virtue ethics as the foundation appears a plausible avenue to explore. The role of virtues is constantly emphasized in early Buddhism. Virtues play an imperative role. The Buddha took a firm stand on the practice of virtues.[1] He seemed aware that virtues have a self-directed and an other-directed role to play. Recently, prominent scholars have started to consider virtues as a basis for evaluating theoretical aspects of Buddhist moral teachings. They also see the myriad ways that Buddhist virtues can be extended to facilitating a concern for the environment quite effectively. Both Alan Sponberg and David Kalupahana have strongly indicated the presence of an environmental virtue dimension in Buddhism.[2] However neither has sufficiently elaborated this position. David Cooper and Simon James also see the strong possibility of this approach in their more detailed analysis.[3] And so, if environmental ethics is approached from this angle, in all probability we shall not only have an early Buddhist environmental theory that is more progressive than others but that is at the same time pertinent to present day ecological conditions. This approach seems promising and therefore deserving of thorough analysis.

Having said this, a general awareness about the limitations of virtue ethics and environmental virtue ethics needs to be maintained at the same time. These are complicated theories in themselves and incorporating them in Buddhism means that a share of these complications is transferred into Buddhism as well. This is notwithstanding the possible allegation of superimposing onto Buddhism the notion of an environment virtue ethics that is a recent construct and is historically and culturally far removed from its core philosophy.

I anticipate these and other objections and will deal with them in due course in this chapter and the next.

Virtue ethics and early Buddhism

Technically speaking, traditional normative ethical theories seek to justify the viability of moral claims that are concerned with the conduct and actions of agents, and for this they consider norms, rules or standards as a measure. Normative ethics thus is that part of ethics whose main objective is to direct action and to offer good reason as to why the action is suggested. Its different forms – consequential, deontological and virtue-based – do exactly this, even though the factors and justifications they are concerned with differ radically. In terms of prevalence and usage, scholars believe that until very recently the consequential and deontological approaches have had an upper hand due to the belief that these were more effectual theories. This inevitably influenced the approaches to environmental ethics too. However, it has been noted that this mind-set appears to be changing, and there is a growing interest in virtue as a basis for ethical theories. As Daniel Statman notes in the opening line of his book on virtue ethics "The most conspicuous development in contemporary ethics is the ever growing interest in virtue ethics."[4] A more intense analysis of virtue ethics does not rule out its more application-oriented stance.

Virtue ethics, as its name suggests, concentrates on the virtues and character of the individual. Since morally correct conduct is evaluated through the virtues, virtue ethics is quite unlike its normative counterparts, consequentialism and deontology, whose attention is solely on the consequences or the act itself respectively. But before we go on to look at its applicability to early Buddhism, a more detailed explanation is required of what a virtue ethics actually is. An illustration of virtue ethics in this section may appear somewhat excessive in the context of the subject being dealt with but is extremely crucial as it paves the ground for acceptance of Buddhist ethics as a virtue ethics and eventually as an environment virtue ethics. The account provides the proper basis for any future agreement and disagreement of the virtue theory within Buddhism, all things considered.

One good way of understanding the nature of virtue ethics is to compare it in a more specific way to consequentialism and deontology. Most actions can be seen as having at least three distinguishable parts. These are concerned with the person who does an action, the action that is actually done by this person, and the results or consequences that follow the action.[5] From the point of view of ethical theories, in simple terms virtue ethics adopts the doer or the agent as central to judging moral value; deontology considers the act as central; and consequentialism takes the consequences as the deciding factor of moral value. This can be explained with the help of an example:

1. Tara feels compassion for suffering animals and is compelled to do something about it.
2. Tara becomes vegetarian and opens an animal shelter.
3. The life of some animals is saved and overall animal suffering is reduced nominally.

A virtue ethics would emphasize (1), which is Tara's compassion for the animals and her will to save their life and reduce the pain they suffer. It would aim to determine Tara's character, the nature of her compassion and maybe even what makes compassion a virtue. Thus this ethics is concerned with determining what a virtue means and its mode of application.

This entire episode can also be looked at from the point of view of the action, that was performed, namely (2) above. Ought Tara to have performed the act of turning away from meat-eating and was this action right? This is the deontological perspective and is concerned with the "ought," "right" and "wrong" of the action itself. It implies that the act must be performed for itself regardless of the consequences. Finally, moving away from the action, the consequences that are expressed in (3) may play a central role in deciding the moral worth of the entire episode. Did the action bring the most excellent consequences or could the consequences have been better if rather than opening a shelter Tara had launched an awareness campaign, set up a fund, or headed a demonstration for her cause in the town square? This is the approach of the consequentialist, whose primary motive is to adjudicate the nature of consequences and then characterize the action as right or wrong. And so each of the three theories offers a structured way or methodology through which actions can be evaluated as moral or immoral. This interestingly forms the basis of differential moral analysis.

Virtue ethics' primary concern is the character of the person. It tries to understand morality by focusing on the nature of the person performing the action. The role of both consequential and deontological theories is crucial in their preoccupation with consequences and the performance of the action according to some duty or rule per se respectively. However, in this the importance of the agent gets trivialized. It appears that the agent is an essential part of the ethical decision making process and determining his position and personality is a matter of some urgency. It is the disposition of agents that virtue ethic targets. The type of persons they are, their circumstances when the decision came to be made, the virtues they hold dear and so on are essential elements when choices are to be made. The agent's dilemma-solving capacity based on character cannot be underestimated and its authority is indispensable in moral situations. Virtue ethics recognizes the role of the agent as extremely significant in any moral evaluation.

It has been observed that virtue ethics interacts in various ways with consequential or deontological theories. Both consequentialism and deontology can acknowledge the virtuous agent in their dealings even though their final analysis relies on other factors. However, in other cases the final decision is to be made on the basis of the virtuous agent alone even while considering the nature of actions and consequences. There are various ways in fact in which virtues, as the final determinant, can be and are considered by various ethicists. Based on such interaction, virtue ethics is seen to be of two types by moralists. However, it can be divided more specifically into three types as I explain below. If a virtue ethics pays no attention to consequences and obligations, it is a radical form. If it pays some attention to other things, but all final decisions depend on the agent's character, then it is a more moderate form of virtue ethics. Finally there may be another version of the moderate form, according to which virtue ethics cannot stand on its own and is supported by deontology, and together they lead the agent to make moral decisions.

Daniel Statman, while introducing virtue ethics states the meaning of virtue ethics as ". . . an approach to ethics, according to which *the basic judgements in ethics are judgements of character*."[6] This, according to Statman is a more radical approach to virtue ethics. It indicates that what must be first considered is not right or wrong behaviour, but rather the virtues or the character of the agent on the basis of which the action was performed. The even more extreme form of radical virtue ethics could reject any support from deontology. G. E. M. Anscombe claimed in her paper "Modern Moral Philosophy" that ethics could be done without deontic notions, and that it would be a great improvement to name a genus such as "untruthful" or "unjust" rather than terms such as "morally wrong" and so on.[7] Thus implying that in the radical version, judgements of character become the measure for determining the moral factor and judgements based on deontology can be neglected or can be subsumed under the former. To summarize, the agent's character – be it upright or unscrupulous – decides the moral worth of action. The calculation of moral worth is thus independent of deontological concerns.

Michael Slote supports a more moderate version of virtue ethics. He says, "The ethical status of actions is not *entirely derivative* from that of traits, motives or individuals, even though traits and individuals are the *major focus* of the ethical views being offered."[8] This view is moderate as it is not focused on virtue alone, but is disposed towards other (deontic) notions as well. It does not follow Anscombe's more radical method of replacing deontic notions with virtues. However, even though some actions by their very nature instigate a deontological evaluation, most appraisals are finally connected with virtue or related to character. To sum up, this view is more accepting of other methodologies and standards than the radical view.

Closely related to the above version is another variety of a moderate virtue ethics. Many would see the two as tacitly similar but in my understanding there is a subtle difference between the two. Where the first moderate version accepts the use of deontic notions, it is not so vociferous in its support of deontology. In its final assessment the second version relies on both virtues and deontic notions together. James Rachels' account of virtue ethics can be seen as one example of the latter version. According to Rachels, who examines both the deontic and the virtue approach, a pure virtue ethics is incomplete as it cannot explain the moral goodness of certain character traits. He disagrees with any radical version when he states:

> . . . radical virtue ethics is committed to the idea that *for any good reason that may be given in favour of doing an action, there is a corresponding virtue that consists in the disposition to accept and act on that reason*. But this does not appear to be true.[9]

He concludes that an approach accommodating virtues and duties, in a way in which both are adequately treated, is needed for moral philosophy to be successful. Robert Louden also supports this version and writes in his essay that we should see the "ethics of virtue and the ethics of rules as adding up, rather than as cancelling each other."[10] He believes that each alone cannot account for the gradation of values, but together they are capable of a more realistic account of moral experience.

Many other aspects of virtue ethics must become clear before the resemblance to Buddhist ethics is discussed. First a virtue ethics must define virtue or at the least make an attempt to say what it consists in. Though this discussion enters the realm of meta-ethics, providing such a definition can clarify the position of the virtue ethicist to a great extent. Admittedly this is no easy task as there can be no one standard definition of virtue to the exclusion of others. Philosophers since ancient times have grappled with this question and have come out none the wiser. It is a disappointment that Plato's *Meno* which starts with the question of what a virtue is does not exactly tackle it and goes on to other things thereby highlighting ever more the problematical nature of this concern.[11] Secondly a virtue ethics must be able to give a list of or at the least a semblance of some virtues that play a vital role in making decisions morally valid. This list can vary and what may count as virtuous behaviour for some, may not for others. However, it can be hoped that there do exist certain virtues that have universal acceptance. Thirdly attention to specific notions such as intention, motivation and wisdom must be included to give shape to the virtue theory. The three aspects are examined here. Since virtue ethics is centred on the individual the question of intention becomes important.[12] Most virtue ethicists believe that agents must be aware of the action they undertake for it to be judged as moral or immoral.[13] Therefore accidental actions or those done under pressure would not really count as virtuous moral actions. Philippa Foot believes virtues concern those things that engage a person's will and character and that virtue belongs to will. She believes this because in her view it is "primarily by his intentions that a man's moral dispositions are judged."[14]

The other related issue is about what motivates the agent to do the virtuous action. Rosalind Hursthouse speaks in detail about the concept of motivation in the case of virtue ethics. She believes that the moral motivation in the case of virtue ethics should be "of acting from virtue – a settled state of good character."[15] This implies that since the action comes from an inherently "virtuous" character, it must be moral and that a virtuous personality would be led to perform the right action quite consistently. So settled is the person in virtue, according to Hursthouse, that there is no dilemma between various inclinations; virtue-directed actions happen quite habitually. Hursthouse also notes that one's acting virtuously cannot really be separable from what is involved in the virtues or from the possession of virtues themselves. This, I think, is an extremely important observation about the general thrust of virtue ethics. Virtue ethics does not remain limited to judging the action alone on the basis of the character of the agent but goes on to make a connection between the agent and the action. The agent happens to be inextricably linked to the action he does. And though Hursthouse does not say anything expressly about this, it seems that her understanding narrows the distance between agent and the actions that follow.

There are virtue ethicists who emphasize the crucial need for moral wisdom. Deciding what constitutes a virtue or deciding between two virtues requires wisdom. For instance humility and acceptance in a situation which requires courage to fight against some form of injustice may lead to undesired consequences. Humility would hardly be considered a virtue in a war torn area where aggression is essential for survival. And sometimes two virtues, say of sympathy and courage may conflict – so that the withdrawing of one becomes essential. For instance a terrorist who was physically abused as a child requires sympathy, however he needs to be contained somehow due to the immediate threat he poses to some innocent hostages. Wisdom is needed urgently here to make a choice. Thus, wisdom becomes essential in virtue ethics. Though the role of wisdom cannot be underestimated in any form of normative ethics, including consequential or deontological theories, it becomes most focused in the case of virtue ethics. For an agent required to take decisions involving the nature of virtue or about dilemmas, knowing that the path chosen will decide the morality of the act, wisdom is absolutely indispensable. So wisdom rather than being just one aspect becomes a principal one in virtue ethics.

No discussion on virtue ethics can be complete without mentioning Aristotle, its earliest progenitor. This is because for him central to ethical action is character. In his most significant writing on ethics, the *Nichomachean Ethics*, he is determined to ascertain what is good for man, and progressively explains that the human good is an activity of the soul in conformity with virtue (*arête*).[16] A virtue, according to Aristotle, is a state of character. This implies that a single act may not necessarily imply a virtue but rather a disposition to act in a certain way. Thus it is the agent's character that dictates his actions and makes him virtuous and in this is also implied that the agent must be able to be virtuous consistently. Aristotle had defined a particular characteristic of (moral) virtue which he explains as a degree to which the action ought to be performed to count as a virtue. Called the mean, he meant for this mean to be relative and to be calculated with the person and circumstances in mind. For instance, the mean between cowardice and foolhardiness is courage but degrees of courage vary from person to person. Aristotle also acknowledged the importance of wisdom by saying that the man of practical wisdom (*phronimos*) determines the mean. Moral virtue, in order to function correctly, had to be conjoined with practical wisdom (*phronesis*) or the virtue of wisdom. Thus, a man's decision to act was to be based on moral virtue and practical wisdom. Coming back to the good of man, Aristotle gives it a name – *eudaemonia*. From his understanding of *eudaemonia* it becomes clear that virtues are an important component of it rather than simply being instrumental to its realization.

Aristotle, according to classical scholar Richard Norman, does not believe that *eudaemonia* is the only end and all else is a means to it. Aristotle, he finds, suggests that some actions are selected for their own sake; some others for themselves and also as means to some different ends. Virtues are ends in themselves and at the same time are means that lead to *eudaemonia*. Though *eudaemonia* is not the only end, it is the only end that is not a means at the same time. This trait gives *eudaemonia* a special status but it does not make it superior to other things, says Norman. In addition for Aristotle *eudaemonia* does not consist of one particular good entity but rather is a combination of many good things. Neither, clarifies Norman, is *eudaemonia* to be considered as one good thing among others. It is composed of other good things and this leads to it being considered a good thing. Thus it is not a detached, unconnected objective, as it is believed to be at times. Norman elaborates "The idea would be that happiness [*eudaemonia*] is more basic than the other goods, not as being something better of the same kind, but as being the framework into which the various particular goods fit."[17] To explain what he means by this Norman gives the example of a man who says that he has a good home, a family and a job but his life has no meaning. This man is not looking for something of the same category as a house and job; he wants these things to add up to something of value and this is similar to what Aristotle means by *eudaemonia*. The most important thing to remember in this discussion is that the other goods are constituents of *eudaemonia* and not means to them.

I would like to claim on the basis of what I have explained so far that early Buddhist ethics is a form of virtue ethics. Like virtue ethics, Buddhism's main concern more than anything else is the character of the agent. It stresses virtue incessantly and there are constant reminders about staying away from vice. The Buddha is portrayed as spending considerable time discussing the virtues that ought to be followed. The doctrine of *kamma*, often considered as one of the most consequentialist aspects of Buddhist philosophy, confirms the stress on the agent's character by saying that it is the agent's intention that makes an action good, thereby making the agent the central focus. Additionally, most Buddhist virtues aim at not only improving the agent's own temperament but at improving relations with others and in this they reach out to all human beings irrespective of cultural or circumstantial differences. James Whitehill, in a paper entitled "Buddhism and the Virtues" was one of the first to speak about a virtue approach to Buddhist ethics. While speaking about the future development of Buddhism in the West he said, "Viewing Buddhist morality and ethics in the light of virtue theory is, I believe, true to the central core of Buddhism."[18] This, he finds, is because Buddhism's key interest and focus is the nature of the agent; the actions that emanate from the agent correspond in quality to this nature. For Buddhist's therefore the dispositions that are created by acts and that are responsible for other acts are more significant than the action itself or the consequences that inevitably follow it. How the agent develops on the basis of his actions is thus a central idea.

However, there is absolutely no way around some obvious instances and arguments that utilize consequential and deontological methodologies in the *Nikāya* literature as well as in other textual sources. Consequences are important and imperatives and rules are prescribed about the nature of actions themselves. In fact, at first sight, early Buddhism makes few claims for identity with virtue ethics. It appears as consequential for it seeks an ultimate end or goal: *nibbāna*. Interestingly though it is hard to rule out Buddhist ethics as consequentialist immediately, it is equally hard to fully identify it with consequentialism as Buddhist ethics does not appear to be about consequences alone. Barbara Clayton finds an obvious utilitarian streak (utilitarianism is a form of consequentialism) in Theravāda Buddhism in the idea that one should give to the *sangha* rather than anyone else because it will bring in more *kammic* rewards.[19] Clayton finds that though it is true that one should give for the sake of generosity, the Buddhists seemingly deviate from this by specifying that generosity towards one rather than another is more fruitful. She sees the above as an example of utilitarian reasoning, for one is aiming to increase rewards; rewards that are after all consequences.[20] Keown, on the contrary, denies that Buddhism is utilitarian. He says that it may seem as if Buddhist ethics is similar to consequential theories for it appears to grade moral action in terms of non-moral consequences produced due to the action. However, Keown finds that this is deceptive for two important reasons.[21] The first reason why a Buddhist theory cannot be utilitarian is that Buddhism does not define the right independently from the good, as is generally done in consequential theories such as utilitarianism. The right and the good are inextricably related. He considers *nibbāna* to be the good that is aimed at and actions are right as far as they participate in this good; the rightness of actions is not dependent on the consequences that follow. The second reason concerns the intention that leads to the action. In

Buddhism the moral value of the action is determined by the agent's intention before the action, namely what is called *cetanā* (intention or volition). The moral value is not decided on the basis of consequences. This means that an action is right if its intention (as based on the character of the deciding agent) is good, it is not right because the consequences of the action are good. I would like to add another reason to Keown's argument. An example can be cited from a Buddhist text that assiduously mentions that the consequences of actions hinge on not only the nature of the acts themselves but also upon the character of the agent. A chronic wrong doer would therefore suffer much more rigorously than a by and large virtue-oriented person in terms of consequences. The Buddha says that a person who has cultivated wholesome habits of mind and body and who has developed insight would suffer less for an evil deed than a person who has committed the same deed but who has not developed wholesome habits and insight. To explain he gives an example: if a grain of salt were to be thrown in a cup of water that water would be undrinkable. Similarly a small offence of an evil person would take him to hell. If the same amount of salt were thrown into the river Ganges, the water would not be undrinkable. Similarly, a small offence of a generally good person would be experienced in the present life through expiation.[22] On this passage Harvey has commented, "This seems to imply that, in a spiritually developed person, a small moral slip will have less effect, as it will be 'diluted' by his or her generally moral nature."[23] Thus consequences differ according to the disposition an individual nurtures. Utilitarianism does not give credence to such a principle of varied consequences directly related to the agent's temperament. The reason why the goal of *nibbāna* cannot be considered consequential either will be dealt with a little later.

Additionally virtues can be looked upon as forming character only once their intentionality is established. The insistence on intention, as mentioned above, plays a central role in early Buddhist ethics just as it does in virtue ethics. By being intentionally willed an act gains the status of a moral act. In Buddhist texts intention is identified with *kamma*, when the Buddha says, "Monks, I say intentional action is *kamma*. Having intended, *kamma* is done by body, by speech, by thought."[24] Thus, the Buddha very categorically identifies *kamma* with intentional actions and extends their scope to every sphere – physical, verbal and even mental. Moreover *kamma*, as has been gathered by many, is as much about the progress and development of the persona of the individual as it is about tangible actions generated by individuals and their inevitable consequences. In Buddhism there is very little gap between the personality of the agent and the actions that emanate from it. The actions would necessarily be of the same nature as the latter. In other words the actions essentially reflect the character of their performer. Thus here too exists a close connection (as in Hursthouse) between being and doing. An agent can be what he is only by doing what he does and by doing what he does he becomes the way he is. This point becomes very important when we speak of any form of applied ethics.

Buddhist ethics must also address the subject of motivation. The motivation is not a selfish one. Buddhism does not imply that the agent seek his own good alone when he decides on a course of action. Buddhism, as has been made clear in a previous chapter, does not have an egoistic approach. Aristotelian virtue ethics as well as Hursthouse's interpretation entail that a virtuous person must always and habitually act from virtue. This appears as the best motivation. The motivation for Buddhism can be believed to be virtue too. It is stated in the *Nikāyas* that one who gives for the sake of giving earns greater rewards than one whose motive is the reward itself. The latter goes to heaven but returns to the drudge of *saṃsāra*. But the person whose motive is selfless and who gives because he values the act of giving goes to heaven and does not so return.[25] Thus here too the highest form of virtue is one whose motivation is virtue itself. As for the question of habitual actions, it must be assumed that actions performed by one who has a virtuous character would always be virtuous; the Buddha's own example should suffice to make this point for he always acted virtuously, habitually. However, this is not to say that a non-enlightened person is not capable of virtues for virtue's sake. Even the striving towards enlightenment must include such motivation, as is clear from the example above.

In that Buddhism prescribes rules and duties, it would not be incorrect for it to lay claim to a deontological temperament as well. Kant, regarded as a leading exponent of deontology, spoke continually of duty while expounding the notion of the categorical imperative in his moral philosophy. In a similar sense, the precepts may also be treated as sundry duties. Additionally the *Sigālaka Sutta* can be seen as an approximate example of specific mutual duties laid down by the Buddha to show how people ought to act towards one another.[26] However, to limit the Buddhist position to deontology would not do justice to its more inclusive philosophy and its employment of varied moral arguments. It may be assumed then that following duties among other things is essential in the aspiration for a high moral character.

Thus it is clear that early Buddhism is neither exclusively consequential nor deontological in its approach. What is deontological or utilitarian within its annals carries within it the weight of virtues as well. Due to this, of all the forms of virtue ethics mentioned earlier, it can be considered as a moderate form of virtue ethics – varying between the second and third versions – rather than a radical one. This means that in Buddhist ethics virtues come before rules and principles, although rules or principles have an important role to play. In his book, *An Introduction to Buddhist Ethics*, Peter Harvey compares Buddhist ethics with the three forms of normative ethics and concludes by saying that by collapsing Buddhist ethics into any one of the three would narrow the vision of Buddhism and that Buddhism agrees with parts of all of them.[27] Though I don't disagree with Harvey's insight of Buddhism being an amalgamation of aspects of all three ethical theories, I do believe that Buddhism is more dominantly a form of a moderate virtue ethics.

Virtues form a very important part of Buddhist philosophy because they play a role in getting rid of the *dukkha* that seems to be eternally linked with the destiny of a human being. Though the origin of virtues (as of other things) is not described, what the practice of virtues can do is explained in much detail, their most important outcome being spiritual elevation. The Buddha's teachings imply that there is too much at stake for those who decide to live a life that is not virtuous. But the exact description of a virtue is not given in any early Buddhist text. No clear definition can be found. Keown, however, finds that the use of *dharmas* by the *Abhidharmists* includes the virtues and vices. Keown explains *dharmas* as "the basic constituents or elements of reality . . . which cannot be further subdivided or analysed." From this he concludes that virtues and vices cannot be regarded as subjective; they are objective and real. On the basis of Keown's findings it can be said that the definition of a *dharma* is the closest thing to the definition of a virtue in Buddhist philosophy. However, the term does not appear in this sense in the rest of the Pali Canon and therefore defies universal appeal and acceptability.[28] Thus a generally accepted definition of virtue is hard to find in early Buddhism. A tentative definition that may be true through implication is as follows: a virtue in early Buddhism stands for certain intentional actions (of thoughts, words and deeds), whose constant practice is a necessity for character building and without which higher spiritual states become impossible. The definition clearly suggests that virtues are those entities whose practice leads people to develop in certain ways, cultivating feelings and dispositions that are conducive to not only virtuous practice but to a higher goal simultaneously. It can be added, of course, that commonsense entails that virtues are highly esteemed and acquire respect inherently. It is also mostly the case that an action based on the opposite of the virtue is looked upon as immoral and gratuitous.

Without clarifying the definition of virtue, scholars have spontaneously utilized the term in relation to Buddhism. Padmasiri de Silva, who is also inclined towards a virtue approach, applies the term as follows:

> . . . Buddhist ethics brings into play a wide variety of virtues for the building up of human character. Some of them are closely welded to the natural feelings humans have for their fellow beings, others apply to the needs of social organization and community living, and yet others are demanded by the path of moral development and self-restraint. Virtues and vices also refer to our emotional aspect . . . the Buddha gave a central place to . . . compassion, generosity and gratitude. . . .[29]

Thus there seems to be no doubt in de Silva's mind that virtues and vices exist and occupy a very important position in Buddhism. Many other scholars have also spoken of Buddhist virtues. Edward Conze speaks of the five cardinal virtues of Buddhism. These, he believes, are faith, vigour, mindfulness, concentration and wisdom.[30] Keown, as seen above, explains virtues and vices in the *Abhidharmic* context and Whitehill has mentioned virtuous practices and virtue-like practices in Buddhism.[31] Though none of the above, except Keown, has attempted to define a virtue, they all appear convinced of the central role of virtues in Buddhist literature. So though some definition is important ultimately the focus in Buddhism clearly ought to be the acquiring of the virtue and what it does to the agent.

The Eightfold Path, especially its division of ethics or *sīla*, signifies value oriented guidelines by adhering to which, it is assumed, an agent can live a virtuous life, cultivate good habits and care for others. *Sīla* includes right speech (*sammā vācā*), right action (*sammā kammanta*) and right living (*sammā ājīva*). The remaining two divisions of the Eightfold Path are meditation or *samādhi*, and insight or *paññā*.[32] The path of meditation encourages the development of mental discipline. Finally, insight is to be cultivated for it alone reveals the real nature of things. Character is in fact developed not only through morality but also through meditation (*samādhi*) and insight (*paññā*). *Samādhi* includes right effort (*sammā vāyāma*), right mindfulness (*sammā sati*) and right concentration (*sammā samādhi*) whereas insight includes right view (*sammā diṭṭhi*) and right resolve (*sammā saṅkappa*). All the components of the Path must be nurtured almost concurrently (rather than one after the other), according to ability. One of the central themes of the Buddhist world-view is morality that governs the behaviour of individuals. But there is no doubt that *sīla, samādhi* and *paññā* together ensure the complete psychological and physiological development of the individual. The three are linked integrally and each facilitates the cultivation of the other two.

Virtues in Buddhism include sympathy (*anukampā*), compassion (*karunā*), universal love (*mettā*), non-injury (*ahiṃsā*), modesty (*hirī*), non-covetousness (*anabhijjhā*), gentleness (*maddava*), tenderness (*soracca*), mindfulness (*sati*) and generosity (*dāna*) among others. As is clear, some virtues are directed towards the agent and the practice of some have an effect on other individuals. For instance, the practice of *ahiṃsā* and compassion affect others whereas mindfulness is more inward directed. By cultivating the virtues the agent can obliterate craving whose constituents are greed (*rāga*), hatred (*dosa*) and delusion (*moha*). All unwholesome acts (*akusala kamma*) have these three as their cause and Buddhists on the whole accept that the highest spiritual state of *nibbāna* can come about only with the permanent eradication of all three. In fact the greatest significance of the Eightfold Path or its three divisions is that it overcomes the vices and suppresses craving or *taṇhā*.

The comparison between virtue ethics and Buddhism also raises questions about ultimate aims: virtue ethics aspires for a virtuous character whereas in Buddhism there is a striving for enlightenment. Ethics (*sīla*), supposedly, has no role to play in the latter. However, most supporters of the virtue approach to Buddhist ethics find this inference unacceptable. Whitehill disagrees with those who find in Buddhism that once a certain level is reached there is no longer a need for morality. He writes:

> The goal of ethics is to become a person who does good or virtuous things freely from the ground of a well-tempered character, supported by a matured, resolute and reasonable knowledge of what one is doing. The path of Buddhism does not dissolve character (which is different from ego and personality). It awakens and illuminates moral character and establishes a "noble" selfhood in the wide, deep, expressive freedom of creative forms of life and its perfections.[33]

Thus at no stage does the importance of morality diminish in Buddhism. Once the tenets of Buddhism become revealed in their true spirit, the dependent relation between enlightenment and morality becomes apparent; ethics is not outside of *nibbāna* at all as is sometimes presumed. In the *Saṃyutta Nikāya* the Buddha says: "Indeed, Rādha, the destruction of craving is enlightenment."[34] Here *nibbāna* means the annihilation of craving (*taṇhā*). Ethics also aims at a similar annihilation. And so rather than leading to *nibbāna*, ethics becomes a part of *nibbāna* itself. Keown, in his groundbreaking research in the area, has pointed out the similarities between Aristotle and Buddhism. He claims that both Aristotelian ethics and Buddhism are teleological and non-consequential for they clearly aim towards an end or *telos* that consists inherently of virtues; virtues are not just an instrumental means for the attainment of the end. He writes "By teleological, then, we should understand the continual expansion of individual capacity towards the goal of complete perfection, rather than the generation of a single transient utility."[35] He suggests that Buddhism is best understood as teleology and finds many other similarities between the two. Both Buddhism and Aristotle rely on the practice of virtues to develop their potential in order to reach their final goal. Furthermore, and importantly, Keown identifies both *nibbāna* and *eudaemonia* as "second-order ends," and says that they are not the only ends aimed at, but include many good things in a harmonious combination. It must be made clear that a concept of teleology is not opposed to virtue ethics, and many virtue ethicists have accepted this. Gary Watson writes:

> For a concept of good *is* primary in Aristotle's view. Thus if teleological theories are those in which the . . . concept of a good is primary, then Aristotle's theory is rightly said to be teleological. It is a mistake, however, to think that the only way of asserting the primacy

> of the good is consequentialism. We should recognize the possibility of a view that is at once teleological and nonconsequentialist. And an ethics of virtue . . . is a theory of this kind.[36]

Keown's findings correlate to this and further confirm Buddhism's similarity to virtue ethics.

Buddhism's stress on wisdom also enhances its virtue character. It has been commented that those among men and gods who have the virtue of wisdom are victorious.[37] Wisdom or insight (*paññā*) in general is considered as an important basis of the moral choice making process but it has a special place in an agent-oriented virtue ethics. Wisdom can be considered to be a virtue in Buddhism (as in Aristotle's philosophy). Support for wisdom as a virtue comes from scholars of repute. While speaking of Buddhist thought Edward Conze has said of wisdom that, "It is regarded as the highest virtue because ignorance, and not sin is the root evil."[38] Harvey, though not expressly acknowledging wisdom as a virtue, gives it a virtue-like status. He speaks of the co-development of virtue (which is, interestingly enough, his translation of *sīla*) with meditation and wisdom. He finds that according to Buddhism a person's first commitment is to develop virtue, which must be followed by "preliminary wisdom." Once virtue is deepened, meditation can follow, with the help of which wisdom deepens and consequently virtue is strengthened.[39] According to *Abhidhamma, paññindrīya* (reason or insight) is a *kusala* state. It is then, on *Abhidhammic* terms, as explained by Keown, to be considered a virtue.[40] In addition to these descriptions wisdom acts as a functional tool that helps the virtues to attain a more defined direction that is crucial always but especially in cases of moral predicaments. It must be reiterated that for early Buddhism *sīla, samādhi* and *paññā* must be all worked on together for the agent to be purged of craving. This is a crucial undertaking for reaching the state of *nibbāna.*

Before we go on to see how a virtue ethics is consistent with early Buddhism in the environmental sphere, one pressing problem that comes up in relation to virtue ethics needs to be addressed. This problem, often pointed out in virtue ethical theory, is that in dealings of applied ethics (connected with methodological guidance on actions) clarity *vis-à-vis* through defining duty or consequences appears to be more important than through imprecise and unclear characterizations of personality. The upshot here is that applying consequentialism or deontology in the various spheres of applied ethics is bound to have more appeal than character assessments. It can be believed that if Buddhism is considered a virtue ethics it is likely to face the same charge. However that this is only superficially the case can be seen with the help of an example.[41] In a very small country called Naturoland there is a severe famine in one corner of the country that faces inland, and people there are on the verge of starvation. The other end of the country is a coastal province and is hit by a typhoon. By clearing the forest in the middle region of the country a dam can be built to help the famine stricken people. But clearing the forest would mean that the force of the typhoon in the coastal region would be more severe. What is to be done? It is hard to see how virtues could provide tangible guidance here. Applying the Buddhist virtue of compassion to the famine-ridden would mean adopting mercilessness against the typhoon-stricken and the same would hold in the opposite case. Buddhist wisdom would be unable to provide a practicable solution. Due to the inability to come up with an answer it would appear that virtue ethics is ineffective in application. This may be the likely argument of the critics. However it is interesting to note how other ethical theories would respond to this dilemma – it is more than likely that they will confront the same indecisiveness and agitation in trying to choose the good of one set of people over that of the others. The consequences of building a dam and of not building the dam are equally bad. Even if Buddhism were to acquiesce to the utilitarian principles of the maximization of happiness making a decision would still be difficult for in ensuring the happiness of one set of people, pain for the other set is assured. This difficulty defeats utilitarian ideology. In the case of deontology which can be taken to mean acting from duty or the rightness of the act a solution is still elusive, for duty to one set would mean neglecting to act from it for the other set of persons. And so the charge against virtue ethics of ineptness in the area of applied ethics is questionable. Ineffective strategy can be the bane of other moral theories as well and so this charge must be exercised with some caution.

It is true, however, that virtues in Buddhism cannot tell the exact course of action to be implemented in situations. Specific guidelines are not laid down for different actions. This ought not to be treated as a failing as Buddhist virtues are framed in such a way that they supply a process or blueprint on how to be and act and what dispositions to cultivate that would be very valuable to the agent facing several choices. This process or blueprint would ensure that the agent acts with fortitude or modesty or sympathy or with whatever else is required such that there is little possibility that the action goes the wrong way. After all there is no force (*bala*) like moral force and moral habit is the supreme weapon (*āvudhamuttama*) – these must be effective somehow in guiding action.[42] The practice of virtues warrants not only the right choice of action but simultaneously ensures progress on the spiritual path towards enlightenment such that the agent gains through virtue cultivation something that touches all aspects of his life.

Virtues approach and the *Abhidhamma*

Before proceeding to discuss the possibility of an environmental ethics in early Buddhism and to describe environmental virtues that can be found in it, a brief discussion of the *Abhidhamma* becomes necessary. The structure of *Abhidhamma*, quite dissimilar from the rest of the Canon, evokes the need for a separate discussion. The reason for inclusion of the *Abhidhamma* (when most studies of this kind tend to neglect it) is that it tabulates certain wholesome and unwholesome qualities, a categorization of which is important in the context of the views that have been suggested in this chapter. Contrary to common opinion that the *Abhidhamma* is too scholastic and interpretive to deserve a place in ethical study Harvey comments that "The *Abhidhamma* literature contains material on the psychology of ethics. . . ."[43] Keown has also noted that in this scholastic compendium:

> . . . basic categories can shed useful light on the nature of Buddhist ethics . . . the *Abhidharmic* ethical classifications are readily intelligible in terms of one of the oldest and most influential concepts in Western Ethics – the concept of a virtue.[44]

It seems, therefore, that mention of the *Abhidhamma* is expedient in any discussion of Buddhism and virtue ethics.

Before going on to examine the nature of the above-mentioned wholesome and unwholesome qualities, however, it is important to understand the aims and theoretical structure of the *Abhidhamma*. The aims of this compendium, even though they remain non-different from those of the rest of the Canon in the ultimate analysis, differ in their approach. The *Abhidhamma* tackles issues differently. Consequently, its structure also differs quite radically from that of the Canon. Harvey understands the *Abhidhamma's* main aims as follows:

> On the one hand, it refines the *khandha* analysis so as to give a fine grained enumeration and characterization of the *dhamma's* (Skt *dharma's*), basic patterns or basic processes, which are experienced as making up the flow of mental and physical phenomena. Among these are included various sets of spiritual qualities. On the other hand, it refines the doctrine of Conditioned Arising by showing how the basic patterns condition each other in a web of complex ways.[45]

The understanding of the *khandhas* (or factors that constitute the so-called self) is central to Buddhism and reveals the self as non-existent. The *Abhidhamma* considers this as the starting point and then undertakes a careful analysis of the ultimate factors of the composition of a person both on the physical level and, more importantly, the psychological level. It, in fact, analyses all of reality in similar terms. An analysis of the interaction and relation of all categories (as expressed in the formula of *paṭiccasamuppāda*) is *Abhidhamma's* second major contribution. Ultimately, in the words of Narada Mahathera "the main object of the Abhidhamma is to understand things as they truly are (*yathabhutananadassana*). One who sees the Abhidhamma is not a surface seer but a seer of reality."[46]

It is with reference to the first aim mentioned by Harvey that I shall trace the presence of what may be termed the virtues within this classificatory system. I shall concentrate on the first book of the *Abhidhamma* – the *Dhammasangani* (Enumeration of the Elements) as it appears most relevant to a preliminary study. The *Dhammasangani* explains the *dhammas* analytically.[47] *Dhammas* are those constituents of experience that cannot be reduced and analysed any further. The *dhammas* are accepted as real but not permanent. As regards this book of the *Abhidhamma*, Keown makes two important observations. First, he points out the close relation between ethics and psychology within this work. Secondly, he finds that even though the ethical terminology this book has adopted is fairly unfamiliar, an understanding of it is crucial because "without an understanding of the ethical function of these *dhammas* it is difficult to provide an analysis of *sīla* at its most basic level."[48] In support of this observation Keown draws attention to a passage in Buddhaghosa's *Path of Purification* where *sīla* is defined with reference to the categories (52 *cetasikas*) recognized by *Abhidhamma*.[49] Keown further states that "*sīla* is a collective point denoting the organization and structuring of the good mental states (*dhamma*) identified in the Abhidhammic system."[50]

Coming back to the *dhammas*, in the *Abhidhammic* classification ultimate (*paramaṭṭha*) *dhammas* are of four types. These are:

1 *Citta*
2 *Cetasika*
3 *Rūpa*
4 *Nibbāna*

The first three *paramaṭṭha dhammas* are treated from the ethical and psychological stand points. *Nibbāna* is different, since it is considered to be unconditioned. It does not arise or disappear as the others do and is established at the time of emancipation. The other three, however, are conditioned and may appear as wholesome (*kusala*), unwholesome (*akusala*) or neutral (*avyākata*).[51] *Rūpa* is always only neutral. Our interest from the virtues' standpoint lies in *citta* and *cetasika*. Accordingly, this remaining section will discuss these in some detail.

The word *citta* comes from the pali "*cinteti*" which means "to think." Thus thinking of an object or even its awareness is *citta*. *Citta* is often also translated as "mind" or "consciousness."[52] Keown finds this definition to be limiting and states:

> While "mind" captures the operation of the conscious process "psyche" is preferable as a translation since it embraces intellectual and emotional life, the conscious as well as unconscious activity of the mind, and encompasses better the dimensions of moral traits, dispositions and character.[53]

Herbert Guenther, on the other hand, understands *citta* as "attitude" and states that "having a certain attitude means to be ready for something, and this readiness . . . is due to the presence of a certain subjective group pattern, being a definitive combination of many factors in the human psyche."[54]

The *Dhammasangani* speaks of 89 classes of *citta*. Of these 21 are of the wholesome variety, which may belong either to the sense sphere, fine-material sphere, immaterial sphere or "unrelated" to the individual existence sphere.[55] The root causes of wholesome states (*kusala mūla*) are non-greed (*alobha*), non-hate (*adosa*) and non-delusion (*amoha*). Of these three roots Nyanaponika has remarked:

> The three Wholesome Roots are the main criteria by which a state of consciousness is determined as being wholesome. The first two of them, Non-Greed (alobha) and Non-Hate (adosa), have to be present in every class of karmically wholesome consciousness if it should have the status. Non-Delusion (amoha) is to be found only in those wholesome states of consciousness which are associated with knowledge (*ñāṇa-sampayutta*).[56]

On the other hand, the unwholesome (*akusala*) states are rooted in greed (lobha), hatred (*dosa*) and delusion (*moha*). Apart from these two (*kusala and akusala*) states, there are certain states that are not conditioned by roots. As mentioned earlier, these are the neutral or *avyākata* states and are of two types – those that are wholesome or unwholesome consequences (*kusala vipāka/akusala vipāka*) and those that are experienced by enlightened beings and from which no consequences follow (*kriyā*). This is, in brief, the classification of *citta*.

Cetasikas, on the other hand, are mental concomitants. These are 52 in number. Of the *cittas* and *cetasikas* Lama Govinda has said "the classification [of *citta*] is like a steel-skeleton of a building into which various materials are to be filled, each at its place according to its nature."[57] Just as with the *cittas*, the *cetasikas* are also divided into wholesome, unwholesome and neutral. Lama Govinda clarifies further that in this threefold division the first two factors are conditioned by wholesome and unwholesome roots, as are the *cittas*. However, the third, though not so conditioned, combines with either the wholesome or unwholesome states and becomes so "according to their combination with other factors."[58] The neutral *cetasikas* are important, however, as they contain elements that are constant factors of consciousness (*sabba-citta-sādhāraṇā*).[59] Some instances that he gives are sense-impression (*phassa*), feeling (*vedanā*) and volition (*cetanā*).

From the point of view of virtue ethics there are two important outcomes of the discussion of *cittas* and *cetasikas*. The first is an ethical one and concerns the listing of wholesome and unwholesome qualities. The second is a psycho-ethical one and relates to the connection and play between *citta* and *cetasika*, which together explain the psychological functioning of a person. These two points are discussed below.

The first listings of what may be considered the virtues and vices in early Buddhism appear in the *Abhidhammic* discussion of the *cittas* and *cetasikas*. Keown appears convinced that the qualities discussed in *Abhidharmic* literature can be accepted as virtues and vices and that "these good and evil qualities (*dharmas*) are perhaps best understood as corresponding to the Western notion of virtues and vices."[60] He adds that the root states (*kusala mūla* and *akusala mūla*) are similar to the Christian Cardinal Virtues of Hope, Faith and Charity, from which all other virtues originate. However, even if one finds it hard to draw such a comparison, the listing of the various *kusala* (and *akusala*) factors appear to be in close harmony with the definition of virtue given earlier in this chapter and it therefore appears as reasonable to look upon them as forms of virtues (and vices).

Though it must always be remembered that the *cittas* and *cetasikas* together compose the psychological set-up of an individual and therefore are responsible for the proper functioning of what can be understood as the virtues and vices, only the *cetasika* list will be discussed herewith, as it should suffice in giving an idea of why such qualities can be considered as virtues. There are 14 *akusala cetasikas* and they form five groups. They are as follows:

1 Delusion (*moha*)
  Immodesty (*ahirika*)
  Unscrupulousness (*anottappa*)
  Restlessness (*uddhacca*)
2 Greed (*lobha*)
  Erroneous views (*diṭṭhi*)
  Self-conceit (*māna*)
3 Hatred (*dosa*)
  Envy (*issā*)
  Egotism (*macchriya*)
  Worry (*kukkucca*)
4 Sloth (*thīna*)
  Torpor (*middha*)
5 Doubt (*vicikichā*)

There are 25 *kusala cetasikas* and these are divided into four classes:

1 Faith (*saddhā*)
  Mindfulness (*sati*)
  Modesty (*hirī*)
  Scrupulousness (*ottappa*)
  Greedlessness (*alobha*)
  Hatelessness (*adosa*); and 13 others[61]

2 Right speech (*sammā vācā*)
Right action (*sammā kammanta*)
Right livelihood (*sammā ājīva*)
3 Compassion (*karunā*)
Sympathetic joy (*muditā*)
4 Reason or insight (*paññindrīya*)[62]

Lama Govinda draws attention to how certain wholesome and unwholesome states are opposed to each other and tend to eliminate each other. For instance, faith (*saddhā*) is in direct opposition to doubt (*vicikicchā*) and to delusion (*moha*). Modesty (*hirī*) eliminates immodesty (*ahirika*) and selflessness (*alobha*) eliminates greed (*lobha*).[63]

The second outcome of the discussion of *citta* and *cetasika* is from the psycho-ethical point of view and is derived from the actual process of interaction and the arising and fading of these factors. Both *citta* and *cetasika* arise at the same time but they are different and have different duties to perform. However, they condition each other. As Harvey explains "The precise cluster of 'mental states' [*cetasikas*] accompanying a moment of *citta* determines (and is determined by) its nature. At each moment in time, another cluster of *citta-with-cetasikas* arises, thus accounting for the subtle moment-to-moment changes in a person's experience."[64] It also becomes clear that at any given time only one *citta* arises, but it may be accompanied by many *cetasikas*.

Nina van Gorkom gives a very interesting account of the interaction between *citta* and *cetasika*. She draws attention to the importance of *cetasikas*. A person cannot, she understands, think, act or speak without the *cetasikas*. She takes the example of "seeing." Seeing is a *citta* that perceives colour and so on. However, in order to perform its function correctly it needs the support of the *cetasika* of contact and of one-pointedness. Thus in all cognition there is a close association of *citta* and *cetasika*. This association is extended to the fact that when *citta* is *kusala*, the *cetasika* will also be *kusala*; and similarly when the *citta* is *akusala*, so will the accompanying *cetasika* be. The *cetasika* itself, in turn, conditions the *citta* and other *cetasikas*: van Gorkom gives the example of the *cetasika* of *pañña*, that conditions *citta* and other accompanying *cetasikas*.[65]

The importance of knowing the way *cittas* and *cetasikas* function cannot be underestimated in the case of a virtue ethics for they clarify the process by means of which virtues arise. It is constantly reiterated by scholars (such as van Gorkom) working on the *Abhidhamma* that since there is no substantial self in Buddhism it cannot posses these states as is commonly presumed to be the case. So instead of attributing greed to the self it simply must be accepted that the *citta* and corresponding *cetasikas* of greed have arisen. And it is only when these qualities are recognized in this sense can the vices be overcome and the virtues established. The essence of *Abhidhamma* philosophy is to throw light on this process and on how to overcome *akusala* qualities that inhibit the higher spiritual quest. Lama Govinda has rightly remarked that morality in the *Abhidhamma* is directional – it directs one towards wholesomeness, away from unwholesomeness.[66] Thus the *Abhidhamma* not only lists certain virtues and vices, it also discusses the manner in which virtues and vices arise and therefore, can be encouraged or constrained as required by one in quest of liberation. In this way a virtue ethics would appear to be supported in the *Abhidhamma*. Though this section has dwelt on the matter in brief, it has attempted to interpret the *Abhidhamma* in the light of a virtue ethics. Even though more will not be said on the *Abhidhamma*, the list of environmental virtues that are drawn up in this and the next chapter appear as a positive reminder of the *Abhidhammic* list of qualities as have been mentioned above.

Environmental virtue ethics: A comparison

Once reasonably established that early Buddhist ethics corresponds to a virtue ethical approach, the idea of an environmental ethics in Buddhism as a form of virtue ethics becomes plausible. Buddhism deals effectively with the ethical question about the type of character to be nurtured through a description of the virtues.[67] However what kind of personality needs to be cultivated to take into account the well-being of the environment remains unanswered in the Buddhist context so far. That this is a very complex issue is to say the least. I will next consider how a case can be made based on portions of the Pali Canon for an environmental virtue ethics and how a virtuous character in Buddhism can also be proved to be an environmentally virtuous character. I will consider the nature of an environmental virtue ethics and indicate the similarities that exist between it and early Buddhist ethics as a virtue ethics. As a more detailed follow-up to this I will demonstrate in the next chapter how some specific Buddhist virtues can be extended to the environment. At the same time I will examine in the next chapter some genuine problems that arise in such a pursuit.

The meaning of an environmental virtue ethics must be clarified to begin with. I put it simplistically. When the virtue ethics approach functions with reference to matters of the environment and focuses on what motivates environmental choices of the independent agent we have an environmental virtue ethics. Thus the character of the agent is as essential here as it is in a virtue ethics, in such a way that a subtle shift occurs displacing the centrality of environmental consequences and environmental duties themselves. In all the focus of an environmental virtue ethics is on identifying character traits that affect the natural world such that not only does the environment gain, but also that the character of the agent gets transformed in a positive manner in general. This is not suggesting that an environmental virtue ethics is more superior or effective in its methodology – only that its methodology is different and that it may be as adept (or incompetent) as other approaches.

Identifying an environmental virtue ethics in Buddhism is indeed a monumental task and would involve an intrinsic transfer of focus from actions and consequences and whatsoever other aspects to character and virtues. A simple and effective way to begin would be to ask an alternative set of questions as have been asked by Geoffrey Frasz. He writes:

> Rather than asking questions like "Do animals have rights?" or "Why is it wrong to wantonly destroy natural entities . . . the questions are "What sort of person would wantonly destroy natural entities?" or "What sort of personal qualities are needed for the humane treatment of nonhuman creatures?"[68]

Similar questions can be raised in Buddhism. Where there is an almost negligible prospect of finding answers to the first set of questions in Buddhism, the second set afford some hope as all questions to do with personal qualities are questions central to Buddhist philosophy. However it remains to be seen if the fostering of particular virtues that are recommended by early Buddhism impact the environment and whether early Buddhism contains principles that are able to convince the moral agent to act for the sake of the environment. Consequently whether virtues similar to environmental virtues and qualities can be found in early Buddhism is debated below.

Environmental virtue ethicists lay down certain virtues or qualities that are required for cultivating a healthy respect for nature. One of the first accounts of an environmental virtue ethics was presented by Thomas E. Hill Jr. in an article where he spoke of the ideals of human excellence that were needed to preserve natural environments. His method was to consider virtues that were commonly accepted and then match them with certain environmental virtues in order to garner support for the latter. Hill connected the caring and valuing of nature thus with virtues such as humility and self-acceptance to make them more appropriate. According to Hill a person who is "a short sighted one, or one with very little concern for others or ones that don't love nature enough" would be unable to act for the sake of environment. He goes on to say:

> The main idea is that though indifference to non-sentient nature does not *necessarily* reflect the absence of virtues, it often signals the absence of certain traits which we want to encourage because they are, in most cases, a natural basis for the development of certain virtues. It is often thought, for example, that those who would destroy the natural environment must lack a proper appreciation of their place in the natural order, and so must be ignorant or have too little humility. Though I would argue that this is not necessarily so, I

> suggest that, given certain plausible empirical suggestions, their attitude may well be rooted in ignorance, a narrow perspective, inability to see things as important apart from themselves and the limited groups they associate with. Or reluctance to accept themselves as natural beings.[69]

Going by what Hill has to say I believe that what is required is for the agent to understand his place in the scheme of things. This is important and acts as the base for building a virtue framework. But, as indicated by Hill above, one of the factors that obstructs this knowledge is the lack of humility. Hill mentions the virtue of humility as an important corollary to environmentally virtuous behaviour and it occupies a central part in his argument. To explain Hill's point, an individual who lacks humility would be most predisposed to wreck and devastate the natural world. The attitude of arrogance would justify to this person the horrific harm he unleashes on nature in order to meet his needs; his needs would appear as his most pressing objective compared to those of others. Such a person would encourage the sacrifice of natural resources to meet his short term and selfish ends. Only once humility is cultivated will this individual be open to recognizing and respecting the value of the natural world and undoing his selfish attitude.

The cultivation of humility is suggested in early Buddhism in many contexts, and is one of the defining characteristics that are sought by monks. The virtue of humility, undoubtedly, figures in a significant sense in early Buddhism. It gets indicated through the term *hirī* which represents a sense of humility or modesty.[70] It is said that if this virtue is not cultivated (*hirī natthi*), monks will not be able to attain wholesome states, and will only decline in this respect.[71] It is also said that those who are not restrained by modesty (*hirī niṣedhā*) will not reach the end of suffering.[72] From this the role of modesty and humility in promoting a virtuous character becomes clear. *Hirī* is also considered an important virtue in the practice of effacement by monks. It is said, "Others will be without modesty; we shall be modest in heart in this matter."[73]

The arrogance (*ahaṃkāra* or *māna*) that hinders modesty is condemned too.[74] In the *Sutta-Nipāta* it is said that a bhikkhu who has destroyed arrogance as utterly as a flood annihilates a frail bridge of reeds is truly on his way to liberation.[75] Human beings are seen as full of arrogance in the *Aggañña Sutta.* Due to this arrogance they forget humility. Such arrogance causes a great change in their natural environment. It is stated in this *Sutta*, "By reason of conceit about their appearance and conceit about their birth, fine earth disappeared."[76] Early Buddhism also contains much on the facts of life such as disease, decay, old age, sickness and death and life is in no sense romanticized. The body is described as full of filth and mire and so not really an object of pride. Such reality checks are supportive of humility as well. Buddhism does not find all of nature to be attractive and thus seems more willing to accept "real" facts about self and nature. Additionally the idea of the composition of a human being in Buddhism makes clear that human beings are not removed from nature or superior to it. This is because physical material (*rūpa*) that makes up the corporeal self contains the five material elements of which all of nature is also made.[77]

The doctrine of no-self or *anattāvāda* in Buddhism breaks down arrogance inadvertently by suggesting that there is no self that is an enduring and eternal entity. The self is simply a combination of five factors or *khandhas*, which disintegrate or separate on the death of the person. A Buddhist scholar has commented:

> According to the Buddha, the idea of self is an imaginary, false belief which has no corresponding reality and it produces harmful thoughts of "me" and "mine," selfish desire, craving, attachment, hatred, ill-will, conceit, pride, egoism and other defilements, impurities and problems. It is the source of all troubles in the world from personal conflicts to wars between nations. In short, to this false view can be traced all the evil in the world.[78]

The sense of self leads to an ego which in its turn leads to pride. The Buddha himself suggested that clinging to the idea of the permanent self could act as a hindrance to perfect insight.[79] Further while discussing right view, Gotama expounds that when the monk has understood wholesome and unwholesome actions for what they are, it would lead to the abandoning of lust and aversion, wrong view and the conceit of "I am."[80] The above passages attack notions of a permanent self and of the arrogance that arises due to its ownership. Buddhist philosophy aims to shatter the selfishness and conceit that human beings often automatically adopt. This is the way Buddhism sustains humility. At this point it would be advantageous to remember that Buddhism never speaks of the cultivation of humility as leading to an awareness of or respect for nature. But respect for nature as a by-product of the virtue cannot be ruled out once it is internalized. It would also become apparent that arrogance towards and misuse of natural resources undermines humility. We can presume that by encouraging humility and the absence of arrogance Buddhism subtly corroborates Hill's thesis.

Another virtue that Hill mentions is self-acceptance. To Hill self-acceptance is not just limited to intellectual awareness about life as such – that is about similar natural laws of living, feeding, dying and so on shared by human beings and nature. It is more about accepting and knowing such facts, which very few persons are able to do. Hill writes:

> My suggestion is not merely that experiencing nature causally promotes such self-acceptance, but also that those who fully accept

> themselves as part of the natural world lack the common drive to disassociate themselves from nature by replacing natural environments with artificial ones.[81]

Hill's suggestion here is that merely intellectually understanding similarity, common laws and so on would not alter attitudes. What is actually needed is an internalization and acceptance of this fact. With this the disassociation from nature would cease. The question whether such acceptance can be seen in early Buddhism remains. It can be assumed that such acceptance can indeed be seen as expressing itself through two unique aspects. Though these aspects of Buddhism are almost unrecognizable when compared to Hill, their essence is quite the same as his. First, it can be shown that in one sense Buddhism did not encourage disassociation through replacement of the natural with the artificial environment; this then simultaneously proves that Buddhists accepted themselves as part of the natural world. The Buddha appears as deeply connected to natural living. He ensured that a good amount of his time and that of his monks was spent in wilderness on meditation exercises. True to form he is never shown in the literary texts as demanding artificial surroundings or requesting palaces, ornamental parks and so on to be built for his gratification. It has been noted that ". . . there is a contention among some scholars that the earliest phase of Buddhism was one in which the Buddha and his disciples lived an eremitic lifestyle wandering in the wilderness, coming into urban centres only to gather alms."[82] Based on such evidence it can be said that the Buddha valued and accepted wilderness and showed no signs of disassociating himself from it. Even though there are references to artificiality in the Canon (as mentioned in the last chapter) these are never ascribed to the Buddha. Such instances have been relegated by many scholars as only a lure to Buddhist followers for doing good deeds and so are connected with virtues and not with artificiality per se. It can thus be appreciated prima facie, without delving too deeply into this debate, that the Buddha's natural sojourns were of great importance to his spiritual practice and that he never really in his personal capacity either revered or identified with artificial environments.

Secondly, Buddhism increases the power of the understanding of the basic notions of reality through practice of the Eightfold Path – especially the category of *samādhi*. What immediately becomes clear is that though this angle can be seen as important in the Buddhist quest for *nibbāna*, questions may be asked about its relation to ecology in the religion. The importance of Buddhist meditation in the ecological context must be discerned. No doubt *samādhi* (or *bhāvanā*) is the channel that transforms attitudes but does nature stand to gain by this transformation as well? According to Walpole Rahula, the ways of meditation do not separate but connect persons to life, joys and sorrows and other activities that sustain life. He adds:

> The word meditation is very poor substitute for the original term *bhāvanā*, which means "culture" or "development," i.e., mental culture or mental development. The Buddhist *bhāvanā* . . . aims at cleansing the mind of impurities and disturbances, such as lustful desires, hatred, ill will, indolence, worries . . . and cultivating such properties as concentration, awareness, intelligence, will . . . leading finally to the attainment of highest wisdom which sees the nature of things as they are . . . Nirvāṇa.[83]

From general accounts we can gather that the idea of meditation is to build a temperament that guides the practitioner towards enlightenment. But while doing so, it also increases the power of understanding (and therefore of self-acceptance). Mindfulness or *sati* is often spoken of in the *Nikāyas*. Its constant and dedicated practice leads to the revelation of the real nature of entities – both physical and psychical. Once the real nature of things is realized by the agent the mind becomes ever purer; the pollution of ignorance is dispelled. With the benefit of such realization agents can imbibe and accept what they truly are. The barrier to knowledge that the egoism had created dissipates and agents are able to truly accept the "co-evolution, causality and continuity" they share with the rest of creation. Thus, the experiential angle of self-acceptance that Hill's account entails exists in Buddhism in this way.

To Hill's account Frasz, in his paper on environmental virtue ethics, adds another virtue that he calls "openness." He finds that Hill's argument is unable to measure out the range of proper humility, that is, a humility that would be a proper character trait for good environmentalism. And so Frasz adds a virtue to it called "openness" which would help to decide the exact range of humility. Like Hill, he criticizes both arrogance (too little humility) and false modesty (too much humility). By focusing on these two he thinks that it is possible to determine "proper humility." Frasz claims:

> In a positive sense, openness is an environmental virtue that establishes an awareness of oneself as part of the natural environment, as one natural thing among many others. A person who manifests this trait is neither someone who is closed off to the humbling effects of nature nor someone who has lost all sense of individuality when confronted with the vastness and sublimity of nature . . . We value openness to other people as an esteemed quality of character since it fosters feelings of love and appreciation for other persons. It may be that this quality as it has developed between persons, when coupled with an understanding of human beings as they exist within nature, will foster similar openness toward nature.[84]

Even though there is no exact equivalent to the term "openness" in early Buddhism Frasz's understanding of the concept is similar to what is to be attained through the practice of the sublime attitudes (*Brahma-vihāras*). He describes openness as something that "fosters feelings of love and appreciation." The sublime attitudes have a similar aim in Buddhism. These inculcate in the practitioner an outward-reaching attitude more than any other virtues found in Buddhism in addition to the development of personal character. Their intention is to recognize both the love and compassion individuals desire for themselves and that they ought to feel at the same time for others. They ensure that agents who practice them are not arrogant or lacking self-worth and are concerned with developing love and sympathy for all other beings.

The four sublime virtues are universal love (*mettā*), compassion (*karunā*), sympathetic joy (*muditā*) and equanimity (*upekkhā*).[85] The Buddha returned to the world of people after his enlightenment, and the *Suttas* often mention his kindness in doing so for the sake of those suffering beings striving for or on the verge of enlightenment and yet unable to attain it without his guidance. The *Ariyapariyesanā Sutta* tells the story of Brahma approaching the rather hesitant Buddha with the request to share his teachings with those who had little dust in their eyes. The Buddha is said to have agreed from compassion.[86] In agreeing to share his teachings however it has been observed by scholars that the Buddha had nothing to gain and so a selfish motivation can be ruled out. In a different context it is said that the Buddha shows compassion for the welfare of living beings.[87] *Karunā* or compassion is the virtue that the Buddha was steeped in; all his teachings have compassion as their support. It is compassion that gives Buddha's moral teachings a special essence. From the Buddha's example it thus becomes clear that his motive was more than a concern for his own benefit because he had already gained what he set out for, and that the teachings included *all* living beings without exception.

The point to be noted is that the Buddha continued to practice these attitudes even after his enlightenment (as has been discussed earlier in this chapter). The reason for this appears to be that he took both wisdom and compassion as indelible in the idea of enlightenment. One without the other was incomplete. In reference to the Buddha, Keown says:

> What we are seeking to discover is whether the Buddha's ethical perfection was underpinned by a sentiment of moral concern. By "moral concern" I mean non-self-referential concern for the well being of others. By "sentiment" I mean a non-cognitive state as distinct from the intellectual understanding or acceptance of validity or rationality of a set of moral rules or principles. It is this principle which animates moral life and its absence which reduces morality to prudentialism or self-interest. On the view put forward here, moral appreciation means caring about others and the effects one's omissions will have upon them.[88]

Keown finds that the Buddha's moral concern can be found in his sympathy (*anukampā*) for others and that this was not a result of his enlightenment; rather it "preceded it and, indeed, motivated it." Harvey Aronson too has identified an interesting phenomenon regarding the occurrence of *anukampā*.[89] He finds that Gotama uses the term *anukampā* at least 20 times and the others more rarely. Aronson claims that the reason for this is that "sympathy is the fraternal concern that is present in an individual and does not require cultivation or meditative development. Gotama's audience required no experience in meditation to have a sense of this attitude."[90] This points to the fact that *anukampā* as a virtue is found in all intrinsically even though its amount may differ.

The sublime virtues were laid out for personal advancement. Meditation practices focus on universal love, sympathetic joy, compassion and equanimity as tools for attaining higher mental states. Thus the Buddha says, "Thus monks, you must train yourself. We will develop liberation of mind through universal love. We will practice frequently, master, exercise thoroughly, experience, increase and scrupulously undertake."[91] The same is then repeated for the other three attitudes. The *Majjhima Nikāya* also contains a description on how to gain insight through practicing the sublime attitudes.[92] Speaking further on the various developments of the mind, what each attitude does is mentioned specifically – universal love gets rid of ill will, compassion of cruelty, sympathetic joy of discontent and equanimity of aversion.[93]

The *Suttas* also make a point of repeating that the sublime virtues were to be applied to others and were not just restricted to personal meditative progress. Gotama tells his monks that they must also think in such a way that they would suffuse a person with friendliness, and then go on to suffuse the whole world, reaching out, without ill will and malevolence.[94] Thus the practice of the virtues was to be extended beyond the immediate neighbour, in fact, to the whole world. That the whole world was to be included can be seen from Gotama's own example:

> . . . with a heart filled with universal love, I continue pervading one quarter, then a second, then a third and a fourth. So above, below, horizontally, in all directions, everywhere, I continue to pervade the whole world with a heart filled with universal love, abundant, great, endless, free from hate and injury. With a heart filled with compassion . . . with a heart filled with sympathetic joy . . . with a heart filled with equanimity. . . .[95]

Each sublime virtue can also be seen individually to have an effect on others. *Mettā* is often also translated as friendliness and is also taken to mean a feeling of brotherhood or a wish for the welfare of all. Of love in general it has been said

> Love is an *other*-centered emotion. To love something is in part to

> see it as having value that goes beyond 'what it can do for you.' Certainly it does serve our interests . . . But to love something is in part to deny that its value is *just* a matter of its serving your interests.[96]

Thus love or *mettā* by its very nature selflessly encompasses other beings. Monks are asked to develop *mettā* towards all beings despite suffering hardships themselves.[97] The *Mettā Sutta* of the *Sutta-Nipāta* analyses its nature further.[98] Here it is suggested that the practitioner should ensure that all beings, no matter what their size or strength or birth be happy (through the practice of virtues). The *Sutta* wills all beings to be content and protected and happy-minded.[99] Sympathetic joy is also extended to all. Compassion towards others, as seen above, is mentioned constantly. Of *upekkhā* it is said that it is "an even minded serenity towards beings, which balances concern for others with the realization that suffering is an inevitable part of being alive."[100] Thus, the sublime attitudes have many benefits that can be clearly related to the cultivation of openness or "love and appreciation" towards others. Based on Buddhism's cosmological vision of nature, openness that is caused by the sublime attitudes can be extended to all of nature. Such openness towards nature is not an entirely alien idea in Buddhism as can be gathered from the discussion above; the sublime attitudes include all beings and the world, of which nature is an essential part.

Conclusion

Many scholars can protest that categorizing Buddhism as a virtue ethics is a rather limiting idea. Buddhism has its own peculiar nuances and these do not tune in with those of a modern day virtue ethics. There is danger that the cultural, historical and philosophical dimensions of this ancient religion would be compromised by such appropriation. However all I argue for here is that the spirit of the religion be considered. There is an overwhelming presence of virtues in Buddhism that have a wide application. It may be true that the context of these virtues is entirely different and difficult to classify in terms of virtue ethics and contemporary environmental discourse. The classification becomes all the more difficult when considering the seemingly final objective of the religion. But the virtues also point to a way of life. They point to character building and appeal to that which is good and noble and honourable in man. They provide a universal formula for thought and action very simply that is about being "good" and doing the right thing. I have sought to make this point my focus and have built on the virtues aspect essentially around this. Thus rather than treating the comparison with virtue ethics as a limiting possibility I find that it widens immediate horizons considerably and allows space for a modern day problem to be treated in a modern day manner. So even though the immediate aim of none of the virtues is ecological, they parallel ecological virtues described by environmental ethicists ensuring that actions based on them would also benefit the cause of nature. It is in this spirit that the comparison I have made ought to be considered; my aim was never to find a perfect match.

This attitude alone will lead to a positive outcome that can counter some of the charges that were outlined in the first and second chapters against a Buddhist position on the environment. I also believe that the Buddhist form of environmental virtue ethics is a moderate one, just as virtue ethics is. This means that duties and consequences may be recognized as legitimate, but only once the underlying disposition is a virtuous one. Thus environmental actions are as important as environmental character, but must necessarily follow it. By implying moderation the motivation to action is not dulled but rather action becomes empowered by inner conviction and character. Moderation brings to mind the "middle path" often mentioned in Buddhist philosophy. As the next step forward the next chapter will attempt to understand some virtues in an independent context to determine whether they are able to positively contribute to and sustain the environment. The concerns that trouble any environment virtue ethicist will also be addressed in the hope that the hypothesis presented becomes more real, substantial and inherently transforming.

5

THE ENVIRONMENTAL VIRTUES OF EARLY BUDDHISM

Virtue consists in fleeing from vice, and is the beginning of wisdom.
Horace, *Epistles*

The central aim of this chapter is to give examples about how some specific virtues in Buddhism can be seen as supportive of nature. However before determining what these virtues are, the nature of an environmental virtue needs to be more accurately defined to avoid any possible misunderstanding and ambiguity. An environmental virtue in the Buddhist context, simply put, ought to be no different from a virtue but with a specific essence. A virtue, as seen previously, is an intentional deed or action whose constant practice necessarily has the ability not only to lead to a certain character but also to a higher goal. An environmental virtue typically would epitomize an intentional deed or an action as well but one that is directed towards the well-being of the environment such that those who possess it, and other qualities like it, would be disposed to being compassionate and proactive towards the environment. Another important point to be noted about environmental virtue generally is that:

> . . . environmental virtue is not merely instrumentally valuable as the disposition to identify and then perform proper actions; it is also valuable in itself. It is life-affirming and life-enhancing. Those who possess it are better off than those who do not, for they are able to find reward, satisfaction and comfort from their relationship with nature. . . .[1]

Thus environmental virtues are not only the means but also the ends; and they benefit not only nature but also their possessor. They ought to be sought then for their own sake as well as for the moral advancement of the practitioner. There are no known environmental virtues in Buddhism fitting the definition given above exactly or in the sense in which they are framed in present day environmental virtue theories. Some environmental ideas can be spotted here and there in early Buddhist texts as has been made adequately clear in previous chapters but these are obviously underdeveloped and thus deriving nature related virtues from them is very difficult. In the absence of a clear demarcation between what is or is not an environmental virtue in Buddhism the best option remains to focus on existing virtues laid down for either the enhancement of spiritual practice or human to human relations (and sometimes for human relations with other beings) and extend these to the environment as a whole. The nature of the virtue and the function assigned to it would largely determine this process and it would be interesting to note whether such extension can be validly endorsed in early Buddhism. The final argument is that once the virtues are accepted and applied in their true spirit the person in possession of them would be unlikely to harm the environment.

Having discussed the virtues of humility, self-acceptance and openness and their possible Buddhist equivalents in the previous chapter and determining the latter's environmental prospects, attention now moves to numerous other traits mentioned in early Buddhism that define a virtuous person. We get such a sense from the Canonical precepts, which can be seen as an embodiment of the virtues. That the precepts were such an embodiment can be gathered from the fact that they are referred to as the perfection of virtue (*sīlasampadā*).[2] Buddhism lays down five precepts (*pañcasīla*) to be followed by lay people. These are abandoning the taking of life (*pāṇātipāta verāmaṇī*), abandoning the taking of what is not given (*adinnādānā verāmaṇī*), abandoning unchaste behaviour (*kāmesu-micchācāra verāmaṇī*), abandoning false speech (*musāvāda verāmaṇī*) and refraining from intoxication of any kind (*surā-meraya-majja pamādaṭṭhānā verāmaṇī*). The eight precepts (*aṭṭhangasīla*) include the first five and three new ones, that are refraining from eating or drinking at wrong times (*vikāla-bhojana verāmaṇī*), refraining from music, dancing, shows from using garlands and other finery (*naccagīta-vādita-visūkadassana-mālāgandha-vilepana-dhāraṇa-maṇḍana-vibhūsanaṭṭhānā verāmaṇī*) and from high and large beds (*uccāsayana-mahāsayana verāmaṇī*). Other precepts (namely, the *dasasīla*) include refraining from the use of gold and silver (*jātarūpa-rajata-paṭiggahaṇa verāmaṇī*). The *dasasīla* are looked upon as precepts for novices. Then there are 227 precepts for monks enlisted in the *Pātimokkha*.[3] The *Brahmajāla Sutta* of the *Dīgha Nikāya* contains additional observances. These include abstaining from the destruction of seed and vegetable growth (*bījagāma-bhūtāgama-samārambhā paṭivirato*) and abstaining from frivolous chatter, from accepting raw grains, raw meat, women, slaves, livestock, elephants is also advised. Involvement in business, bribery, fraud, murder and robbery are also cautioned against.[4]

The laity are advised to follow the first five precepts at all times, and are expected to follow the rest at some special times. Monks are expected to follow all the precepts at all times. Though each precept has a specific task to accomplish, together they can be looked upon as discouraging immoral actions and supporting that which is upright and virtuous. Contemplating precepts and their steady intentional practice leads invariably to the dissolving of the *āsavas* (greed, hatred and delusion) as well as of egoism.[5] However the question arises whether these precepts and others suggest virtues that have an influence on the environment and can be classified as environmental virtues. Some of the guidelines given above are immediately relevant to the environment such as not harming other living beings, the protection of seeds and vegetable growth, and abstinence from accepting raw meat, whereas others are indirectly environmental such as shunning luxury, the promotion of simple living and abstaining from fraud. Thus by following the dictates of the precepts closely, environmental behaviour becomes naturally included. It appears that not only does the intentional and consistent abiding by the precepts and other guidelines clear the mind of impurities and make grounds for a virtuous disposition but it simultaneously makes the agent act in ways that enhance the state of nature. Thus the outcome of this initial survey appears optimistic.

However, at the same time the above explanation is vague and the feeling that acting for the sake of the environment is fortuitous in early Buddhism cannot be shaken off. More vindication and exactitude is needed in framing the environmental virtues in the Buddhist context. Accordingly, in the remaining chapter I shall identify more specifically some Buddhist virtues with environmental value and discuss their character and application. The listing here is somewhat reminiscent of the *Abhidhamma*.[6] These virtues are enumerated as follows:

1 The virtue of respecting all life (*ahiṃsā*)
2 The virtue of simple living and contentment (*arāga, santuṭṭha*)
3 The virtue of generosity (*cāga or dāna*)
4 The virtue of responsibility (a derived virtue, based on the doctrine of *kamma*)
5 The virtue of wisdom or insight (*paññā*)

In general terms there is no doubt that virtues such as a respect for life and contentment contribute to a sound ecology by restricting unnecessary and meaningless loss of life and by reducing the pressure on natural resources. The virtue of generosity implies sacrificing in the interest of nature that itself has been generous. On the other hand, the virtues of wisdom and responsibility are more intellectually poised. Responsibility draws attention to the accountability of human beings and their obligation to the environment. Wisdom plays an essential role in the ecological choice making process. In this context, the singling out of vices is important too, e.g. greed (*rāga*), hatred (*dosa*) and delusion (*moha*); unfulfilled desires and endless craving are often seen as the foundational causes of the environmental crisis. The development of the individual along these virtues is bound to have an environmental impact as it encourages kindness, concern for other, charity and the reduction of craving. All these attitudes can be be seen as environmentally friendly.

Environmental Virtues (and Vices)

The respect for life is one of the most important and effective environmental virtue that can be identified in Buddhism. It corresponds with the definition of an environmental virtue in that a person who truly accepts it will, as a matter of course, protect the valuable entities of nature as also enhance and affirm his own life. By accepting a respect for all life an individual concedes that other beings can experience sensations just like him or herself as a result of certain actions. By following this virtue needless pain from intentional actions to such beings can come to an end. It is bound to strengthen and calm its practitioner as well. The first precept speaks of *ahiṃsā* or non-violence and categorically implies that all life must be respected. Gotama himself is often praised for adopting non-violence and it is said, "Having forsaken the destroying of life, the ascetic Gotama abstains from destroying life, without stick, without weapon, humble, with kindness, he lives with compassion for the welfare of all living beings."[7] In the *Dhammapada* it is stated that the life of each and every being is dear to it and all tremble at the thought of pain. Therefore one should never harm others for they too can suffer like one's own self.[8] Virtues of non-violence and non-hurting are exhorted in the *Theragāthā* too. Herein the monk Sankicca admits that he has lived in forests and caves amongst many wild creatures but the thought of harming them has never crossed his mind. He says that it was never his quest that living beings receive *dukkha* – through being killed or slaughtered – and finds such malice and hatred undignified.[9] Respect for life thus is a constant theme in the *Nikayās* and in other texts and its practice is reiterated over and over again. This acts as a reminder of its importance.

The virtue of respect for life is also suggested in the Eightfold Path under right action and right livelihood. Right action and livelihood specify how an individual ought to act and live in this world. He must act such that all life is respected. Under right action (*sammā kammanta*) Buddhism suggests, just like the first precept, abstinence from killing (*pāṇātipāta verāmaṇī*, D II 312). Right livelihood (*sammā ājīva*) also supports respect for all life. By adopting the correct means of making a living, a person can ensure that no being is hurt and protection is extended to everything that can suffer. This sense is conveyed by specifying that certain forms of making a living are to be avoided at all costs. The Buddha says, "Monks, a lay disciple ought not to indulge in five trades. Which five? Trade in weapons, trade in human beings, trade in flesh, trade in spirits and trade in poison."[10] Especially to be noted is a ban on the professions of hunters and butchers and others, who may physically harm other living being.[11] The *Therīgāthā* also mentions that certain professions generate evil results – pig and sheep butchers, hunters, thieves and murderers – and no amount of splashing of holy water can free them of their destiny.[12] People who injure their fellow creatures are admonished by being warned that they too will suffer ill consequences of their actions for the effects of the latter are never lost.[13] Thus, a respect for all life was emphasized in Buddhist literature. Respect extends to plant life as well. It is true that one is unable to establish that plant life is sentient on Buddhist principles, however this does not rule out respect for plants derived from precepts such as "non-injury to seeds and plants" (even though the motivation in such cases, as discussed earlier, is unclear).[14]

Since a respect for life is so strongly suggested in all texts it allows nature analogies that appear to support violence towards non-human beings (and defy conservation in the process as mentioned in Chapter 2) to be looked at in a different context. For instance, the training of the mind during meditation was compared to the skilful elephant trainers hook when he restrains a wild elephant from his savage ways.[15] But rather than taking this metaphor to mean an allowance of violence towards elephants it now appears that it is bringing to mind only the violence and aggression with which the practitioner has to restrain his mind and cut out from the root worldly desires. The metaphor is really about the intensity and finality of the getting rid of ill-passions and it must convey this vision completely. The virtues outlook ensures that the value of natural objects ought not to be drawn out from such specific examples; it must rather be seen in the idea of virtuous conduct as such that Buddhism upholds. Thereby this understanding gives a certain amount of legitimacy to limiting meaning by relegating such instances to specific contexts.

Another factor in Buddhism that contributes to a good environment is the indirect endorsement of simple living. Simple living is essentially articulated through non-greed (*arāga*) and contentment (*santuṭṭhi*) and corresponds with the definition of an environmental virtue as well. The Buddha appears to approve that living simply would advance the agent's quest by providing an impetus towards liberation. The virtue does not have a direct ecological motive in Canonical literature, but can be seen to support ecology implicitly. That simplicity is a foundational virtue for an environmental virtue ethics is not in doubt. As an environmental virtue it recognizes that such living plays a positive role in reducing the demands made on the natural world and consequently in protecting the environment. Thus any philosophy that supports a simple life and contentment not based on material possessions is bound to be inherently environmental.

Simplicity in the Pali Canon is advocated in a number of ways. First, following the path of sense desires was discouraged fervently. Sense pleasures (*kāma*) to the Buddha were beset with many drawbacks. Not only did they give limited satisfaction, they caused a great amount of anguish and disillusionment.[16] To drive in this point sense pleasures are compared with gross similes such as those of a skeleton (*aṭṭhikaṇkalūpamā*), a lump of meat (*maṃsapesūpamā*), a torch of dry grass (*tiṇukkūpamā*), etc., and in each comparison the result of indulging in sense pleasures is macabre.[17] A nun in the *Therīgāthā* explains that for her sense desires are like daggers and sharp pointed weapons and what appears as enjoyment now are causes of discontentment.[18] To the Buddha the path of sense desires was one that always led to misfortune and unhappiness. Thus in any way he could the Buddha's advice was to follow the path of simple living guided by morality and as opposed to one guided by desires. Secondly, monks and nuns were told to consume no more than was necessary. The monk is asked to be content (*bhikkhu santuṭṭho hoti*) with whatever food, robes and lodgings be given as alms but not to admire or be repulsed by them.[19] Equanimity towards material things was to be practised. Buddhism did recognize in a practical sense basic material needs – robes, food, lodgings and medicines – but nothing beyond such a simple existence. The monk was told to live and be content with little, referring to his alms and robes, as a means of cultivating and practicing morality. Thirdly, we know from the precepts that luxury items such as high beds, gold and silver, garlands and so on were not to be used. These objects and others like it put unnecessary pressure on precious natural resources. The shunning of luxury items points to the encouragement of a simple living.

At the same time supporting some luxury for the laity ensures that Buddhism is not excessively ascetic; enjoying material success as a result of *kamma* seems to be quite a common theme within the Canon and has attracted much scholarly curiosity. The *Cūḷakammavibhanga Sutta* says that the good result of *kamma* may make one wealthy. Here Queen Mallikā asks the Buddha why some women are born poor and deformed. The Buddha explains that if a woman is good tempered, a giver of charity and not jealous or vengeful then she will be reborn with great beauty and wealth. However, if she is the opposite then she is poor and deformed.[20] The reward of an ethical life is shown to be wealth. But at the same time as acknowledging material prosperity there were stringent guidelines for how one attained such prosperity – these were to do with virtuous behaviour. The wealth had to not only be ethically earned but honourably spent as well and there are many examples of how this may be done.[21] Many scholars agree that it is entirely possible that when Buddhist philosophy is looked at as a whole it becomes apparent that wealth (and the praise of artificiality to some extent) was displayed only to ensure virtuous behaviour and not to encourage the unnecessary use of luxury goods. Thus such examples do not negate the virtue of simple living. In fact they ensure virtue. In any case a person on the path of spirituality soon came to realize the worthlessness of such things.

One appropriate use of wealth suggested in the scriptures is the pursuit of generosity (*dāna*). Generosity was one of the more important virtues for Buddhists and has an important role to play in an ethics of nature. An agent who possesses the environmental virtue of generosity would be inclined and disposed in equal measures to act for the sake of nature. He would be receptive to nature's generosity and would want to be generous in return. He would realize that his own welfare is indelibly connected with such generosity. The possession of generosity also overcomes selfishness and preoccupation with one's own interests. These latter attitudes are devastating in relation to the environment and by eradicating them the value of generosity increases even more. The attitude of generosity can thus be an important environmental virtue. There are many examples in the Canon where offerings made to the *sangha* by resourceful laypersons are treated as excellent *kamma* which undoubtedly would lead to a good rebirth.[22] It was also believed that giving for the sake of the virtue was nobler than giving for some gain.[23] It is assured at one place that a man who has much property, who has gold and food and does not want to share his things, is a loser and not a gainer in this world.[24] Householders were expected to have a greater amount of material objects so as to be able to give them as alms and share them with monks. In fact, there is a constant reiteration of the interdependence between monks and householders; householders were imperative in their role as material supporters of the *sangha*. The monks in their turn had to be generous by imparting the true meaning of the Buddha's teachings to lay disciples. Thus generosity is encountered through this mutual give and take or mutual dependence. Generosity in this form towards nature would benefit the latter immensely. Once again even though generosity is not directly related to ecology it is said in the *Aṅguttara Nikāya*:

> As for me Vaccha, I say thus: even if one throws dish-scourings or cup-scourings into a pool (which is either at the out-skirts of a village or near a village) for creatures there – by which these creatures are caused to be kept alive – this giving is a source of merit, I say, [not] to talk of feeding human beings.[25]

This is just one example to show that the rewards of generosity did extend to non-human beings and did count for something. (This may appear as an example of consequentialism, in that the consequences of feeding a human beings are superior to those of feeding other creatures and in this sense the act is done and judged based on its consequences. However, I believe that, rather than endorsing consequentialism this example reconfirms early Buddhism's hierarchical structure of the value of beings. Human birth is more privileged due to the possibility of liberation it contains and therefore more merit is attained by providing food for human beings. What this example clarifies is that such hierarchy does not allow for unethical treatment of others. Other creatures are deserving of generosity as well and good consequences accrue from deeds of generosity done towards them. In this context the example upholds virtues.)[26]

The next virtue to be considered is that of responsibility. Extending an attitude of responsibility towards nature entails a certain moral commitment to nature and ensures that certain obligations to nature are fulfilled. Such responsibility is often looked upon as an invaluable asset of environmental consciousness and can be accepted as an environmental virtue. Early Buddhist texts do not contain any direct references to responsibility towards the environment. One arena where the sense of responsibility could be possibly derived would be that of the nature of duty in Buddhist texts.[27] This is because duty and responsibility are closely related; one who is bound by a sense of duty would be inextricably shouldering some amount of responsibility and vice versa. The *Sigālaka Sutta* elaborates various forms of duties, but unfortunately no environmental ones are mentioned here.[28] The *Sutta* contains a code of conduct laid down for the laity who must maintain relations with the others who share their life. It mentions six groups towards whom an individual has duties and who have duties towards that individual; the individual is told how to treat mother and father, teachers, wife and children, friends and companions, servants and helpers, finally, ascetics and Brahmins. Each of these groups in turn is assigned some duties that are to be directed towards the individual. For instance, the *Sutta* suggests that parents are to be looked after and supported, the family honour maintained and their duties are to be performed by the individual who is the offspring and who in turn ought to be kept away from evil by parents, be given good skills and inheritance and be found a suitable wife. In his role as a pupil the individual must serve his teacher, be attentive and study wholeheartedly. The teacher should instruct properly, ensure that the pupil learns good skills and provide him with security. As a master the individual should ensure that the servant is given work according to strength, is paid rightfully and is looked after in general. The servant in his turn ought to work hard, take only what is given and uphold the master's good reputation. Of the relation between employer and employee (or master and servant) in the *Sutta*, P. D. Ryan says that this defines, by extension, all relations in which one group is stronger than the other. This is increasingly the relation between man and the environment. He finds that this idea of mutuality has been absent in most of our dealings with the natural world.[29] However, I find that this extension is not really applicable, as the idea of mutuality is practically non-existent in cases of human and non-human interaction. Such an extension would be fraught with difficulty and is overstepping the limits of the *Sutta's* intentions. (It has been suggested that actually the relation between parents and children is possibly the one that ought to act as the blueprint for the human-nature relation. This is a non-reciprocal, non-negotiable relation. There is no contract between parents and children, this being a natural relation; parents act from unconditional love, not motivated by selfishness; even though there may be some sense that children will take care of them in their old age this is not a factor that affects a parent's love for a child.)[30] To account for responsibility towards the environment as based on mutuality of duty between employer and employee is not very viable.

On the contrary, responsibility towards nature (without corresponding mutuality of course) can be based on the doctrine of *kamma* and I shall now attempt to show how. Tracing the virtue of responsibility, as emanating from *kamma*, is a complicated process especially as early Buddhist literature does not mention the "virtue of responsibility," *per se*. It must be remembered that this, at best, remains a derived virtue. To begin with the nature of responsibility itself must be clarified. In his book delving into the notion of responsibility Hans Jonas states:

> The first and most general condition of responsibility is causal power, that is, that acting makes an impact on the world; the second, that such acting is under the agent's control; and third, that he can foresee its consequences to some extent. Under these necessary conditions, there can be "responsibility," but in two widely differing senses: (a) responsibility as being accountable "for" one's deeds, whatever they are; and (b) responsibility "for" particular objects that commits an agent to particular deeds concerning them. . . . The one is formal, the other a substantive concept, and we really speak of two different things when we say that someone is responsible for what happened (which is neither praise nor blame), and that someone is a responsible person, that is, honours his responsibilities (which is praise).[31]

That actions that are under the control of the agent or are intentional actions are the ones whose moral worth is determined allows early Buddhism to meet the second condition of responsibility quite adequately. Support is also garnered from the definition of *kamma* ("Monks, I say intentional action is *kamma*") as mentioned earlier. The notion of *kamma* makes clear that the responsibility of intentional actions rests with the agent himself or herself whose consequences the agent must subsequently enjoy or suffer. Thus as for point (a) in the above quote that the agent is responsible for the deeds he commits voluntarily there is plenty of literary support in Buddhism.

However, enquiries about actions making an impact on the world are more difficult to address. Whether early Buddhist literature considers the impact that actions can have on others (including the environment) is questioned. For instance, when an agent aggressively and undeservingly usurps someone's house with the intention of doing so, not only is he breaking a precept (the precept to refrain from taking what has not been given, *adinnādānā veramaṇī*) and exposing himself to unfavourable consequences, he may also be affecting someone else's life in that the owner of the house may become homeless due to his action. A positive acknowledgement of the latter would substantially cover point (b) in the above quote. However it is often legitimately alleged that the consequences of the agent's actions on others hardly gets mentioned and that *kamma* mainly concentrates on how actions affect the agent himself. From this point of view one condition of responsibility remains unfulfilled. However, the effect of actions on others is not an invisible idea in Buddhist literature. Further it is interesting to note that the instances where repercussions of moral actions on others have been discussed are environmental situations.

The *Aṅguttara Nikāya* contains two examples where the consequences of *kamma* on the external world have been pointed out. When Gotama is asked to explain why the population of the world has decreased to such an extent he traces the reason to the perverted and immoral desires of people and their mistaken beliefs. This has led them to slaughter one another. General immorality has also affected the natural world. This has led to a shortage of rainfall, food becoming scarce, and famine and starvation.[32] Thus, non-virtuous actions are acknowledged as causing havoc in the natural world. In a similar example in the same *Nikāya* an unrighteous king is held responsible for environmental catastrophes. When the king was unrighteous his entire realm lived unhappily and the order of nature was disturbed for the rains came out of season. His unrighteousness filtered down to all in society and adversely agitated the balance of the natural world. It is said:

> . . . the sun and moon go about disharmoniously; . . . the constellations and stars go about disharmoniously; . . . day and night go about disharmoniously; . . . the cycle of seasons are disharmonious; . . . winds blow disharmoniously; . . . the multitude is disharmonious. When the winds and multitude are disharmonious, the gods are very agitated. Thus they do not give proper rain showers. Due to this, crops ripen disharmoniously. When crops ripen disharmoniously, men who use such crops are short-lived, ugly, weak and sickly.[33]

The *Sutta* goes on to say that the exact opposite happens when the king is righteous. It ends by saying that the "whole realm dwells in happiness if the ruler lives aright" (*sabbaṃ raṭṭhaṃ sukhaṃ seti rājā ce hoti dhammiko ti*).

These passages have been interpreted in various ways and many scholars see them as an example of group *kamma* more than anything else.[34] However in a paper looking exclusively at the concept, James McDermott writes that though such isolated cases can be found "their nature and infrequency in this literature make it clear that a systematic concept of group karma was in no sense operative in early Theravāda. Instead, the repeated emphasis is . . . on the individual as heir to his own deeds."[35] Rare and contextual as they might be, however, and not really instances of group *kamma*, such examples have other more important implications. They authenticate and give substance to the prior unfocused feeling that internal values and intentions have an unmistakable connection with "objective" factors, a feeling that has only been hinted throughout the course of early Buddhist literature. In environmental terms, they highlight the connection between *kamma* or human actions and the state of the natural world. Sue Hamilton has arrived at a similar conclusion. She finds:

> . . . whatever state one is in subjectively is correlated objectively. Thus one is responsible not just for neutrally cognitive structural aspects of objectivity, but also for its qualitative aspects. Indeed *whatever* is part of objectivity is subjectively dependent, even if it be a hurricane, desertification or a famine. . . . what Buddhist teachings suggest is that the correlation is connected primarily through the matrix of subjective states of mind, what today would be called attitude.[36]

The examples indicate that the more immoral human actions are the more the physical environment will be harmed. They also show that not only is the individual responsible for his actions but that the responsibility "for" the state of the environment lies with him to a great extent through his actions. (I use the words "to a great extent" deliberately as human beings are responsible for the crisis but not entirely. It has been scientifically proven that some disasters in nature are necessarily "natural" that is, not man-made, and a wearing away may be happening in the natural progression of things. Buddha's understanding of *kamma* allows for this, since the Buddha admitted that not everything that takes place is due to *kamma* or intentional action. Thus the *kammic* approach was very practical.)

As for foreseeing the consequences of action (the third aspect of responsibility) early Buddhism says even less in concrete terms. All it reiterates constantly is that wholesome actions will have good results and unwholesome actions bad. Things are also complicated at the environmental end. There must be awareness that there are many environmental decisions and actions whose consequences cannot be foreseen. It has been stated:

> When men act on nature, they do not simply modify a particular quality of a particular substance. What they do, rather, is to interact with a system of interactions, setting in process new interactions. Just for that reason, there is always a risk that their actions will have consequences which they did not predict.[37]

There are cases where the action cannot be specifically related to an agent or agents and this creates further problems for the notion of environmental responsibility for no one as such can be held responsible. This can be best understood with an example. The increase in demand for housing increases the consumption of wood and leads to the cutting down of old-growth forests. Mr X's demand for a luxurious ten bedroom house (when he already has a perfectly functional house that protects against the weather and other natural hazards) does not make him directly responsible for the cutting down of forests. In fact, he might not be aware of where the wood for his house building activity is coming from. Even if he does have some information, he could be completely ignorant of how much harm he has caused the ecological balance in a remote Ecuadorian forest where his demand for wood has endangered many species of animals, caused mudslides, displaced and caused the death of numerous thriving and rare plants and added to global warming. These consequences are unintentional and unplanned and if he were to be held responsible he could react by being distraught or by going into denial for he did not foresee them at all. How, and on whom, is responsibility to be pinned here? This matter is complicated, of course, by the fact that it was never Mr X's intention to harm the Ecuadorian forest.

Buddhist tenets would allow for this issue to be approached from a different angle. The agent cannot be held responsible for the diminishing forest and so on (for he acted unintentionally) but he can be held responsible for his immediate desires and actions. And he ought to be able to foresee that the consequences of unnecessary and excessive desires and connected actions would be bad. When unscrupulous desire (*taṇhā*) underlies action, the latter becomes objectionable. The Buddha constantly reminds his disciples of the entangling and clinging nature of craving which is the cause of unwholesomeness.[38] It is interesting also to note that the stain or pollution (*abhilepana*) of the world is referred to as desire.[39] So when the desire and action are unwholesome then its consequences will also most likely be unwholesome and awful even though they cannot be specifically pointed out in some cases. Therefore in the case of the deforestation of an Ecuadorian forest, in one sense, responsibility of unseen consequences cannot be denied for the agent is responsible directly for his desires. And this is how Buddhism deals with the environmental crisis. External nature can be altered through the desires that are nursed by individuals. An individual in this unique way is thus thrust with responsibility for nature – he is responsible for his own actions and the formation of his own character, he can be held responsible for the consequences of these actions on others, and he continues to be responsible even when he is unable to foresee the effect of these actions.

The above discussion on unwholesomeness leads to further questions about the nature of vices and of desire. So before going on to the virtue of wisdom, some vices and the nature of *taṇhā* in early Buddhism are examined in more detail. The presence of vices (even though environmental vices per se cannot be found in early Buddhism) is contraindicative to good environmentalism and another way in which Buddhism supports an environmental virtue ethics is by advising the ethical agent to get rid of them. An environmental vice, as defined by many scholars, is directly opposed to an environmental virtue and exemplifies a disposition wherein the agent acts intentionally to harm or destroy natural resources in some way. This definition can be extended to certain vices mentioned in early Buddhism. These vices encourage the development of arrogance and conceit such that the environmentally virtuous character so painstakingly described above is suppressed. In other words the possession of vices does not allow virtues such as humility, openness, respect for life and generosity to develop.

In a number of places in Pali texts character defects or vices appear. Some of these are covetousness (*Abhijjhā*, M III 50), greed (*giddhilobha*, M I 360), ill-will (*āghāto*, D I 3), avarice (*macchariya*, M I 281), laziness (*ālasa,* Dp 280 and also *tandī*, Sn 926), sloth (*manda*, Th 17, 101) and egoism (*ahaṃkāro*, M III 18). These match environmental vices. Covetousness reinforces exploitation of nature's bounties for it implies increasing and holding on to one's own possessions irrespective of the harm and havoc such an attitude may play upon the existence and property of others. Greed points to single-minded attention to the one's desires, however banal and trivial they may be. Ill will and avarice are also qualities whose possession would not allow a person to act on behalf of another and are reminiscent of a malevolent spirit. Similarly laziness and sloth point to the agent being unwilling to act for nature's sake out of either sheer indifference or low enthusiasm or little focus. Egoism or treating one's own self as above everything also leads to a diminished nature; it is an attitude that justifies lack of responsibility and makes selfish behaviour an acceptable norm.

Not only are the vices identified, their possession is also discouraged in many ways in the texts. Many *Suttas* contain warnings about the consequences of non-virtuous behaviour. Evil doers lament everywhere due to the tarnished nature of their acts.[40] The *Bālapaṇḍita Sutta* of the *Majjhima Nikāya* speaks of the distinction between a wise and a foolish man. The foolish man breaks the five precepts and therefore suffers bad consequences. He suffers in knowing that people in assemblies are discussing his breaking the precepts, that criminals are punished by the king and that his evil-doing is going to lead him to a bad rebirth.[41] It is also said that greed for the pleasure of life lead to the neglect of the good that brings true happiness.[42] Punishments that accrue to evil actions are described graphically, as in the *Devadutta Sutta* where it is said, "Monks, overwhelmed by the eight wrong states, Devadutta, with his mind overcome, suffered greatly in a state of misery after death, in purgatory, staying there for an aeon."[43] The literature under consideration thus does not waver to spell out what comprises immoral *kamma* and leads to severely painful results. That the effect of vices can be felt beyond the individual also becomes clear in the discussion on responsibility. Therefore it can be believed that vices affect the agent, his community and his environment and by the same extension also the present and the future.

However, *taṇhā* or craving is yet the greatest impediment to the cultivation of virtues. It is interesting to note that though craving is not connected obviously with ecology in the *Nikāyas*, it is always closely linked with material desires. This becomes clear from the following, "Due to craving there is search; due to search there is acquisition; due to acquisition there is decision; due to decision there is desire and lust. . . ."[44] And since material desires are one of the greatest causes of the devastation of nature, the latter appears to have an essential connection with craving. Materialism, ever-growing desires and non-satiated needs would most likely initiate the processes that deplete the environment. Thoughtless acquiring of goods is also directly opposed to the virtues of contentment and simple living that were mentioned previously. Human experience in general is witness to the fact that desires never end and this fact is often acknowledged in the texts. At one place it is said that if one could magically transform a single mountain into two mountains of solid gold it would still not provide lasting satisfaction to any one individual.[45]

However the *taṇhā* or craving of early Buddhism has a much more insidious meaning than simply material desires. It is that which underlies all the vices. The Second Noble Truth explains the cause of eternal suffering or *dukkha* as craving. G. P. Malalasekera understands craving as follows:

> *Tanhā* is, rather what might be called thirst, the craving of the limited, individual living creature seeking to gratify itself in its separateness and to use the external world as a means to satisfy its self centred needs. The evil in man's life is man-made and, therefore, eradicable by man, without outside interference.[46]

The *āsavas* of greed (*rāga*), hatred (*dosa*) and delusion (*moha*) have craving as their foundation. Once the agent allows craving to define his character immoral action is sure to follow. Buddhism subsequently aspires to show how to restrain inclinations borne out of craving. There are numerous discourses on the controlling of the *āsavas*. A follower of Buddhist teachings is on his way to liberation and final freedom when the true significance of craving is understood by him.[47] As an additional reason for his followers to overcome craving the Buddha admonished them to perform actions of merit for they brought happiness and long term consequences filled with joy.[48] Much was to be gained by a craving-free outlook – a good life, heaven hereafter and finally even absolute liberation.

Some concerns addressed and the virtue of wisdom

Having discussed the nature of some virtues (and vices) that have environmental significance in early Buddhism, problems may still be faced about how to identify environmental virtues and to determine what constitutes an environmental disposition. Scholars have often pointed out problems faced by virtue and environmental virtue ethics in general. Some of these have been adapted here in anticipation. One possible objection is that Buddhism's definition of a virtuous disposition may not reveal the most environmentally favourable action. Early Buddhist texts have devoted much to understanding and explaining what constitutes a right action and the intentions of the actor; but these texts do not specify the nature of an environmental action.

Cultivation of environmental concern appears as a secondary development. As a result ambiguity may be extensive and could pose as an obstacle to guiding and directing environmental actions. Added to this, since the Buddha does not specify environmental virtues, the agent can harm the environment and yet be virtuous; he may follow the five precepts meticulously, for instance, but continue to supervise the building of a hotel in an environmentally sensitive area. Secondly, there is an equal possibility that some Buddhist virtues may be completely neutral or indifferent towards nature. For instance, the fifth precept of refraining from intoxication of any kind seems irrelevant where the environment is concerned. This complicates the matter of classifying virtues as environmental. A third objection is that there may be some vagueness about how a dispute is to be settled amongst two environmentally virtuous men. Disputes of this nature can become quite serious and there are not enough examples and arguments in Buddhist scriptures on the basis of which these can be analysed and settled. On the basis of all these objections it may be charged that the idea of establishing an environmental virtue ethic in Buddhist literature is unachievable and unfounded.

However this conclusion can be challenged. All the above objections can be successfully countered to some extent in the Buddhist context. Admittedly Buddhism does not define an environmental disposition that reveals to the agent the most beneficial environmental action. However a careful study of the life of the Buddha reveals that an individual steeped in virtue would be unable to act violently against nature. Notions of environmental despoliation do not touch his persona despite the absence of an obvious environmental ethics at the Buddha's time. The Buddha is never personally described as harming animals or damaging nature in the *Nikāyas*. It may be pointed out that sometimes events are described in the early literature (as illustrated in Chapter 2) that do not appear supportive of the cause of nature but these are not ascribed to the Buddha himself. Furthermore all the major events in his life are connected with natural surroundings (birth, enlightenment, first sermon and death). A description of Gotama as one who is limbed like an antelope, who is slim and lean, taking in little or no food, with few material demands and not distracted (presumably by desires) from his meditation in the forest supports the belief in his intermittent environmental character.[49] Based on this it can be said even though acting for the sake of nature is not primarily on his agenda a virtuous person is unlikely to undertake actions that damage nature. There is a sense here that the pursuit of ecology happens simultaneously with the pursuit of virtues. Furthermore, a virtue that leads to enlightenment, the supreme state of spirituality, and also causes environmental destruction appears absurd to commonsense. The second objection, that a virtue may be indifferent towards environmental causes, can be doubted too for the virtue still plays a role in enhancing the character of the agent in Buddhism. For instance while agents are contemplating whether a dam ought to be built or not they indulge in intoxicants. In an inebriated condition they would hardly be able to come up with a reasonable solution. So though the precept on the use of intoxicants does not have a direct impact on the environment it affects the overall state of the agents and makes them incapable of sound decisions.

The third, and most serious, objection is when virtues conflict. This is where the virtue of wisdom comes in. That the virtue of wisdom must function in almost every case, but especially in resolving disputes is demonstrated below. Disputes of a general nature may arise for Buddhists when they must decide between one categorical virtue or another. The precept "Abandon false speech" tells the Buddhist to inform a dying mother that her son has been implicated in a murder and is imprisoned for life, whereas the virtue of "compassion," after taking stock of her painful and sickly situation, dictates that it may be better to withhold such information to spare her further agony. Making choices between virtues is a difficult thing and there seems to be no fixed formula in early Buddhism for deciding which one to pick – no virtue is specified as more superior or less so and neither is any special insight or figure appealed to. This problem extends to environmental virtue ethics in Buddhism too. Not only Buddhism but environmental ethics itself constantly encounters the problem of choosing one virtue over another. In the context of the natural world there may be tensions among various virtues; for instance respect for life extends to tigers whereas the virtue of sympathy tells us to cull some for the sake of depleting deer populations. These virtues are all equally important in the virtues, Buddhist and ecological worldviews.

It is significant however that though the Buddha is portrayed in the Pali Canon as having framed precepts to hold categorically and does not explicitly state how a dispute between two mutually conflicting virtues is to be settled, he made some subtle allowances when faced with dilemmas. He was sensitive to the fact that at times some principles in life may have to be forsaken for others. One such dilemma is noticeable in the case of eating meat. Meat-eating may be taken as an environmental case study and an example of how further dilemmas may be looked at and solved within the Buddhist context. To begin with, three reasons can be cited as to why the Buddha did not support the killing of animals and the eating of meat. The first reason is the frequent mention of the precept of *ahiṃsā* or non-violence. The second is that the professions of a butcher and hunter and so on were denounced. And the third is the Buddha's indefatigable and relentless capacity for compassion and kindness, which extended to animals. Putting all these three together, one may be led to saying that meat-eating was clearly not permissible according to early Buddhist scriptures.

Doubts about this conclusion begin to appear, however, when the Buddha allows his monks to eat meat as part of their alms. The only qualification is about why the animal was killed. In the *Jīvaka Sutta* the Buddha states that if it is seen, heard or suspected that the animal was killed for the sake of the monk, then it would be an unwholesome action to eat such meat.[50] The repercussions would affect not only the monk but also the person who killed the animal for the sake of feeding the monk. An elaborate list of actions that involve the killing of the animal for the sake of the monk are described and to each a sin is ascribed. Demerit is incurred for the five following reasons:

> When he says: go fetch that living being. Indeed this is the first condition that produces much demerit. When that living being is fetched with a pain in its neck and undergoes distress of the mind and body, this is the second . . . When he says, go and kill that living being, this is the third . . . when that living being undergoes distress of the mind and body in being killed, this is the fourth . . . when he offends the *tathāgata* or his disciple with this [food] which is not proper, this is the fifth. . . .[51]

This Discourse clarifies that what really is important are the circumstances under which the eating of meat are allowed. If the circumstances were favourable then the monk could indulge in eating meat but not under others. The *Vinaya* appears to agree with the *Sutta* and in addition allows monks to eat meat when they are ill.[52] Some may take this to mean that the Buddha had no objection to the eating of meat. Since there is no specific adage in the scriptures saying that the Buddha supported vegetarianism (it is sometimes said that the *Mahāparinibbāna Sutta* contains an example of the Buddha himself eating pork, though this is a controversial issue), Buddhism must be seen to accept the eating of meat. Little help for resolving this issue comes from the *Vinaya* and it contains no clear-cut solution. However, the *Jīvaka Sutta* is not as straight-forward as it appears to be. A meticulous reading of it reveals that an alternative virtue is being pursued here. The Discourse is promoting the cultivation of non-attachment; the monk had to be non-attached to and unaffected by the alms (including meat) he received in order to attain higher spiritual states.

On account of the discussion above it emerges, first, that the Buddha supported non-violence towards animals on the one hand and allowed his monks to accept and eat the meat as alms on the other. The implication is that the virtue of non-violence exists but is not categorical. Secondly, it also appears that the Buddha, given a choice between non-violence and non-attachment, chose the second. What do these two (or three) quite perplexing claims amount to? Things begin to fall in place with the acceptance that the *Sutta* is not about the loss of compassion in monks but about disciplined release from attachment. Since the meat that is consumed is specifically qualified this example must not be treated as infringing the categorical nature of non-violence. But what about the blatant support for the cultivation of non-attachment over non-violence? This question, somewhat forcefully framed, may not be quite the right one to ask. Rather the question of what this *Sutta* can be taken to imply more subtly ought to be asked: the *Sutta* entails the possibility that the value of situations can be measured through several different lenses always to ensure that the development of a virtuous disposition is not impeded in any sense. As Rupert Gethin sees it:

> Ultimately Buddhism teaches that the nature of good conduct is subtle and complex – so complex that it precisely cannot be solved by reference to precepts and rules of conduct. It can only be solved by following a path of training that ends in rooting out greed, aversion and delusion.[53]

In the light of this observation, the message here is not that an act (the eating of meat) can be justifiably dictated by non-violence but rather that the monk must categorically pursue a virtuous character through spiritual non-attachment. The focus thus undergoes a complete transformation. And in the spirit of non-attachment alone the eating of meat is allowed. It is not, then, that non-violence is given much less importance. The very fact that the viciousness of killing animals is described in some detail should be indication enough that Buddhism did favour non-violence and compassion and therefore vegetarianism. Understanding this example's true significance in such a way reinforces the worth of cultivating virtue and its quite ingenious configuration in Buddhism even more. Other examples where similar dilemmas can be found could also be understood and contextualized in a similar way.

In the above case arguments appear easily as to why meat-eating was not a favoured activity. But arguments are hard to come by in contemporary environmental dilemmas. For instance, out of sympathy for the children who are dying from some rare blood disease extremely painful experiments on animals to discover a cure could be conducted. On the other hand a blanket ban on vivisection, whatever the circumstances, for the sake of *mettā* or *ahiṃsā* could be imposed. But clearly the latter would be unsympathetic to these children. Early Buddhism contains no information about these issues as such. However in such dilemmas the close association of ethics with other factors in Buddhism must be kept in mind. *Samādhi* and *Paññā* are essential in their support to resolving ethical dilemmas. For instance, non-vegetarianism in any form appears contrary to the first precept of respect for all life. However when all three factors evaluate the act, it gains some ground. Thus ethical judgements are to be made only once *sīla*, *paññā* and *samādhi* are considered. Together they will lead to moral action. Thus if, after deliberation, wisdom dictates that animal experimentation be allowed in a most humane way, ensuring adequate use of painkillers and anaesthetics, until the moment a hint of a cure is found, out of compassion for the children, then so be it. If on the other hand wisdom dictates that conducting tests is searching for answers in the dark and there is little likelihood of a solution then the experiment can be cancelled out of compassion for the animals. Or any other solution wisdom thinks ought to be adopted. Even though the above formulation is rather simplistic, there is no denying that the worth of virtue can come through only when the weight of wisdom is combined with it. This ought to work in all cases, no matter how complicated. In this sense the role of wisdom is inimitable.

The two constituents of wisdom – View (*diṭṭhi*) and resolve (*saṅkappa*) – must be right (*sammā*) and are seen as means of understanding the situation fully and rightly and ultimately of motivating actions based on convictions that develop through this process. Reflection or careful thought about actions and their consequences is also an ingredient of such wisdom. The Buddha stressed deep thought and reflection on an action before and whilst doing it. No action was to be undertaken without considering all alternatives equally. An action which obstructs and impairs the happiness of self, other or both is to be considered an evil, unwholesome action according to the *Ambalaṭṭhikārāhulovāda Sutta* and was to be avoided at all costs. The Buddha is believed to have explained this beautifully through the use of a metaphor. He asks monk Rāhula about the purpose of a mirror and Rāhula's response was that this was reflection. The Buddha then advises him to do any action of body, speech and mind after repeated reflection that it caused no injury or damage to anyone:

> So Rāhula, when you are desirous to do an action with the body then you should reflect on the bodily action thus: would the action I desire to do with the body, my bodily action lead to hurting myself, lead to hurting others, lead to hurting both? Is it an unwholesome bodily action with grievous consequences, with grievous results?[54]

This reiterates not only the importance of freedom of choice but also of deliberation and pause before doing an action so that the choice made would be the most beneficial one. It obviously rules out acting impulsively or for the sake of instant gratification without considering all consequences.[55] The *Dhammapada* adds in a similar sense that by withdrawing from a less significant happiness if there is a probability of a greater one then the wise man should abandon the less significant for the sake of the greater one.[56] I think that this is an extremely relevant guideline for environmental action; the course an action takes must be predetermined by a certain amount of reflection about the damage or good it can do. The choice of virtues must be directed by wisdom. On this understanding there is no doubt that an appeal to wisdom is an important addition to morality and virtue ethics.

The problem of practical orientation comes up repeatedly.[57] Many theories of environment virtue ethics are contested on the grounds that though they give plenty of information about the agent's character and virtue-oriented disposition they are unable to say how these have to be put into practice. This has led Louke van Wensveen to comment that environmental virtue ethics turns out to be a "curious phenomenon of a discourse committed to social change without a developed theory of social change."[58] Observations such as these are deeply problematic. However, in reply it may be said that an environmental virtue ethics does not imply a search for guidance on practical actions alone. It has been said:

> Virtue ethics reminds us that providing us with a decision procedure covering all possible situations is not the main purpose of moral theories (if it is even a purpose at all). The people for whom moral theories are intended are people already in the midst of living their lives. They come to philosophy hoping that it can help them reflect on their lives. A moral theory is successful if it provides that assistance and unsuccessful if it does not.[59]

Thus the main purpose of a moral theory (and so of an environmental virtue ethics) is to train the mind to carry out the right action (or the right environmental action) through a reflection on life and its meaning. This early Buddhist philosophy does flawlessly – not because it wants only to attain a far-reaching goal but because it understands how inextricably linked our present lives are to that goal. Therefore, a lack of practical guidance is not something that goes against early Buddhism's environmental character.

Conclusion

An important concern yet remains to be addressed. Though all the virtues discussed so far can be seen in Buddhism in one sense or another to support environmental thinking there is no direct connection between them and ecology. For instance, it is difficult to demonstrate in concrete terms with the help of examples from the *Nikāyas* and other texts how, say the virtue of contentment or *santuṭṭha*, is directly relevant to the natural world. It must be admitted that not much evidence can be gathered in the literature, except in rare cases. All the arguments by extension in this and the previous chapter can be rejected through this single challenge alone. However, when this quandary is seen in the light of the attainment of a final aim it can be countered effectively; that is, through the suggestion that the eventual aim of Buddhism (attained through the virtues) and the final aim of environmental ethics (attained through environmental virtues) are not unconnected. This leads to the question of teleology.

In the previous chapter early Buddhism was shown to be a non-consequential teleology. It is a teleology as its end remains the attaining of *nibbāna*. It is also non-consequential as *sīla, paññā* and *samādhi* partake of and not only lead to *nibbāna*. However, their focus is not some ideal form of environmental virtue ethics. It is unmistakably the individual and his spiritual flourishing. On the other hand, for an environmentally virtuous person the end seems to be environmental concern and other related issues such as establishing the intrinsic value of natural goods. Thus at least on teleological grounds the aims of the two – early Buddhist ethics and environmental virtue ethics – appear unconnected. This dilemma disappears once it is realized that environmentally virtuous behaviour is a part of virtuous behaviour (as has hopefully become clear in the course of this chapter). Since virtuous behaviour is not only a means to *nibbāna* but also intrinsically related to it, environmentally virtuous behaviour is also intrinsically linked to *nibbāna* through being an essential part of virtuous behaviour. And by accepting the presence of an environmental virtue ethics in Buddhism problems of teleology do not arise, for the aim of early Buddhism, of Buddhist ethics and of environmental virtue ethics are not opposed, and in aiming for one the others are attained. In this context the words of Sponberg are very apt. He writes:

> . . . Buddhism has seen no need to develop a special and separate position on nature and ecology. And indeed we might as well be justified in concluding that in fact Buddhism *has* no particular environmental ethic at all. By the same token, however, we would have to conclude also that Buddhism *is* an environmental ethic, in that it cannot be put into practice without completely transforming one's every response to nature and the environment.[60]

It is true in Buddhism that no motivation exists that is evocative of a concern for environment. But environmental good happens through the practice of virtues. This, then, is the Buddhist position.

Support for an environmental virtue ethics also comes from the *Jātaka* tales. These will be looked at in the next chapter. I am convinced however that yet more comprehensive work is required and anticipate that new specifics will be revealed as the analysis of both Buddhist philosophy and virtue ethics deepens along these lines. But I hope that I have been able to show that "in the absence of an environmental virtue ethics, environmental ethics itself is incomplete and unbalanced," and at the same time to have introduced a substantial vindication of its prospect.[61]

6

ENVIRONMENTAL VIRTUE ETHICS IN THE *JĀTAKAS*

The Buddha makes use of the story
. . . To expound his doctrines

Lotus Sutra

My investigation in this chapter focuses on the *Jātakas*, which are a part of the *Khuddaka Nikāya* of the *Sutta Piṭaka* or the first basket of the Pali Canon. The *Jātakas* are a collection of over five hundred stories that in common parlance are called folklore. Each story conveys a moral that is considered as the basis of righteous conduct by early Buddhists. In the first part of this chapter I will discuss my reasons for selecting the *Jātaka* books for the development of my thesis despite the presence of some uncertainty about their importance in scholarly Buddhist traditions and despite caution from scholars about their use. I will demonstrate that the evaluation of these texts is significant in defining a sense of environment in early Buddhism, and that recent research indicates that I am justified in including them as a source of information. Following this some of the stories contained herein will be assessed for their factual and ethical content to establish how an environmental perspective, both affirmatively and negatively, can be elaborated. The general outcome of this exercise is the non-contentious revelation of an environmental virtue ethics component in them (similar in theme to the one developed in the rest of the Canon). In conclusion, the contradictions that the search for an environmental ethics in the *Jātakas* may generate as well as other obstacles that have to be faced along the way will be highlighted. My final analysis seeks to ascertain the role of the *Jātakas* in the formation and development of the position of early Buddhism on nature not only through their framework of virtues but also through their innate pragmatic nature. Ultimately, I include the *Jātakas* here not only because they are fairly expressive of the thesis I have advanced in the last two chapters, but also because they draw attention to some possible limitations of this position in early Buddhist philosophy.

Why the *Jātakas*?

The renowned Buddhist scholar T. W. Rhys Davids, in his book *Buddhist India*, writes, "When the original *Jātaka* was being gradually formed most of the stories were taken bodily over from the existing folklore of northern India."[1] It is mostly undisputed that the *Jātaka* stories originated not from specific Buddhist thought and culture but rather from the already prevalent folk tradition of India. This is one of the reasons why the *Jātaka* collection was showered with prejudice and considered secondary Buddhist literature. Scholars, as has been noted often, rejected these stories for not being philosophically and intellectually significant and therefore undeserving of deeper exploration. James Whitehill, in a recent work says, ". . . we should probably resist calling them 'narrative' because they display a narrow range of the Buddhist reality picture, and we should hesitate to call them Buddhist, because the stories are from a pre-Buddhist tradition."[2] Comments such as the latter highlight the general prejudiced attitude towards the *Jātaka* stories.

However, not all stories are subject to such prejudice. K. R. Norman believes that "Although many Jātakas can be regarded as being non-Buddhist, or even pre-Buddhist, there are some which are certainly Buddhist."[3] Furthermore though it is true that all the *Jātakas* are not purely Buddhist in origin, more recent research also shows that they did assimilate Buddhist principles in all seriousness and so cannot be so easily overlooked due to their origin. This is the position taken by Nirmala Salgado in her dissertation entitled "The Structure of Evil and Ethical Action in the *Jātakatthavaṇṇanā*."[4] Salgado demonstrates admirably that the underlying motivation of these tales was a Buddhist one and this became evident to her in her comparisons of the *Jātakas* with other Indian folklore of the time. This comparison points to the fact that certain Buddhist themes present in the *Jātakas* were not present in other Indian folklore such as Brahmanical based *Pañcatantra* leading her to say:

> Buddhist scholarship of the nineteenth and twentieth centuries has often neglected a systematic investigation . . . influenced by prevailing prejudices. These prejudices have led to the denigration of non-canonical literature – including the *Jātakatthavaṇṇanā*, as well as the formation of the distinction between the great tradition of canonical Buddhism and the learned elite, and the little tradition of folk and popular local religiosity, in which the former enjoyed a largely undeserved position. . . .[5]

Salgado is disturbed by the dismissing of the *Jātakas* as of little importance in the philosophical corpus. She adds that disparagement of the *Jātakas* is a limitation of contemporary scholarship rather than an acknowledgement of their true status at the time of their conception.

And so it can be assumed that a generic Indian origin and prior historic prejudice are not enough reason for neglecting the *Jātakas* in present day research as they cannot reject out of hand that Buddhist tendencies in these tales exist. I have focused on the *Jātakas* in my study for two reasons. The first is that these tales not only express an environmentalism reflective of the one contained in the remaining Pali Canon, they also contain a reaction to nature which adds in some way to the thesis I am advancing in this book (here one has to be aware as in the rest of the Canon that environmental issues, at the time the *Jātakas* originated, did not exist the way they do today). The second reason for the incorporation of the *Jātaka* collection is that it possibly expresses virtues that were transmitted to the laity – and therefore express environmental ideas from their point of view. A majority of the Pali Canon is directed towards ethical instructions for monks in search of liberation. There are only modest accounts of ethical instructions for lay persons who were great followers of Buddhism too. The *Nikāyas* are often accused of not saying enough about lay virtues. The *Jātakas* stories on the other hand are devoted mostly to the questions of ethical advancement concerning laity. This is reflected by the fact that the stories chart the quest of the Buddha in a distant past where he found himself in life situations comparable to those of a commoner. Notions of community interaction and relations with others that arise in everyday living are stressed both in Buddha's appearance as a human being or even as an animal. Furthermore the Buddha's choices are underlined as always based on some virtue or other. If this is accepted as a possibility, the *Jātakas* can be seen as giving added insight into lay Buddhism. Thus, together with sections of the Pali Canon the *Jātakas* would help determine the comprehensive stand on virtues of Buddhism by embracing both the monks and laity. I will not be distinguishing between the views and beliefs of monks and laity as the idea is beyond the scope of this work; my focus is just to be aware of and to reflect on this suggestion. However it is interesting to note from my discussion below that most virtues in the *Jātakas* resemble those found in other literature. This draws attention to the universal nature of virtues irrespective of the stage of life, profession and final objective of the practitioner.

The importance of the *Jātakas* and the role they can perform in ascertaining an ethics of the environment in Buddhism has not gone unnoticed. Their influence has been felt in most environmental literature on Buddhism. Lambert Schmithausen and Alan Sponberg, two eminent Buddhist scholars of the environment have indicated that the *Jātakas* are essential for any future research.[6] In his seminal study *Buddhism and Nature* while speaking of determining the position of animals in Buddhism Schmithausen mentions the *Jātakas* and says of them in a footnote, "A systematic investigation of the matter in this text and in others of this genre may be rewarding."[7] And in the foreword to his paper dealing with the sentience of plants he says, ". . . a comprehensive treatment of the issue should perhaps, with due caution, also investigate similes, poetical imagery, narrative literature and artistic representations etc., referring to plants;. . . ."[8] Schmithausen also mentions that in the *Jātakas* animals were more like their real selves and therefore not particularly unhappy and finds that these tales show an affinity to the hermit strand.[9] However, despite this awareness even scholars who have used the *Jātakas* have done so with great trepidation. This has resulted in a smattering of information on the *Jātakas* within environmental literature but no specific and in-depth analysis devoted to these tales.

Perhaps one exception to this general trend is Christopher Key Chapple's essay "Animals and Environment in the Buddhist Birth Stories" which attempts a more focused approach and examines some specific *Jātakas*.[10] Chapple finds a strong environmental message within these stories, although he is aware that the *Jātakas* contain a lot of negative imagery. He points out that animals are included in the six categories of beings of Buddhist cosmology. That animals can be seen as potential human beings in the *Jātakas* makes the boundary between animals and human beings much more fluid than it is in the West. Chapple's work can thus be considered a good starting point to any investigation on the *Jātakas* and the environment.

Moving away from scholarly discussions, the *Jātakas* have been extensively used by some Buddhists and environmentalists seeking to paint a positive picture by taking for granted that Buddhism is environmental. I termed these works "Partisan" in the first chapter. Due to a lack of in-depth analysis such versions are often open to severe condemnation. It is within this framework that I came across an essay on the *Jātakas* called "Thoughts on the *Jātakas*" by Rafe Martin, in which he says:

> . . . the *Jātakas* simultaneously validate and give credence to our own natural feelings of compassion and our own spontaneous acts of selfishness. These tales ideally show us how to live in a suffering world, as well as offer us a noble and deeply spiritual vision of the nature of the universe.[11]

However, in his short essay Martin is unable to deal with the immensity of his claim. He merely skirts around the issue, describing ideas that are found in the *Jātakas*, without explaining in detail how they can be logically derived and defended.

As for the historical dimensions of the *Jātakas*, as mentioned earlier, the Buddha's teachings were recorded a long time after his death and survived only due to a live oral tradition. Historians have determined that the *Jātakas* were part of this tradition based on the third century B.C.E. sculptures at Bharhut which depict some stories and their verses. Ananda Coomaraswamy maintains, "We learn from these sculptures that folk-tales and secular fables were adapted to an edifying purpose quite early in the history of Buddhism precisely as popular and secular art is adapted to Buddhist purposes in the sculptures themselves."[12] Thus it appears that the Buddhists realized that stories were a good medium to spread their philosophical and moral message and so did not hesitate in using them to their advantage. It is believed the stories gained much popularity and so may have been effective in their aim.

As mentioned earlier, the *Jātakas* contain over 500 birth stories.[13] Each of these *Jātakas* focuses on some compelling episode in the life of human beings or non-human beings (animals, trees, spirits and others). These human beings and creatures are then admitted as being incarnations of the Buddha and others of his generation in a previous life. The *Jātakas* are set within *nipātas* or books depending on the number of verses or *gāthās* quoted in each story. Each story has parts and includes an introduction or *paccuppannavatthu* that explains some situation in the Buddha's life that made him tell the story of a previous life. The story that follows the introduction is the *atītavatthu* and this contains one or more verses or *gāthās* that are recited by the *bodhisatta*.[14] In some cases these verses are included in the introduction rather than the previous-life story. The final section or *samodhāna* of every tale consists of the Buddha identifying the different characters of the stories with him and other human beings who existed and interacted with him in his life as the Buddha. For the most part I will be primarily concerned with the subject matter of the story or *atītavatthu* and the verses or *gāthās* except in some instances where I have discussed the *paccuppannavatthu* for its overwhelming environmental content.[15]

Rhys Davids believes that the story or parable is the oldest among all the parts of the *Jātakas* and may even be older than Buddhism itself. However, of the canonical *Jātakas*, it is accepted by most historians that the oldest probably are the verses as their language is much more antiquated. There is some vagueness about the dating of the verses as they are preceded by a long oral tradition. It was traditionally believed in Sri Lanka that the original *Jātaka* collection consisted of verses alone and so confusion also exists about when the word commentary to the verses was added. Together with the word commentary with its division into parts the *Jātakas* are referred to as *Jātakatthavaṇṇanā*. Some *Jātaka* stories also appear in other parts of the Canon, sometimes word for word, suggesting that stories pre-existed in some sense. There is also uncertainty about the author of the preserved and now available Pali *Jātakas*. Some historians believe that the original was written in Singhalese in Sri Lanka, and translated into Pali by Buddhaghosa around 500 C.E., after which the original Singhalese commentaries went missing. Many also believe Buddhaghosa to be their author but Rhys Davids categorically denies this.[16] Thus many questions remain regarding the historical antecedents of this collection.

Some tales analysed

A study of the ethical and factual content of the *Jātakas* reveals both supportive and negative aspects of importance in determining the nature of environmental discourse. Factually, environmental actions such as the protection of trees and banning of hunting can be identified in these tales. At the same time, actions that have a negative effect on ecology can be found. The content of many stories includes the glorification of unnatural surroundings, indiscriminate use of resources and depravation of animals. On the level of ethics the *Jātaka* stories contain virtues that may be seen to have environmental significance. The *Jātaka* narratives are full of instances of Buddhist moral beliefs; the virtues they embody as mentioned earlier are quite similar to the ones present in other portions of the Pali Canon. Some of the virtues are non-violence towards all beings, a spirit of sacrifice on one's own part for a greater good, and loyalty to those things that have served one. All these can be seen as supportive of the cause of nature. Additionally while examining both dimensions I especially consider a few stories where animals and trees are the main actors. The reason for selecting them is to reconfirm how far they represent the natural dimension. In all, my intention is to simultaneously draw attention to the (environmentally) positive and negative and virtuous aspects of the tales. Practical dimensions such as the electing particular virtues when faced with difficult environmental choices and some other observations peculiar to the *Jātaka* stories will be dealt with in the penultimate section of this chapter.

In the *Kusanāḷijātaka*, the *Bodhisatta* was born a deity and was dwelling in a clump of *kusa* grass (*kusanāḷigacche devatā*).[17] He became friendly with a tree deity that dwelt in the nearby tree. The tree was beautiful and received great attention from the king of the land. It so happened one day that the king's palace needed a strong pillar as the old one had rotted and this tree was the only tree that seemed strong enough to hold up the roof. Under these circumstances the king gave permission for the tree to be cut down. On hearing this, the deity of the tree burst into tears for her home would be destroyed. The *Bodhisatta* promised to help her out of her predicament. He assumed the shape of a chameleon (*kakaṇṭaka*), worked his way up the tree and made it appear full of holes. On seeing the holes, the woodcutters declared the tree to be rotten and unfit to be cut and this averted the tree being chopped. The explicit moral outlined in the story itself is that the wise should be respected and befriended irrespective of their position. However on closer examination the tale also has many indirect environmental implications. It brings awareness about the protection of trees, even though the protection comes from a simple spirit living in a clump of grass. Of this tale Chapple has said that in it "the salvation of the tree stands for the preservation of both remarkable trees and the larger ecosystem in which they thrive."[18] In addition the deity of the *kusa* grass employs dexterous means to protect his friend's home and for this is considered virtuous. Attention is also drawn simultaneously to two facets of human beings – their enjoyment of the aesthetic and their adoption of any means to meet their singular selfish ends. The second overpowers the first and the tale implies that this is not a commendable step. The theme of tree protection is also echoed in the *Pucimandajātaka* where the *Bodhisatta*, as a Nimb-tree deity (*nimbrukkhe devatā*), saves the tree from destruction.[19] In this way he saves his home. Both tales, however, also raise questions about the motive behind protecting trees. It appears that the trees were protected only so far as they were the abodes of the tree deities, and thus, not for the sake of themselves. Since environmental discourse focuses on value for its own sake this interpretation (also mentioned in Chapter 2 under Plants) is problematic. Another added implication is that if certain vegetation is not considered to be the home of a deity it can be cut down or harmed in some other way. Hence no incentive to act purely for the sake of the environment can be reasonably drawn.

The *Jātakas* also allow for harmful things to be destroyed. The *Palāsajātaka* suggests the uprooting of those things that are harmful.[20] The *Bodhisatta*, a golden goose in this lifetime, struck up a friendship with the guardian deity (*nibbatadevatā*) of a Judas tree (*palāsarukkha*). There sprang up a Banyan sapling in the ground below the tree. On seeing the sapling, the goose advised his friend to destroy it for fear that it would destroy the Judas tree, the home of the deity. The deity did not heed the advice and decided to act as a saviour of the Banyan tree by allowing it to grow unchecked. As a result the Banyan tree eventually grew and broke down the Judas tree. The general moral of the story is that that which causes harm should not be supported and ought to be uprooted as early as possible. The indication is towards those harmful attitudes that are nurtured due to attachment. Since such attitudes only lead to bad consequences they ought to be forsaken sooner than later. From the point of view of virtues the story has a clear purpose. Environmentally, however, the tale is ambiguous – it may be seen to be negative in that it suggests interference with the workings of nature and as positive in that it apparently encourages protection of the endangered.

There is also good evidence that can be gathered from various *Jātaka* stories that points to a comfortable acceptance of non-natural environments. These appear as things to be striven towards. In the *Kulāvakajātaka* are mentioned some of the good works that the *Bodhisatta*, as *Magha*, the young Brahmin did, such as charity and the keeping of the five Buddhist precepts.[21] By his example others around him were inspired to do the same. However, a description of these works glorifies artificial surroundings as becomes clear from the following passage:

> . . . with clubs they tear out stones that lie on the four highroads and other roads, they destroy the trees that strike against the axle of

> wheels of carriages, the uneven they make level, lay bridges, dig small lakes, build a hall, give gifts and uphold moral conduct. . . .[22]

The context of the story implies that the taming of wilderness is the way of the wise. In another tale called the *Saccaṃkirajātaka*, the *Bodhisatta*, in order to repay the kindness of a rat, a snake and a parrot, had a golden tube made for the snake to live in, a crystal casket to house the rat and a cage of gold for the parrot.[23] Though the tale is expressly about the virtue of gratitude, it points to something else as well. Animals are pulled out of natural surroundings, put in the lap of human luxury and are portrayed as happy. The *Jātakas* hence tilt towards artificial comforts rather than natural surroundings. Many stories, in fact, lend their approval and positive encouragement to an overuse of resources through praising exaggerated luxury, boundless amounts of food and the like and armies of animals hanging about without any purpose. Such stories have a distinct non-ecological flavour. For instance the *Kāliṇgabodhijātaka* tells the story of the king who worshipped the Bo tree with 60,000 carts of flowers.[24] And in the *Mahākapijātaka* the *Bodhisattva's* body was cremated with full honour by King Brahmadatta, whose ministers "made a funeral pile with a one hundred wagon loads of timber!"[25] However one has to be aware at the same time that in the *Saccaṃkirajātaka* the welfare of animals is sought. So though environmentally the tale is disagreeable, the virtue of caring for animals and being grateful appear to be its foremost implications and in this sense it has a valuable environmental orientation.

Of the virtues, charity or generosity draws much interest. The *Arakajātaka* tells the story of the *Bodhisatta* as Araka, who became a teacher of the virtues and lived in the Himalayan region.[26] Araka tells his disciples that following the path of virtues would lead them to Brahma's heaven. Virtues such as charity, sympathy and equanimity are mentioned by him; the nature of the virtues described is such that they appear to benefit others extensively rather than having just a limited effect and in this are somewhat reminiscent of the *Brahma-vihāras* that were discussed in the fourth chapter. Charity (*dāna* or *cāga*), also referred to as liberality and generosity, is more directly alluded to in many instances. The *Akittijātaka* is the story of the *Bodhisatta* as young Akitti who leaves his luxurious home to become an ascetic.[27] Sakka, disguised as a Brahmin, comes begging for alms to test the resolve of Akitti. Such is the generosity of Akitti that he gives the Brahmin all his food for three consecutive days keeping none for himself. He is joyous at such an opportunity to practice giving. It is clear that generosity contributes to an environmental character as the virtue of generosity implies forsaking benefits for the sake of a nature that has been generous itself.

Extreme generosity may even transform into self-sacrifice. Environmental scholar Holmes Rolston III has pointed out that:

> Sometimes we ought to make sacrifices, at least in terms of what we presently value, to preserve species. On such occasions humans may be duty bound to be losers in the sense that they have sacrificed values and have adopted an altered set of values, although they would still be winners for doing the right thing. Ethics is not merely about what humans love, enjoy, find rewarding or about what they find wonderful . . . it is sometimes a matter of what humans *ought* to do. . . .[28]

The spirit of sacrifice is somewhat glorified as a particularly gallant sentiment and many instances describe its practice. Sacrifice can be interpreted to mean acceptance of jeopardy to one's self for the welfare of something else. This can be well illustrated through the especially popular *Nigrodhamigajātaka*.[29] In order to avoid being killed by a king who was very fond of hunting, the deer living in the royal forest decided that each day one amongst them would be handed over to the king. This meant that all of the deer were not continually terrified. Unluckily, once a doe expecting a fawn was selected. On her request to be spared until she had her fawn, the king of the deer, no other than the *Bodhisatta*, offered himself as a substitute. When the king of the land heard of this sacrifice, he spared the life of this deer as well of the others and gave up hunting. Similarly, in the *Mahākapijātaka* the *Bodhisatta*, a monkey king, saves the lives of his following of 80,000 monkeys by making his body into a bridge for his beloved subjects to cross over into safety.[30] Not only are the tales environmentally relevant in pointing out the value of animal life and sacrifice for their sake they hint that the political ruler ought to be harbinger of such sacrifice. The dying monkey king utters the verses:

> I am not tormented by bonds; death will not torment me,
> Happiness was acquired for them whose kingdom I ruled.[31]

The well-being and satisfaction of his liege ought to be crucial to an ideal king, even if it implies sacrificing his life. The *Jātakas* are akin to the *Nikāyas* here as the responsibilities of the king are mentioned in a similar way in the latter.[32]

The thoughtful use of things is also advised by the *Jātakas* and this can be an important environmental value.[33] The *Jātakas* share in the appreciation of many virtues present in the rest of the Canon such as universal love/friendship (*mittā/mettā*), gratitude (*kataññutaṃ*), generosity (*cāga/dāna*), non-violence (*ahiṃsā*), perseverance (*viriya*) and modesty/humility (*hirī*) and have numerous stories centred around them. The *Mahāukkusajātaka* describes the friendship or love (*mittā/mettā*) between some animals due to which they are willing to sacrifice and do much for their friends.[34] There are undertones of friends protecting friends in their bad times and the sense of shelter and security that friendship invokes can be a virtue that can be applied to the protection of the environment. Again, cultivating gratitude was seen as an important aspect of environmental virtue ethics in the previous chapter and as mentioned in the story of Akitti above. The *Jātakas* especially contain innumerable stories praising this virtue. Another story that exemplifies generosity is the *Godhajātaka*. It tells the story of a king who refused to show gratitude to the kindness of his wife.[35] But once he is reminded of her virtues he feels gratitude (*katañ̃nuta*) and gives her all he has. Generosity thus results in selflessness and altruism. Perseverance (*viriya*) is also a virtue that can be seen as environmental for courage and perseverance (as opposed to sloth and laziness) are needed to recognize and deal with the environmental crisis. The virtue of perseverance can be seen in the *Vaṇṇupathajātaka* where the *Bodhisatta* is a merchant who is lost in the desert with his fellow merchants.[36] They are without water but through the perseverance of the *Bodhisatta* are able to find water and reach their destination safely. The virtue of humility or modesty (*hirī*) is also praised in the *Jātakas*. It has already been seen in the fourth chapter how this virtue helps in the development of an environmental character. The *Devadhammajātaka* revolves around the life of a demon that has lost his sense of humility. Not only does the *Bodhisatta* restore this but also teaches him the benefits of following the path of virtues, thereby converting the demon to virtue.[37]

Other than this, much is said about vices as well. The vice of greed (*lola*) can be seen as one of the leading sources of environmental destruction and therefore, these stories can be understood as promoting ecological thinking indirectly by suggesting limited use of resources and self-control. The *Godhajātaka* tells the story of a greedy monk who developed a taste for the flesh of lizards.[38] In order to fulfil his yearning he tries to kill the *Bodhisatta*, who is a lizard in this lifetime. The monk does not succeed and is warned by the *Bodhisatta* that he will go into the realm of suffering for not practising self-control (*asaññataṃ*). Other than greed, various forms of craving (such as the craving for delicious food or *rasataṇhā*) are criticized in the tales.[39] Craving for hugely wasteful and exotic foods may harm health, have no added nutritional value and be produced through severe environmental costs. Hurtful behaviour and selfishness are advised against. A man contracts leprosy for his ingratitude (*akataññutaṃ*) to an animal that had served him with kindness in the *Mahākapijātaka*.[40] Most of the above were shown to be ecological virtues and vices in the previous chapter; their presence in the *Jātakas* is indicative of the presence of an environmental virtue ethics here as well.

That the Buddha cherished non-violence (*ahiṃsā*) is also expressed in various ways – through his own utterances or as the moral of stories. The virtue of respect for life is reflected quite compellingly. Therefore acts such as hunting bear the brunt of much criticism and their consequences are described as unavoidably morbid. The *pañcāvudhajātaka* is the story of how the *Bodhisatta* converted an ogre from his violent ways through his own fearlessness and by showing the ogre the sufferings that will come upon him as a consequence of his violent acts.[41] The Buddha also qualified acts of violence with the feature of intentionality. Only those acts that were intentionally violent were to be judged as immoral and as deserving the most dire repercussions. This stress on intention brings to mind the morality of the *Nikāyas* and *Vinaya*, which repeatedly insist that destiny, good or bad, is created only when actions are intended. The following story reflects on this intentionality. In the *Telovādajātaka* the *Bodhisatta* is an ascetic who eats fish given to him whilst begging for alms.[42] The tale goes on to state that he commits no sin for he is not responsible for the killing of the fish. The verse in the story says:

> Having unrestrainedly killed their wife and son, [the wicked] give them as gift
> Even by the eating of this, the wise are not defiled by sin.[43]

Once again it can be drawn from this that the eating of meat with qualification was permitted by the Buddha. But clearly the acquiescence to eat flesh unreservedly cannot be seen. This story gives a sense that the eating of meat may have attracted much discussion at the time of the Buddha for it to have filtered down through the literature of the *Nikāyas* and the *Vinaya* and also the *Jātakas*. However, once again, as with the former, these tales provide no clear conclusion to the debate and scholars must rely on other evidence to reach an acceptable solution.[44]

Interestingly enough, the idea of the external consequences of *kamma* reflected in the *Nikāyas* is seen in the *Jātakas* as well. The *Aṅguttara Nikāya*, as mentioned in Chapter 5, speaks about the effects of non-virtuous actions on the environment. Actions that are influenced by unwholesome desires, greed and so on are seen to affect the natural world by causing famine, desertification, hunger and other problems. The reign of an unrighteous king is seen as causing similar upheavals. The same idea (garbed in more positive terms however) forms the central theme of the *Kurudhammajātaka* and the *Manicorajātaka*. The former concludes by saying that the practice of the five precepts of non-violence, not taking what is not given, not being lustful, speaking no lies and drinking no strong drink, are useful in assuaging a drought.[45] It is the correct practice of *dhamma* that brings the rains. In the *Manicorajātaka* virtuous conduct transforms a natural adversity.[46] Herein it is said:

> If a king is unrighteous, god sends rain out of time, in time there is no rain; the fear of famine, fear of disease, and the fear of weapons – these three fears overpower . . .[47]

Thus, as in the *Nikāya* example, it is pointed out here that the unrighteousness of a king would lead to natural calamities. This once more indicates that Buddhists possibly believed that internal values have a connection with external factors and the state of the natural world. This reinforces the virtue of responsibility and strengthens the claims of an environmental virtue ethics even more.

Much on the treatment of animals can also be derived from the *Jātakas*. There is a diversity of animals contained within the tales; some 70 animals in all are mentioned, with monkeys and elephants topping the list.[48] In the *Jātaka* stories animals are the actors. Scholars working on the *Jātakas* have observed that animals are shown as beings capable of extreme altruism and at the same time animals are seen as depraved; some tales look down upon certain species of animals such as jackals, whose characteristics are described as those to be avoided. It has been also noted that sometimes the same animal is both altruistic and depraved.[49] Since the *Jātakas* do not follow a consistent approach it becomes difficult to classify animals as one or the other of these things. What this entails for the *Jātakas* (and the morality of animals) will be brought out in due course. The ambiguity is further sharpened through the distinct difference between the real condition of animals and their (rather fictitious) setting in these tales. The two do not coincide in many instances. More will be said on this over the following pages.

The sacrifice of animals, an accepted practice of the time, appears to have greatly perturbed the *Bodhisatta* of the *Jātakas*. Animal sacrifice was deplored and intentional injury in this form became especially unacceptable to the Buddhists. There appears to have been an underlying awareness that the precept implying respect for life was compromised due to such acts. In the *Matakabhattajātaka* a goat that was to be sacrificed by a Brahmin showed signs of great joy and great sorrow.[50] The goat explained the reason for each emotion. In a previous life the goat had been a Brahmin who had sacrificed a goat, due to which he was born a goat in the last 500 lifetimes and each time had to have his head chopped off. He had laughed because this was his last birth, but he had cried for the Brahmin would be doomed for killing a goat. The sacrifice was stopped. In another story the *Bodhisatta* was born a king and vowed to stop the sacrificing of living creatures in his land.[51] He devised a clever strategy for this. He announced in his kingdom that any being that indulged in animal sacrifice would, in turn, be sacrificed to a certain Banyan tree. The result of this was that none of his subjects, during his reign, harmed another living creature for fear of being sacrificed themselves. Scholars identify two reasons for the general Buddhist opposition to animal sacrifice. One could be seen as compassion, that the Buddha did not want animals to suffer (and so having an indirect bearing on the environment).[52] The other reason is metaphysical, that sacrifices were a waste of time leading to no greater good. It is unclear which position (compassion or kamma) the *Jātakas* seem to support, and arguments for both can be deduced in different instances.[53]

A tale that is of considerable ecological significance and also concerns animals is the *Kāsāvajātaka*, where the *Bodhisatta* is an elephant himself.[54] The tale revolves around the deceit of a man who dresses as a Brahmin in order to lure elephants and then kill them for their ivory. The *Bodhisatta* realizes his true intentions and drives him out of the forest. Attention is drawn to this particular tale only to illustrate that there was some awareness about the pain suffered by animals and there is acknowledgement that killing an elephant for material gain (ivory) is not an acceptable act. Thus this story relates directly to present day ecological problems.

Another story that is based around animals and may be seen as containing some environmental value is the *Vyagghajātaka*.[55] This *Jātaka* is a particular favourite among many scholars who have written on ecology and nature in Buddhism and has been recounted and analysed a number of times.[56] It tells the tale of a lion and a tiger driven away from the woods by a foolish tree deity (*andhabāla*) because it did not like the way they used to kill and eat creatures and leave the forest full of rotting carcasses and a foul stench. The *Bodhisatta*, another tree deity, warned him not to do so for these animals kept men away and therefore safeguarded the forest. But his warning was given no attention by the foolish tree deity. Woodcutters, realizing that they no longer saw animal footprints, chopped the trees and cultivated the land. The explicit moral of the story is that the advice of the wise must be respected and the unattractive must not be interfered with for usefulness that may not be immediately recognizable. However, in terms of animal life, the story suggests that the natural presence of animals should evoke more than just aesthetic sentiments and sometimes even when they appear unattractive, they ought to be left undisturbed for their value may rest elsewhere.

Though many see this story as merely an environmental tale, Florin Deleanu claims that to its authors it was more of a "moral lesson."[57] Deleanu obviously means this in the sense of a moral lesson or teaching to the readers of the tale. However, the term "moral lesson" brings to attention another important issue – that animals and other non-humans are portrayed as moral agents who suffer the consequences of their actions. Several stories (such as the *Kāsāvajātaka* described above) depict animals as moral beings. Can it then be said on the basis of the *Jātakas* that animals are moral beings? The answer to this question cannot be anything but positive for animals are active in the practice of virtues and vices and appear to be held responsible for their actions. However this idea has to be reconciled with two related problems that surface consistently in the tales. One problem has to do with the portrayal of animals in factually erroneous (and rather fictitious) ways; the other problem is anthropomorphism.

Christopher Chapple claims that the *Jātakas* give an accurate and detailed account of animals.[58] However, Paul Waldau completely disagrees with Chapple.[59] Waldau cites the example of elephants, which are always portrayed as patriarchal in Buddhist writings, whereas they are actually matriarchal, that is, they are led by the female: "Mature bulls are solitary, they wander in and out of different groups; they are by no means the leaders."[60] Waldau finds that no attention is paid to the complexity of animals. Elephants have a remarkable intelligence; they prefer freedom and suffer in captivity. Furthermore, breaking an elephant requires considerable torture for the elephant. He finds that there is barely an acknowledgement of this in the tales. The *Dubbalakaṭṭhajātaka*, probably the only story in the collection, acknowledges the pain elephants go through while being broken.[61] It tells the story of an elephant that could no longer suffer the pain it was being subjected to, and so broke free of its fetters and escaped to the Himalayas where it lived in constant fear until it was advised by a tree deity to overcome its fear. Despite this awareness, elephants continued to be seen as animals of prestige and no message whatsoever seemed to be given in any other tale to let them live in their natural surroundings. Waldau adds:

> Captivity of elephants is eminently an intentional act which clearly involves harms. Since these harms were recognized by the Buddhists, it might at first seem baffling why instrumental uses were not condemned by someone who had the extraordinary insights which Gotama surely had. The answer lies in the Buddhist view of the relative value of humans, on the one hand, and all other animals, on the other hand.[62]

Waldau notes this lack of information regarding the real nature and behaviour of animals elsewhere too. In another place, whilst discussing monkeys he says that it is believed that these, and in fact all, animals lack wisdom and that these primates are simple characters, so much so that "one might assert that more than a mere belittling of these evolutionary cousins occurs; what arguably takes place is the dismissal of their possibilities and realities, for they are considered stupid and malicious. . . ."[63] Florin Deleanu makes a similar observation. Whilst speaking of the jackal, he notes that this animal is referred to as a vile beast because of its foraging habits and for no other reason than this. Referring to this habit, Deleanu adds "whatever this behaviour maybe, it is sure that it has nothing in it which would justify the epithet 'the vilest of beasts'."[64] With reference to such examples, Waldau brings to attention a very important issue – that Buddhists sometimes left things the way they were in the society of the time for the sake of practical considerations. Examples that downgrade animals or misrepresent them, serve to confirm this point for him. It is difficult to reconcile this aspect with an all-embracing compassionate environmental ethics.

Other problems that are faced in the portrayal of animals in these texts pertain to anthropocentrism and anthropomorphism. Speaking of the former, if the aim of the stories be taken as a refinement of *kamma* then they can be classified as anthropocentric. For instance, the reason for stopping the sacrifice in the *Matakabhattajātaka* mentioned above is that the Brahmin feared bad *kamma* and repeated rebirths. It appears from this that the life of the animal was not important as was what taking it meant for the Brahmin performing the sacrifice. Thus the *Jātakas* swerve towards an anthropocentric ethic by the very fact that their concern largely is the human individual. It can also be said that though protection is extended beyond the human community, such protection is somehow linked to human welfare. On this account therefore the *Jātakas* can be seen as largely anthropocentric and this poses serious problems for an ethics of environment. But, as seen earlier, anthropocentrism is not necessarily incompatible with ecology and so this issue can be resolved amicably. In the case of the *Jātakas* as well most instances of anthropocentrism can be classified as weak rather than strong. As mentioned in Chapter 3, strong anthropocentrism is more selfish and narrow in its concern; weak anthropocentrism tries to correct this deficiency by including an element of altruism. Since the virtues of compassion, altruism and concern for the other figure overwhelmingly in just about all the tales (whether they are directed at human beings or others) the tales seem better defined as weak anthropocentrism. By criticizing selfishness and egoism, the *Jātakas* make their attitude even more distinct and removed in relation to strong anthropocentrism. And, as shown earlier, here too it is by the acceptance of weak anthropocentrism that the environmental doctrine becomes more real and cooperative in applied situations.

As for anthropomorphism, the animals in these stories are clearly not factual animals but the Buddha and his contemporaries playing some role. In this the tales are clearly anthropomorphic. In his brief critique of the *Jātakas* Ian Harris notes that:

> . . . the often highly anthropomorphic character of the essentially pre-Buddhist folk-tradition of the *Jātakas* may be said to empty the stories of any "naturalistic" content, thus defeating the intention of those who bring them forward as evidence in support of an authentic Buddhist environmentalist ethic.[65]

Though in agreement with Harris's assessment that the *Jātakas* are anthropomorphic and that the "naturalistic" content of these tales is compromised due to this factor, I find that limiting the environmental intent of the *Jātakas* in this way is unfair. Through my analysis I have tried to show that those who treat the *Jātakas* as an actual representation of nature can be easily contested. Not having agreeable naturalistic content is indeed a problem as it is suggestive of distorted awareness regarding nature and natural beings and thus contrary to the spirit of environmental ethics. At the same time it does not fully discount an environmental conscience in the *Jātakas*. Once again, on the basis of my discussion above, I believe that the *Jātakas* approach environmental issues at a different level to the factual one. This can be clearly seen in the virtues they extol. (Though Harris does mention this point briefly, it is clear that he does not place too much importance on it.) The *Jātakas*, in fact, can be treated as a pronounced expression of early Buddhism's moral framework. The virtues within these tales can be reasonably extended to dealings with the natural world and non-human beings. The *Jātakas*, just like the

Nikāyas and other texts, can then be said to support an environmental virtue ethics. It is in imparting the virtues that the most important objective – of moral dissemination – of the *Jātakas* is fulfilled and one can hope that this helps in limiting the effect of a detrimental "naturalistic" content.

Determining the possibility of an ethics of the environment in the *Jātakas*

Having discussed the possibility of an environmental virtue ethics in the *Jātakas*, an additional question needs to be addressed to determine, more broadly, the nature and scope of this ethics. The question regarding pragmatic implications for the natural world of an environment virtue ethics is an important one and has been raised earlier. An essential and unique way the *Jātakas* contribute to this area is through suggesting how virtues are to be employed. They are suggestive that choices are to be made after an assessment of the situation. They demonstrate through concrete examples how the different needs of different moral circumstances have to be dealt with. The *Jātakas* go so far as to allow for similar situations to have different results. I shall explain this point with the help of an example. In the following stories, though the situation is similar, very different results are seen. Both stories address moral predicaments and in their own way have environmental concerns in their content. The *Mahāsukajātaka* tells the tale of a parrot that refused to leave a barren fig tree, due to a fierce loyalty to the tree that had served the parrot in its better days.[66] The tale goes as follows. In order to test the loyalty of the parrot Lord Sakka dried up the fig tree where the parrot lived, perforated it and filled it with dust. The parrot lived off the dust but refused to fly away. Sakka then appeared before the parrot in the form of a royal goose and asked him why he hadn't left the dry tree when the other birds had flown away to more fruitful trees. The parrot revealed that he had decided to stay due to gratitude and love for the tree. Sakka was so overjoyed with this reply that he granted the parrot a wish: the parrot wished for the tree to be returned to its former glory. The *Kacchapajātaka*, on the other hand, tells the tale of a tortoise that refused to leave a dried up lake due to his attachment to it.[67] For this he lost his life. It is pointed out that instinct tells fish and other aquatic animals when there will be rain and when there will be drought. One year the creatures sensed a drought and so swam from the lake to the river but the tortoise refused owing to such an attachment to the home where he was born, grew up, etc. He remained buried in the mud of the now dry lake and became a victim of a potter's spade who unknowingly struck him thinking him to be a lump of clay. Due to a fondness for home, one who was unable to leave perished, is the message of this *Jātaka*. The *Bodhisatta* was the potter and exhorted at the end of the tale that attachments bring much sorrow as they did for the tortoise.

The parrot appears to have displayed the following two virtues – loyalty and endurance. And it is also clear that the first *Jātaka* is in addition about the virtues of love, friendship and gratitude whereas in the second the vice of attachment is being warned against. The action of the parrot is looked upon favourably; that of the tortoise is taken as foolish. In the case of a moral impasse – here it is to leave or not to leave – it must be decided, in the context of the situation, what course of action is to be followed. The focus of attention is once again the presence of some virtue or vice on the basis of which an answer must be sought. From the natural point of view, these tales can be understood as environmentally significant as well. One suggests the wisdom of migration where life is endangered.[68] The other suggests loyalty to that which has served one: the object must be tended and damage to it undone so that it is restored to its former glory. Such an attitude may help in tackling the environmental crisis we see today where the loss of species and wilderness is rampant. The *Jātakas* would advise that situations be tackled on the basis of virtues and nothing less.

The *Jātaka* stories make persons more attentive to the method through which choices can be made. And their method is of applying the right virtues so that the correct solutions can then be derived. The presence of a large variety of stories extolling different virtues ensures that endless possibilities can be adopted. That the purpose of the *Jātakas* was additionally didactic is confirmed by Cowell when he says, "These legends were also continually introduced into religious discourses which were delivered by the various teachers in the course of their wanderings, whether to magnify the glory of the Buddha, or to illustrate Buddhist doctrines and precepts by appropriate examples."[69] In fact the larger-than-life expression and animated descriptions the stories contain make an impact that lingers for a long time afterwards and it is not uncommon to see this feature in most didactic literature. Thus imparting lessons of moral methodology appears as the motive of the tales and that these are being communicated through trees and animals strengthens the case for an ethics of the environment.

A direct appeal to virtues in environmental quandaries is a theme that is present in the *Jātakas* as well. The *Vaṭṭakajātaka* tells the story of a quail that was able to put out a jungle fire by an act of truth.[70] The quail remembers all those who have been enlightened and attained perfections. He grasps on to the one truth they relied on saying, ". . . and I too grasp the one truth; I am moved by and fully understand this inherent nature."[71] Through this act of truth the quail makes the flames recede. It is to be noted here that the physical action of the flames dying away is related to the mental act of evoking of the perfections of past enlightened beings. In this analysis of the *Vaṭṭakajātaka* it is seen that the power of the virtues is such that even just evoking them can have a tremendous impact. Thus in following or even thinking of the path of the perfections one avoids calamitous conditions. An interesting analogy can be drawn here: if the perfections are followed, they could lead to a lessening of desires, which in turn would reduce harm being done to forests and the weather conditions, and these in turn could lead to a reduction in the number of jungle fires!

The focus of many contemporary environmental theories is on objects such as mountains and rivers and species and eco-systems. But in the *Jātakas* there is hardly any information relating to their treatment, let alone their conservation; the focus is mostly on how the individual can enhance his moral quotient. Thus the foundations of an environmental ethics begin to look doubtful and questionable again. It also defeats the question of practicality. However, it may be said in defence of the *Jātakas* that their environmental ethics is expressed more in their accounts of virtue than in their references to nature. It is through the virtues that they reach out in the practical sphere. Even though the virtues do not have a direct ecological motive, they parallel environmental virtues as judiciously as they did in the *Nikāyas* and other texts. The virtues lead to the creation of not only a moral character but have an added ecological dimension that ensures that rash environment related crimes become a thing of the past. The virtues would act as a determinant for correcting misdemeanours of all sorts – environmental or otherwise. Under such circumstances the senseless and evil harming of any creature or entity becomes virtually impossible.[72]

Some stories indicate a sense of hierarchy implying that beings have distinct values based on different aspects of their existence. It is not unknown for theories of the environment that support moral consideration of human beings, animals, plants and/or physical nature (rocks and rivers etc.) to accept a notion of hierarchy. By accepting hierarchy such theories acknowledge that the interests and needs of different beings and objects are dissimilar and choices must be made that respond to these differences. This acknowledgement of hierarchy can be quite encouraging when it comes to making decisions in the real world. But the question of making choices is complicated when interests conflict radically. The interest of a flock of migratory birds is respected when their migratory habitat is not destroyed. However this habitat may be required by human beings for vital farming land to feed starving populations. Such questions are hard to solve. Despite such conflicts, these ethicists admit that a hierarchical balance must be reached and all interests, short and long term, considered to some extent. In this their approach is quite unlike some forms of egalitarian environmental ethics that in their insistence on the flourishing of all things disallow the destruction of those that cause harm. Acceptance of a hierarchy of value appears as the most practical path to adopt. This sense is present in the *Jātaka* collection. The *Jātakas* seem to uphold a hierarchical view by not favouring equality and accepting that an entity can be destroyed for the sake of some other thing. For instance, in the earlier-mentioned *Palāsajātaka* the destruction of the Banyan tree is encouraged. Cutting down an overgrowth need not be a negative action under all circumstances and the sense of hierarchy in the *Jātakas* allows for such acts. One has also to be aware that this story does not encourage the destruction of trees *per se*, but only of the select few that cause damage. If a wise, knowledgeable, mindful and compassionate individual were to destroy some weeds or trees after careful consideration, how can this be considered an immoral act? That the situation is not taken lightly can be gathered from the tale when it recommends the advice of a wise person. If the trees were recklessly destroyed without any fair justification then *Jātaka* wisdom would not condone the act. Thus destruction is not rampant because choices are to be made on the basis of strict circumstantial evidence and much virtue and insight. The destruction of higher beings is also suggested. One example among many is the *Dhammaddhajajātaka* where the *Bodhisatta*, a bird in this life, partakes of killing a crow for his lying and deceitful acts.[73] Sometimes there may be good reason to destroy some animal that may be creating havoc in a delicate ecological balance; but this must not be seen as a license for unwarranted killing. However, though environmentally encouraging, it must not be forgotten that these two examples also lead to serious questions about the use of aggression and violence involved in destroying something; in all they are not in tune with the categorical nature of the precept of *ahiṃsā* and contradict what is upheld generally in the rest of the Canon.

In applying the *Jātakas* to environmental issues there has to be therefore an added caution against unanticipated interpretations. Another veiled predicament arises in connection with the *Bodhisatta*. His actions ought to be exemplary in connection with the environment but are not: he is at times responsible for overusing the bounties of nature or is associated with events that are subversive of a respect for nature. As in the *Mahākapijātaka*, the *Bodhisatta*'s greatness is cherished by cremating his body with 100 wagon loads of timber.[74] It has been often noted by scholars that the *Bodhisatta* is not adverse to material opulence and so is quite unlike the simple and austere Buddha of other texts. Even though he strives towards renunciation in many stories, there are instances where he lives among a plethora of grand possessions as in the *Dūtajātaka* where the *Bodhisatta* is a king and enjoys the luxuries of kingship.[75] However in defense of the *Jātakas* one other interpretation must be accepted: that these examples can be relegated to a didactic context. Stories tend to be more effective when the protagonist, in this case the *Bodhisatta*, identifies with his audience and with those to whom he is reaching out. So living a life of luxury for him is not unbeknown or unusual only for this reason.

Conclusion

Contradictions that qualify any search for an environmental ethics in the *Jātakas* have been articulated throughout this chapter. No doubt the *Jātakas* contribute variously to the protection of the environment, but at the same time there are several examples of anti-environmental behavior that resist the formation of a consistent environmental theory. The live tension between the tales' negative natural content on the one hand and their positive content and admiration of virtues on the other is palpable. On a more positive note the *Jātaka* tales contain the possibility of an environmental virtue ethics and at the same time support a boundless wisdom that guides the moral choice making process such as can be extended to the natural world. In the course of this chapter all possible avenues of establishing an environmental ethics within the *Jātaka* tales were investigated. Finally, though I cannot deny that an impeccable environmental ethics cannot be based on the *Jātakas*, I hope that I have demonstrated that an implicit environmental virtue ethics is a unique possible alternative. An irreproachable theory of environmental ethics here is impossible but an environmental consciousness brought out through the virtues the tales exalt and the pragmatic environmental situations they can be envisioned to address is a promising outcome. In conclusion it may be said that the *Jātakas* contain an unconventional environmentalism that can be applied to contemporary environmental matters, provided one is attentive to the distinctive nature of problems that ensue of which some have been presented in the course of this chapter.

CONCLUSION

> *What relationship have we, you and I, to that crisis and how shall we act?. . . we have to assume the responsibility for our own action, that is, we have to understand our own nature, we have to understand ourselves.*
>
> J. Krishnamurti, *On Nature and the Environment*

In his paper "Causation and 'Telos': The Problem of Buddhist Environmental Ethics," Ian Harris shared his concern of choosing between two positions in ecology and Buddhism – he admitted that his heart was drawn to the optimistic position that Buddhism did contain a response to environmental problems, but he also admitted that his mind was more attuned to the other position that rejected such a possibility. Almost every serious scholar who embarks upon a study of Buddhist environmental ethics faces a similar dilemma. Early Buddhist principles inherently suggest a deep-rooted sense of environmentalism and yet they remain intellectually ambiguous with regard to the environment. My aim throughout this book has been to make sense of the former while at the same time expressing such beliefs intellectually.

The genesis of an environmental ethics in early Buddhism lies in the ethical system that Buddhist philosophy contains. Though a defined and palpable environmental ethics continues to elude its principles, a meticulous examination of the virtues of early Buddhist ethics reveals their value to environmental matters. However, this hypothesis begins to make sense only after the significance of nature in Buddhist thought is determined. This again is no easy task as most descriptions of nature are rather limited in import and so in direct conflict with Buddhism's more expansive understanding of the concept. In my analysis I have challenged the former descriptions and have established that early Buddhism's understanding of nature is innately cosmological and it is only in this sense that nature can be recognized in Buddhist thought. My study then goes on to indicate that despite successfully giving form to a sense of nature in early Buddhism, a cosmological understanding is an inadequate basis for an environmental ethics, as it does not provide enough impetus for ethical actions aimed towards the environment. In other words, a cosmological insight undoubtedly paves the way as it acknowledges an awareness of nature, but it is unable to guarantee that moral actions are directed towards the natural world. This gap is filled by the early Buddhist ethical theory and in this its role is crucial.

The Buddhist ethical theory influences and determines the nature of actions. It essentially suggests that the individual is responsible for the life he creates through the choices he makes and the actions he undertakes; it also implies that this individual alone can change the course of his destiny by making alternative choices and then acting on them. To make the "right" ethical choices Buddhism recommends virtuous living and cautions against vices. On the basis of the fundamental concern of early Buddhist ethics with virtuous behaviour, I have demonstrated that early Buddhism is predominantly a virtue ethics. In my analysis I then proceeded to show that an environmental virtue ethics must be looked upon as an inherent part of this virtue ethics in early Buddhism, for general virtues can also be seen as having ecological significance. I indicate further that in this case environmental virtue ethics cannot be cut off completely from other aspects of Buddhist philosophy for by such isolation its very presence is threatened and it may lose its intensity. Therefore it must never be overlooked that it is in acting virtuously that the aim of a Buddhist virtue ethics and an environmental virtue ethics is fulfilled. The two are not separate. In this way then, my study argues, early Buddhism endorses an inimitable environmental ethics as rooted in its virtue ethics.

Based on what has been said throughout this book it can now be seen that early Buddhism's apparent recognition of environmental problems would have a predominantly psychological essence. My enquiry therefore culminates in the observation (also noted by innumerable scholars before me) that in all likelihood the environmental crisis to the early Buddhists is the manifestation of a psychological crisis because most physical actions and outward behaviour are shaped by what is going on in the mind. As long as the mind is influenced by the three unwholesome principles of *rāga, dosa* and *moha* or greed, hatred and delusion the human race will be stricken by environmental and other forms of exploitation, as well as selfish actions, greedy consumer cultures, dissatisfaction and other attitudes that can be looked upon as vices. Though there is no direct information about the relation between these states of mind and their resulting immoral actions to the environmental crisis, there is little doubt that the latter lies deeply embedded in the psyche and is strongly associated with ethical deliberations which are indelibly influenced by greed, hatred and delusion. The Buddha often blamed these for giving rise to hurdles in the path of enlightenment. Unsurprisingly the Buddhist response is singularly focused on eliminating the three unwholesome values. It is within this framework that an environmental virtue ethics finds its place.

The method for obliterating greed, hatred and delusion rests in the teachings of the Buddha. Buddha's identification of these three principles with all the misery and anguish present in the world and his prescription of a technique to hasten their downfall acts as the solution to the spreading environmental epidemic. The Buddha is often likened to a physician or surgeon of unsurpassed excellence (*Sallakaṭṭō anuṭṭarō*) who offers a remedy for *dukkha*.[1] He also ought to be referred to as an environmental surgeon with the power of healing the current environmental crisis. Even though it is true that the Buddha's antidote of rebuilding personal character through virtues may not have the necessary force for removing all environmental evils irrespective, it has the indispensable effect of gradually breaking down those walls that irrationally conceal anti-environmental discourse and action. And this rebuilding is not passive but rather evokes active involvement and struggle. This is environmental virtue ethics, and as my study indicates, it is a position that can be validly based on early Buddhist principles in such a way that the environment is bound to respond positively.

Throughout my book I have demonstrated that early Buddhism can be seen to address environmental problems once its philosophy is interpreted in the right spirit. Additionally even though a vision based on Buddhist literature would possibly treat the environmental crisis primarily as a psycho-ethical one, the value of nature itself adds up to something more. I also trust that I have managed a conciliation between the two approaches mentioned earlier – the one cautiously guarded and the other emotionally optimistic – to Buddhist environmental philosophy. I hope to have added something of significance to environmental deliberations by revealing latent potentialities within the early Buddhist doctrine and by contributing to more innovative ways of regarding nature.

NOTES

1 TOWARDS AN ENVIRONMENTAL ETHICS IN BUDDHISM

1 Clarification of the term "Early Buddhism" will be given subsequently.

2 Alan Sponberg, "Green Buddhism and the Hierarchy of Compassion," in Mary Evelyn Tucker and Duncan Ryūken Williams (eds) *Buddhism and Ecology: The Interconnection of Dharma and Deeds*, Cambridge, Massachusetts: Harvard University Press, 1997, p. 351.

3 David Little, "The Present State of the Study of Comparative Religious Ethics," *Journal of Religious Ethics* 9, 1981, p. 221 [*sic*]; quoted in Robin W. Lovin and Frank E. Reynolds, "In the Beginning," *Cosmogony and the Ethical Order*, Chicago: The University of Chicago Press, 1985, p. 7.

4 No absolute claims however can be made about the Pali Canon and scholars have varied opinions.

5 Ananda K. Coomaraswamy, *Buddha and the Gospel of Buddhism*, London: George G. Harrap and Company, 1916; reprint, rev. New York: Harper and Row Publishers, 1964, p. 279.

6 A. K. Warder, *Indian Buddhism*, Delhi: Motilal Banarsidass, 1970, p. 7.

7 Sue Hamilton, *Early Buddhism: A New Approach: The I of the Beholder*, Richmond, Surrey: Curzon Press, 2000, p. 8.

8 For example, William Lafleur's "Saigyō and the Buddhist Value of Nature" appeared in 1974. Reprinted in J. Baird Callicott and Roger T. Ames (eds) *Nature in Asian Traditions of Thought: Essays in Environmental Philosophy*, New York: State University of New York Press, 1989; reprinted as Indian edition Delhi: Sri Satguru Publications, 1991, pp. 183–209.

9 Lambert Schmithausen, *The Problem of Sentience of Plants in Earliest Buddhism*, Studia Philologica Buddhica Monograph Series, VI, Tokyo: The International Institute for Buddhist Studies, 1991.

10 Sponberg, "Green Buddhism and the Hierarchy of Compassion," pp. 351–76.

11 Alan Sponberg, "The Buddhist Conception of an Ecological Self," in Sallie B. King and Paul O. Ingram (eds) *The Sound of Liberating Truth: Buddhist-Christian Dialogues in Honour of Frederick J. Streng*, Richmond, Surrey: Curzon Press, 1999, pp. 116–18.

12 Ibid. p. 118.

13 David J. Kalupahana, "Toward a Middle Path of Survival," in J. Baird Callicott and Roger T. Ames (eds) *Nature in Asian Traditions of Thought: Essays in Environmental Philosophy*, New York: State University of New York Press, 1989; reprinted as Indian edn Delhi: Sri Satguru Publications, 1991, pp. 247–56.

14 David J. Kalupahana, *Ethics in Early Buddhism*, Honolulu: University of Hawaii Press, 1995. See the chapter entitled "Nature and Morals."
15 Peter Harvey, *An Introduction to Buddhist Ethics*, Cambridge, UK: Cambridge University Press, 2000.
16 P. D. Ryan, *Buddhism and the Natural World*, Birmingham: Windhorse Publications, 1998.
17 Ian Harris, "Causation and 'Telos': The Problem of Buddhist Environmental Ethics," *Journal of Buddhist Ethics* 1, 1994, p. 54, http://jbe.gold.ac.uk (accessed 7 October 1999).
18 Malcolm David Eckel, "Is There a Buddhist Philosophy of Nature?," in Mary Evelyn Tucker and Duncan Ryūken Williams (eds) *Buddhism and Ecology: The Interconnection of Dharma and Deeds*, Cambridge, Massachusetts: Harvard University Press, 1997, pp. 327–49.
19 Paul Waldau, "Buddhism and Animal Rights," in Damien Keown (ed.) *Contemporary Buddhist Ethics*, Richmond, Surrey: Curzon Press, 2000, pp. 81–112.
20 Paul Waldau, "Speciesism in Christianity and Buddhism," unpublished thesis, University of Oxford, 1998, p. 229.
21 Florin Deleanu, "Buddhist 'Ethology' in the Pāli Canon: Between Symbol and Observation," *The Eastern Buddhist XXXII*, no. 2, 2000, p. 117.
22 Mary Evelyn Tucker and Duncan Ryūken Williams (eds) *Buddhism and Ecology: The Interconnection of Dharma and Deeds*, Cambridge, Massachusetts: Harvard University Press, 1997, p. xli.
23 Martine Batchelor and Kerry Brown (eds) *Buddhism and Ecology*, London, UK: Cassell Publishers Limited, 1992; Allan Hunt Badiner (ed.) *Dharma Gaia*, California: Parallax Press, 1990; Stephanie Kaza and Kenneth Kraft (eds) *Dharma Rain*, Boston and London: Shambhala, 2000; Tucker and Williams, *Dharma and Deeds*.
24 Joanna Macy, *World as Lover, World as Self*, Berkeley, California: Parallax Press, 1991.
25 Ibid. pp. 183–92.
26 Padmasiri de Silva, *Environmental Philosophy and Ethics in Buddhism*, Basingstoke, Hampshire: Macmillan Press Ltd, 1998.
27 Tony Page, *Buddhism and Animals*, London: UKAVIS Publications, 1999.
28 Harris, "Causation and 'Telos'."
29 The view that Buddhism negates nature is the position of Noriaki Hakamaya, as is mentioned by Harris. Schmithausen holds a similar opinion of Hakamaya and his writings include a detailed critique of the latter's position. Both scholars base their views on two articles by Hakamaya – "Shizen-hihen to-shite no Bukkyō" (Buddhism as a Criticism of "*Physis/Natura*"), *Komazawa-daiguku Bukkyōgakubu Ronshū*, 1990, p. 21, 380–403; and "Nihon-jin to animizmu," *Komazawa-daiguku Bukkyōgakubu Ronshū*, 1992, 23, 351–78. I will not be considering Hakamaya's position any further. See Harris, "Causation and Telos," 47; and Schmithausen, *Sentience of Plants*, p. 53f.
30 Martine Batchelor, "Even the Stones Smile," in Martine Batchelor and Kerry Brown (eds) *Buddhism and Ecology*, London, UK: Cassell Publishers Limited, 1992, pp. 2–17.
31 Lily de Silva, "The Hills Wherein My Soul Delights," in Martine Batchelor and Kerry Brown (eds) *Buddhism and Ecology*, London, UK: Cassell Publishers Limited, 1992, pp. 18–30.
32 Stephen Batchelor, "Buddhist Economics Reconsidered," in Alan Hunt Badiner (ed.) *Dharma Gaia*, California: Parallax Press, 1990, pp. 178–82.
33 Rita M. Gross, "Buddhist Resources for Issues of Population, Consumption and

the Environment," in Mary Evelyn Tucker and Duncan Ryūken Williams (eds) *Dharma and Deeds*, Cambridge, Massachusetts: Harvard University Press, 1997, pp. 291–312.

34 Ken Jones, "Getting Out of Our Own Light," in Alan Hunt Badiner (ed.) *Dharma Gaia*, California: Parallax Press, 1990, pp. 183–90.

35 Padmasiri de Silva, "Buddhist Environmental Ethics," in Alan Hunt Badiner (ed.) *Dharma Gaia*, California: Parallax Press, 1990, pp. 14–19.

36 Stephen Batchelor, "The Sands of the Ganges," in Martine Batchelor and Kerry Brown (eds) *Buddhism and Ecology*, London, UK: Cassell Publishers Limited, 1992, pp. 31–9.

37 Jeremy Hayward, "Ecology and the Experience of Sacredness," in Alan Hunt Badiner (ed.) *Dharma Gaia*, California: Parallax Press, 1990, pp. 64–74.

38 Ibid. p. 73. *Anattā* refers to the Buddhist theory of no-soul or no-self.

39 Martin Pitt, "The Pebble and the Tide," in Alan Hunt Badiner (ed.) *Dharma Gaia*, California: Parallax Press, 1990, pp. 102–5.

40 Suzzane Head, "Creating Space for Nature," in Alan Hunt Badiner (ed.) *Dharma Gaia* California: Parallax Press, 1990, pp. 112–28.

41 Eckel, "Is there a Buddhist Philosophy of Nature?," p. 329.

42 Kerry Brown, "In the Water There Were Fish and the Fields Were Full of Rice," in Martine Batchelor and Kerry Brown (eds) *Buddhism and Ecology*, London, UK: Cassell Publishers Limited, 1992, pp. 87–99.

43 Ibid. p. 99.

44 Donald K. Swearer, "The Hermeneutics of Buddhist Ecology in Contemporary Thailand: Buddhadāsa and Dhammapitaka," in Mary Evelyn Tucker and Duncan Ryūken Williams (eds) *Dharma and Deeds*, Cambridge, Massachusetts: Harvard University Press, 1997, pp. 21–44.

45 Susan Darlington, "Tree ordination in Thailand," in Stephanie Kaza and Kenneth Kraft, (eds) *Dharma Rain*, Boston and London: Shambhala, 2000, pp. 200–1. Also, see details of the Thai Ordination Procedure 4, where the novice has to state he is human, in www.thailandlife.com/ordination_004.htm

46 Macy, *World as Lover*, 60. The recognition of the shift in meaning isn't new to Macy and has been noticed by others. One example is David J. Kalupahana, *Causality: The Central Philosophy of Buddhism*, Honolulu: The University Press of Hawaii, 1975, p. 71.

47 Macy, *World as Lover*, p. 63.

48 The shorter formula goes as follows – When this is, that comes to be; with the arising of this, that arises; if this is not, that does not come to be, from the stopping of this, that is stopped. (M III 63)

49 Mutuality is found in one place in the formula (Macy gives the example of S II 103) but it may not necessarily extend to other levels of dependent origination as Macy takes it to. Lambert Schmithausen has criticized Macy on similar lines. See "The Early Buddhist Tradition and Ecological Ethics," *Journal of Buddhist Ethics* 4, 1997, http://jbe.gold.ac.uk (accessed 7 October 1999).

50 Macy, *World as Lover*, pp. 68–9.

51 Joanna Macy, *Mutual Causality in Buddhism and General Systems Theory: The Dharma of Natural Systems*, Albany: State University of New York Press, 1991; reprinted, India: Manohar, 1992, p. 75.

52 Macy, *World as Lover*, p. 86.

53 Ibid. p. 88.

54 Ibid. pp. 89–92.

55 Ibid. p. 92.

56 Ibid. p. 184.

57 Ibid. pp. 187–8.
58 Ibid. p. 190.
59 Ibid. p. 192.
60 Ibid. p. 191.
61 Ian Harris, "Buddhist Environmental Ethics and Detraditionalization: The Case of Eco-Buddhism," *Religion* 25, 1995, p. 206.
62 Ian Harris, "Buddhism and Ecology," in Damien Keown (ed.) *Contemporary Buddhist Ethics*, Richmond, Surrey: Curzon Press, 2000, p. 125.
63 Harris, "Causation and Telos," 53. Also in Harris, "Buddhist Environmental Ethics and Detraditionalization," p. 206.
64 Ian Harris, "Getting to Grips With Buddhist Environmentalism: A Provisional Typology," *Journal of Buddhist Ethics* 2, 1995, p. 178, http://jbe.gold.ac.uk (accessed 7 October 1999). Also in Harris, "Buddhist Environmental Ethics and Detraditionalization," p. 202.
65 Harris, "Buddhism and Ecology," p. 125. Also in Harris, "Buddhist Environmental Ethics and Detraditionalization," p. 205.
66 Harris, "Causation and Telos," p. 46.
67 Schmithausen, "The Early Buddhist Tradition and Ecological Ethics," 6.
68 Lambert Schmithausen, *Buddhism and Nature*, Studia Philologica Buddhica Occasional Paper Series VII, Tokyo: The International Institute for Buddhist Studies, 1991, p. 1.
69 Ibid. p. 4.
70 Schmithausen, "The Early Buddhist Tradition and Ecological Ethics," 10.
71 Ibid. pp. 11–12.
72 Ibid. p. 22.
73 Schmithausen, *Buddhism and Nature*, p. 44f.
74 Ibid. p. 50.
75 Schmithausen, *Buddhism and Nature*, pp. 29–32. These pages contain a discussion on *ahiṃsā*.
76 Ibid. p. 32f. These pages contain Schmithausen's discussion on Buddhist attitudes towards species and eco-systems.
77 Schmithausen, "The Early Buddhist Tradition and Ecological Ethics," p. 24.
78 Ibid.
79 Schmithausen, *Buddhism and Nature*, p. 16.
80 Schmithausen, "The Early Buddhist Tradition and Ecological Ethics," 26–8. Also see Schmithausen, *Buddhism and Nature*, pp. 18f.
81 Schmithausen, *The Problem of Sentience of Plants*, pp. 3–4.
82 Ibid. p. 5.
83 Ibid. pp. 8–10. The examples given include D I 5, D I 64, M I 180, M I 268, A II 209, etc.
84 Ibid. p. 11f.
85 Ibid. p. 13.
86 Ibid. pp. 14–15.
87 Schmithausen does not consider acting from virtue to be the motive. More on this in Chapter 4.
88 Schmithausen, *The Problem of Sentience of Plants*, pp. 31–2. The reference to Vin IV 205f.
89 Ibid. pp. 34–5.
90 Ibid. p. 64. The passage is M II 196.
91 Ibid. p. 67.
92 Ibid. pp. 67–9.
93 Ibid. p. 69. Also in Schmithausen, *Buddhism and Nature*, 6f.

94 Ibid. p. 72.
95 Ibid. pp. 16f. Also in Schmithausen, "The Early Buddhist Tradition and Ecological Ethics," p. 28f.
96 Schmithausen, "The Early Buddhist Tradition and Ecological Ethics," p. 30.
97 Ibid. pp. 7–8.
98 Ibid. p. 34.
99 Schmithausen, *Buddhism and Nature*, p. 11.
100 Ian Harris, "How Environmentalist is Buddhism?," *Religion* 21, 1991, pp. 103–4.
101 Ibid. p. 104.
102 Ibid.
103 Harris, "Causation and Telos," p. 15.
104 Ibid. pp. 15–16.
105 Harris, "Buddhism and Ecology," pp. 114–15.
106 Ibid. 120.
107 Ian Harris, "Buddhism," in Jean Holm with John Bowker (ed.) *Attitudes to Nature*, London, New York: Printer Publishers, 1994, p. 17.
108 Harris, "How Environmentalist is Buddhism," 107. This reference is from Vin II p. 194f. It can be noted that the Sanskrit equivalent of *Mettā* is *Maitri*. My discussion of *Mettā* is in Chapter 4.
109 See Harris' "Buddhism and Ecology," pp. 119f; "Buddhism," pp. 18–19; and "How Environmentalist is Buddhism," pp. 106–7 for discussion of *mettā* and the treatment of animals.
110 Harris does move away from his insistence on the instrumentalist nature of *mettā* in his later works on Buddhism and ecology. See Harris, "Buddhism and Ecology," p. 120.
111 Harris, "Causation and Telos," p. 46.
112 Ibid. p. 53.
113 Harris, "Buddhism," p. 19.
114 Both Schmithausen and Harris have discussed these ideas to a limited extent. In addition to the above see Lambert Schmithausen, "Buddhism and the Ethics of Nature – Some Remarks," *The Eastern Buddhist New Series* XXXII, no. 2, 2000; and Ian Harris, "Buddhism and the Discourse of Environmental Concern: Some Methodological Problems Considered," in Mary Evelyn Tucker and Duncan Ryūken Williams (eds) *Dharma and Deeds*, Cambridge, Massachusetts: Harvard University Press, 1997. An exception is the more recent book by David E. Cooper and Simon P. James, *Buddhism, Virtue and the Environment*, U.K.: Ashgate, 2005. This book contains a detailed examination of the virtues approach in Buddhism and of an environmental virtue ethics. The authors speak of environmental virtues divided into the categories of self-regarding and other-regarding. Though I have not included a detailed review here, I do believe that this work serves to highlight not only the relevance of this interpretation but also that this particular dimension of Buddhist environmental ethics has been neglected and requires far more attention and research than previously accorded.
115 Since I have devoted a full chapter to the *Jātakas* I have not included their analysis in earlier chapters.

2 NATURE: A "CONSERVATIONIST" ANALYSIS

1 *Oxford Latin Dictionary*, 1982 edn, s.v. "natura," pp. 1158–9.
2 One example is the *English Greek Dictionary*, 1964 edn, s.v. "physis," p. 483.
3 Yrjo Haila and Richard Levins, *Humanity and Nature*, London: Pluto Press, 1992, p. ix.

4 John Passmore, "Attitudes to Nature," in Robert Elliot (ed.) *Environmental Ethics*, Oxford: Oxford University Press, 1995, p. 129.
5 Angelica Krebs, *Ethics of Nature*, Berlin, New York: Walter de Gruyter, 1999, p. 5.
6 Ibid. p. 6.
7 Ibid. pp. 8–9. Emphasis in original.
8 Ibid. p. 7 and p. 5 respectively.
9 Conveyed in personal communication on 19 September 2003.
10 R. Descartes, *Key Philosophical Writings*, Enrique Chavez-Arvizo (ed), trans. Elizabeth S. Haldane and G. R. T. Ross, Hertfordshire: Wordsworth Editions Limited, 1997, p. 92.
11 John Cottingham, *Descartes*, Oxford, New York: Basil Blackwell, 1986, p. 112.
12 Ibid. p. 181.
13 Descartes, *Key Philosophical Writings*, p. 109.
14 Tom Regan, *The Case for Animal Rights*, new edn, London: Routledge, 1988, p. 5.
15 Passmore, "Attitudes to Nature," p. 136.
16 This sense of marginalizing nature as such is by no means a new development. Many others have spoken of it without labeling it so (including John Passmore in his paper "Attitudes to Nature").
17 For a critique of Platonic attitudes see Robin Attfield, *Environmental Philosophy: Principles and Prospects*, Avebury: Aldershot, 1994; and John Passmore, "Attitudes to Nature."
18 Timothy A. Mahoney, "Platonic Ecology, Deep Ecology," in Laura Westra and Thomas M. Robinson (eds) *The Greeks and the Environment*, Lanham: Rowman and Littlefield Publishers, 1997, p. 45.
19 Gabriela Roxana Carone "Plato and the Environment," *Environmental Ethics* 20, no. 2, 1988, 117.
20 This point has been supported by Carone as well. Carone "Plato and the Environment," p. 118.
21 John Burnet, *Greek Philosophy*, London and Basingstoke: The Macmillan Press Ltd, 1914; reprint and reset 1964, p. 280.
22 I rely heavily on the very excellent translation and commentary of *Plato's Cosmology: The Timaeus of Plato*, Francis M. Cornford, Routledge, 1935; reprint, Indianapolis, Cambridge: Hackett Publishing Company, 1997, p. 165.
23 Ibid. p. 165.
24 Ibid. p. 40. The reference is 30 c, d and 31.
25 Ibid. p. 52. The reference is *Tim.* 32 c and 32 d.
26 Ibid. pp. 140–3. The reference of *Tim.* 41 c, d is just one instance.
27 Ibid. p. 57. The reference is *Tim.* 41.
28 Ibid. p. 105. The reference is *Tim.* 77.
29 Carone "Plato and the Environment," p. 120.
30 John Rist, "Why Greek Philosophers Might Have Been Concerned About the Environment," in Laura Westra and Thomas M. Robinson (eds) *The Greeks and the Environment*, Lanham: Rowman and Littlefield Publishers, 1997, p. 28.
31 Nevertheless, awareness must be maintained about the unfortunate denigration of women and lower animals. Cornford, pp. 356–8. The reference is *Tim.* 91–2 c.
32 Gregory Vlastos, *Plato's Universe*, Oxford: Clarendon Press, 1975, p. 3.
33 Madonna Adams "Environmental Ethics in Plato's *Timaeus*," in Laura Westra and Thomas M. Robinson (eds) *The Greeks and the Environment*, Lanham: Rowman and Littlefield Publishers, 1997, pp. 57–8.
34 W. K. C. Gutherie, *A History of Greek Philosophy: The Later Plato and the Academy*, Vol. V, Cambridge and London: Cambridge University Press, 1987, p. 256.

35 Chapters 4 and 5 include a discussion of environmental virtue ethics. Buddhism's cosmological understanding of nature is discussed in the next chapter. A source that led me to consider some important questions in this section was Allan Greenbaum's "Environmental Thought as Cosmological Intervention."
36 Krebs, *Ethics of Nature*, p. 9.
37 Allan Greenbaum, "Environmental Thought as Cosmological Intervention," *Environmental Values* 8, 1999, pp. 488–9, emphasis in original.
38 Scholars translate *mettā* variously as love, universal love, loving kindness or friendship.
39 *Apādakehi me mettaṃ mettaṃ dipādakehi me*
Catuppadehi me mettaṃ mettaṃ bahuppadehi me
Mā maṃ apādako hiṃsi mā maṃ hiṃsi dipādako
Mā maṃ catuppado hiṃsi ma maṃ hiṃsi bahuppado (A II 72)
40 Lambert Schmithausen, "The Early Buddhist Tradition and Ecological Ethics," *Journal of Buddhist Ethics* 4, 1997, pp. 18–19, http://jbe.gold.ac.uk (accessed 7 October 1999), emphasis in original.
41 *Tasmiṃ kho Brāhmaṇa yaññe n'eva gāvo haññiṃsu na ajeḷakā haññiṃsu na kukkuṭa sūkarā haññiṃsu, na vividhā pāṇā saṃghātaṃ āpajjiṃsu, na rukkhā chijjiṃsu yūpatthāya, na dabbhā lūyiṃsu barihisatthāya . . . Sappi-tela-navanīta-dadhi-madhi-phāṇitena c'eva so yañño niṭṭhānam agamāsi.* (D I 141)
42 A II 42–3.
43 S I 75.
44 Sn 310.
45 S I 76.
46 S I 75.
47 However, I believe, it could act as a premise on the basis of which a conclusion that reiterates respect for all life can be drawn. This aspect will be highlighted in Chapters 4 and 5.
48 M I 343.
49 *Ahaṃ kho 'mhi bhikkhave bhuttāvī pavārito paripuṇṇo pariyosito suhito yāvadattho. Atthi ca me ayaṃ piṇḍapāto atirekadhammo chaḍḍiyadhammo, sace āhaṅkhatha bhuñjatha, sace tumhe na bhuñjissatha idānāhaṃ appaharite vā chaḍḍessāmi appāṇake vā udake opilāpessāmīti.* (M I 13)
50 *gahanaṃ h'etaṃ Pessa yadidaṃ manussā uttānakaṃ h'etaṃ Pessa yadidaṃ pasavo* . . . (M I 341).
51 M III 169.
52 Paul Waldau, "Speciesism in Christianity and Buddhism," unpublished thesis, University of Oxford, 1998, p. 189.
53 This weakens the arguments of the marginal-ist who would never regard animals as moral beings. Many other scholars have also arrived at the conclusion that animals are moral beings or at least can make choices. See P. D. Ryan, *Buddhism and the Natural World*, Birmingham: Windhorse Publications, 1998, pp. 39–40; and Christopher Key Chapple, "Animals and Environment in the Buddhist Birth Stories," in Mary Evelyn Tucker and Duncan Ryūken Williams (eds) *Buddhism and Ecology: The Interconnection of Dharma and Deeds*, Cambridge, Massachusetts: Cambridge University Press, 1997, p. 144.
54 Waldau, "Speciesism in Christianity and Buddhism," p. 161.
55 Ibid. p. 231.
56 Ibid. p. 237, emphasis in original.
57 Florin Deleanu, "Buddhist 'Ethology' in the Pāli Canon: Between Symbol and Observation," *The Eastern Buddhist XXXII*, no. 2, 2000, pp. 118.
58 Ibid. p. 121.

59 Ibid. p. 124.
60 *Bījagāma-bhūtagāma-samārambhā paṭivirato.* (D I 5)
61 Vin III 155.
62 Some of these reasons have already been mentioned in the survey of literature on Buddhism and ecology: I repeat them here once more to make my point.
63 See Chapter 1 for details on Schmithausen, who has done detailed research in this area.
64 A III 369.
65 Conveyed by Dr Kate Crosby in personal communication on 19 September 2003.
66 Vin III 155. For detailed analysis and references see the Schmithausen section in Chapter 1.
67 *The Buddhist Monastic Code: Chapter 8: Part Two: The Living Plant Chapter* (16 May 2001), p. 1, http://www.accesstoinsight.org/lib/modern/bmc/ch8–2.html (accessed 13 July 2001).
68 The 75 is one example.
69 Sacred is used metaphorically here. The *Therīgāthā's* tone is slightly different possibly because isolation in the case of nuns exposed them to other dangers.
70 M I 213–214.
71 One example is M I 274.
72 D III 54.
73 A III 101.
74 Th 31 and 1097.
75 Schmithausen, "The Early Buddhist Tradition and Ecological Ethics," pp. 27–8.
76 *Ārāmaropā vanaropā . . . tesaṃ divā ca ratto ca, sadā puññaṃ pavaḍḍhati . . . te janā saggagāmino ti.* (S I 33)
77 D III 182.
78 *Asīti-vassa-sahassāyukesu bhikkhave manussesu ayaṃ Jambudīpo iddho c'eva bhavissati phīto ca, kukkuṭa-sampātika gāma-nigama-rājadhāniyo. Asīti-vassa-sahassāyukesu bhikkhave manussesu ayaṃ Jambudīpo Avīci maññe phuṭo bhavissati manussehi seyyathā pi nala-vanaṃ vā sara-vanaṃ vā.* (D III 75)
79 Peter Harvey, *An Introduction to Buddhist Ethics*, Cambridge, UK: Cambridge University Press, 2000, p. 183.
80 Ibid. Harvey is referring to Ian Harris's paper "How Environmentalist is Buddhism?" See Ian Harris, "How Environmentalist is Buddhism?," *Religion* 21, 1991, p. 108.
81 Maurice Walshe, "Notes," *The Long Discourses of the Buddha: A Translation of the Dīgha Nikāya*, Boston: Wisdom Publications, 1995, p. 602.
82 *viññanaṃ anidassanaṃ anantaṃ sabbato pahaṃ ettha āpo ca paṭhavī tejo vāyo na gādhati. . . .* (D I 223)
83 For instance, the *Dhātuvibhanga Sutta* of the *Majjhima Nikāya, Sutta* 140.
84 Examples are M I 423 and M III 240–242. I have deliberately not brought up the Buddhist discussion on space as it has no direct significance to the present discussion.
85 *Taṃ: n'etaṃ mama, n'eso 'ham- asmi, na mēso attā ti evam. . . .* (M I 185)
86 A II 164.
87 M I 1f.
88 M I 228.
89 A. Berriedale Keith, *Buddhist Philosophy in India and Ceylon*, India: Chowkhamba Sanskrit Series Office, 1963, p. 94.
90 M I 13.
91 For details of Schmithausen's discussion and references see Chapter 1.
92 M I 500.

93 The 140–41.
94 The 466–68.
95 The basic requisites of food, clothing, shelter and medicines are described for the endurance and protection of the body in M I 10.
96 M I 81.
97 M I 341.
98 D III 113.
99 M I 212.
100 *Tassa mayhaṃ bhikkhave etad-ahosi: Ramaṇīyo vata bho bhūmibhāgo pāsādiko ca vanasaṇḍo, nadī ca sandati setakā sūpatitthā ramaṇīyā, samantā ca gocaragāmo; alaṃ vat' idaṃ kulaputtassa padhānatthikassa padhānāyāti.* (M I 167)
101 Balkrishna Govind Gokhale, *New Light on Early Buddhism*, Mumbai, India: Bombay Popular Prakashan, 1994, p. 87.
102 Th 13, 211–12, 523–25, 1062–1071 and many more.
103 Mrs. Rhys Davids, "Introduction," *Psalms of the Early Buddhists: Psalms of the Brethren*, London: Pali Text Society, 1913, p. xli.
104 S V 64, M I 26. For the philological discussion of *subha nimitta* see Bhikkhu Bodhi, *The Connected Discourses of the Buddha: A New Translation of the Saṃyutta Nikāya*, Vol. II, Boston: Wisdom Publications, 2000, pp. 1899–1900.
105 *Nāhaṃ bhikkhave aññaṃ ekadhamam pi samanupassāmi yena anuppanno vā kāmacchando uppajjati uppanno vā kāmacchando bhiyyo bhāvāya vepullāya saṃvattati yathayidaṃ bhikkhave subha-nimittaṃ.* (A I 2)
106 Colin Edwards, "Response to Letter: The Buddha: Friendship and Beauty," *Buddhist Studies Review* 17, no. 1, 2000: p. 60. The author here is replying to an objection raised by Laurence Khantipalo Mills.
107 Ibid. p. 62.
108 An exception is story XLV of *Theragāthā* where the name *ramanīya-vihārin*, is given to a monk for his attachment to sensual pleasure and not for praises of natural beauty. This makes the use of "*ramanīya*" ambiguous.
109 J. Baird Callicott and Roger T. Ames (eds) "Introduction: The Asian Traditions as a Conceptual Resource for Environmental Philosophy," *Nature in Asian Traditions of Thought: Essays in Environmental Philosophy*, New York: State University of New York Press, 1989; reprinted as Indian edn Delhi: Sri Satguru Publications, 1991, p. 15.
110 David E. Cooper, "Aestheticism and Environmentalism," in David E. Cooper and Joy A. Palmer (eds) *Spirit of the Environment*, London and New York: Routledge, 1998, pp. 110–11.
111 A II 112–113.
112 *Seyathāpi bhikkhave dakkho go-ghātako vā goghātakantevāsī va gāviṃ vadhitvā cātummahāpathe bilaso paṭivibhajitvā nisinno assa, evam eva kho bhikkhave bhikkhu imam eva kāyaṃ yathā-ṭhitam yathā-paṇihitaṃ dhātuso paccavekkhati. . . .* (D II 294)
113 Ryan believes that the Buddha is "honouring" the skills of the butcher in this passage. I would be cautious about such a rendering. Ryan, *Buddhism and the Natural World*, p. 48.
114 My methodology is inspired by Kathryn Blackstone's. However, her context is different. See Kathryn R. Blackstone, *Women in the Footsteps of the Buddha*, Richmond, Surrey: Curzon Press, 1998, pp. 83f.
115 *Tass' eva kho pana bhikkhave mahato migasaṅghassa kocid- eva puriso uppajjeyya atthakāmo hitakāmo yogakkhemakāmo, so yvāssa maggo khemo sovatthiko pītigamanīyo taṃ maggaṃ vivareyya, pidaheyya kummaggaṃ, ūhaneyya okacaraṃ,*

nāseyya okacārikaṃ; evaṃ hi so bhikkhave mahā migasaṅgho aparena samayena vuddhiṃ virūḷhiṃ vepullaṃ āpajjeya. (M I 117)

116 M I 225–226. This example is very reminiscent of the stewardship tradition that has often been seen in the Bible.

117 Dp 82.

118 A I 134–35.

119 Th 77.

120 Dp 244.

121 M I 124.

122 Deleanu, "Buddhist Ethology," p. 121.

123 Ryan, *Buddhism and the Natural World*, p. 62. Ryan has used nature descriptions and metaphors quite extensively to promote the cause of ecology in Buddhism as well. However, his positive conclusions are diametrically opposed to my readings of ambiguity and uncertainty.

3 NATURE: A "COSMOLOGICAL" APPROACH

1 A more detailed discussion is given in the section "*Saṃsāra.*"

2 John Ross Carter, *Dhamma: Western Academic and Sinhalese Buddhist Interpretations: A Study of a Religious Concept*, Tokyo: The Hokuseido Press, 1978, p. 6.

3 Damien Keown, *A Dictionary of Buddhism*, Oxford: Oxford University Press, 2003, p. 74.

4 One example is D II 152, where it is said that a monk goes for refuge to the Blessed Lord, the Buddha, the *Dhamma* and the *Sangha.*

5 See D I 86 and D II 16.

6 S III 132.

7 Mrs Rhys Davids, *Buddhism: A Study of a Buddhist Norm*, London: Williams and Norgate, [1912], p. 33.

8 I. B. Horner, "Introduction," *Middle Length Sayings: A Translation of the Majjhima Nikāya*, London: Pali Text Society, 1954, p. xix.

9 M. Hiriyanna, *The Essentials of Indian Philosophy*, London: George, Allen and Unwin Ltd., 1949, pp. 13–14

10 I am aware that not all scholars agree with tracing the origin of *dhamma* to *ṛta*. However, I shall not be dwelling on this debate and, in general, agree with those who take *ṛta* as expressive of the same ideas as *dhamma.*

11 A. L. Basham, *The Origins and Development of Classical Hinduism*, Kenneth Zysk (ed. and annotated) Boston: Beacon Press, 1989, p. 102.

12 A. T. Embree, [ed.] *The Hindu Tradition*, New York: Vintage Books, 1972, p. 9.

13 *Atharva Veda*, Vol. V, trans. Muir (Original Sanskrit Texts) 64 iv. 16. pp. 1–5; quoted in Radhakrishnan, *Indian Philosophy*, Vol. 1, London: George, Allen and Unwin Ltd, 1940, p. 78.

14 S. Tachibana, *The Ethics of Buddhism*, Oxford: Clarendon Press, 1926; reprinted, London: Curzon Press, 1975, p. 257.

15 Some examples are S I 35, S III 132, M I 161–62 and M I 167.

16 In fact it has categorically been said that, "whoever sees *paṭiccasamuppāda* sees *dhamma*, whoever sees *dhamma* sees *paṭiccasamuppāda.*" (M I 190–91)

17 See Joanna Macy in Chapter 1. Partisan scholars have also used *Paṭiccasamuppāda* as a foundation of ecology.

18 *Imasmiṃ sati, idaṃ hoti; imass'uppādā idaṃ uppajjati imasmiṃ asati, idaṃ na hoti; imassa nirodhā idaṃ nirujjhati; . . .* (M III 63)

19 In S II 101–103 the lust for edible food is taken as the first link.
20 The *Mahānidāna Sutta* of the *Dīgha Nikāya*, for instance, does not contain the link "*saḷāyatana*" or the six-sense basis.
21 S II 25.
22 See the *Mahānidāna Sutta* of the *Dīgha Nikāya*.
23 See the section on animals in the previous chapter for details of animals as moral beings.
24 Ramakrishna Puligandla, "What is the Status of the Doctrine of dependent Origination?" in Frank Hoffman and Deegalle Mahinda (eds) *Pali Buddhism*, Richmond, Surrey: Curzon Press, 1996, p. 175.
25 S I 134.
26 A I 223f.
27 A I 135–136.
28 David J. Kalupahana "Toward a Middle Path of Survival," in J. Baird Callicott and Roger T. Ames (eds) *Nature in Asian Traditions of Thought: Essays in Environmental Philosophy*, New York: State University of New York Press, 1989; reprinted as Indian edn Delhi: Sri Satguru Publications, 1991, p. 252.
29 Ibid. p. 252. The reference here is to A V 313.
30 I am aware that Ian Harris is particularly sceptical about Kalupahana's rendering, but when this issue is looked at from the cosmological perspective rather than the conservationist one, it begins to make sense.
31 Paul Williams (with Anthony Tribe), *Buddhist Thought*, London and New York: Routledge, 2000, p. 63.
32 See T. W. Rhys Davids and William Stede, *Pali-English Dictionary*, s.v. "*saṃsāra*," p. 659.
33 S III 149.
34 M I 74.
35 M I 38–39.
36 D III 234 and M I 73 mention five, the realm of titans is missing here. D III 264 refers to all six realms.
37 M III 165–67.
38 M III 169.
39 *Petās* are mentioned in S II 255. *Asurās* are often spoken of in the *Nikāyas* as being defeated by the gods in war (D II 285, *Bhūtapubbaṃ bhante devāsura-saṃgāmo samūpabbūḷho ahosi . . . devā jiniṃsu, asurā parājiṃsu*).
40 M III 172–78.
41 There is a realm of heaven called Pure Abode or *Suddhāvāse* after which *nibbāna* is attained directly. (M I 81–82)
42 Avner De-Shalit, *Why Posterity Matters*, London and New York: Routledge, 1995, p. 6, emphasis in original.
43 Winston King, *In the Hope of Nibbāna*, La Salle: Open Court, 1964; and Melford E. Spiro, *Buddhism and Society: A Great Tradition and its Burmese Vicissitudes*, Berkeley: University of California Press, 1982.
44 Critics include Harvey Aronson, *Love and Sympathy in Theravada Buddhism*, Delhi: Motilal Banarsidass, 1980; and Damien Keown, *The Nature of Buddhist Ethics*, Basingstoke, Hampshire: Palgrave, 1992, reprinted (with minor alterations) 2001.
45 Aronson, *Love and Sympathy in Theravada Buddhism*, p. 79.
46 James Boyd, "The Theravāda view of Saṃsāra," in Somaratna Balasooriya *et al.* (eds) *Buddhist Studies in Honour of Walpola Rahula*, London: Gordan Fraser, 1980, p. 32. The reference here is to A II 48.
47 Ibid. The reference is S IV 93.
48 Ibid. Boyd is referring to S IV 95.

49 Ibid. p. 37. His reference is S V 8.
50 Ibid. p. 37.
51 *Oxford English Dictionary*, Vol. II, 1970 edn, s.v. "cosmogony," p. 1031.
52 *Dīgha Nikāya, Sutta* 27.
53 Frank E. Reynolds, "Multiple Cosmogonies and Ethics: The Case of Theravada Buddhism," in Robin W. Lovin and Frank E. Reynolds (eds) *Cosmogony and Ethical Order*, Chicago: University of Chicago Press, 1985, pp. 203–24.
54 Under this are discussed (1) Buddha's life, (2) *thūpa* architecture, and (3) lay and monk interaction.
55 *Anamataggāyam bhikkhave saṃsāro pubbakoṭi na paññāyati avijjānīvaraṇānam sattānaṃ taṇhāsaṃyojanānaṃ sandhā vataṃ saṃsarataṃ.* (S II 178)
56 Arthur Fabel, "Environmental Ethics and the Question of Cosmic Purpose," *Environmental Ethics* 1, no. 3, 1994, p. 307.
57 Michael Carrithers, *Why Humans Have Cultures: Explaining Anthropology and Social Diversity*, Oxford: Oxford University Press, 1992, p. 82.
58 Richard Gombrich, "The Buddha's Book of Genesis?" in *Indo-Iranian Journal* 35, 1992, pp. 159–178.
59 Richard Gombrich, *How Buddhism Began: The Conditioned Genesis of the Early Buddhist Teaching*, N.J.: Athlone, 1996, p. 82.
60 *Khattiyo pi kho Vāseṭṭha kāyena duccaritaṃ caritvā, vācāya duccaritaṃ caritvā, manasā duccaritaṃ caritvā, miccha-diṭṭhiko, micchā-diṭṭhi-kamma-samādāna-hetu kāyassa bhedā param maraṇā apāyaṃ duggatiṃ vinipātaṃ nirayaṃ upapajjati. Brahmano pi kho . . . Vesso pi kho . . . Suddo pi kho . . .* (D III 96)
61 Thomas Fawcett, *The Symbolic Language of Religion: An Introductory Study*, London: SCM Press, 1970, p. 109.
62 An extensive discussion of Buddhist cosmogony and the evolution of elements has been undertaken by P. D. Ryan. For a more detailed analysis of the myth see P. D. Ryan, *Buddhism and the Natural World*, Birmingham: Windhorse Publications, 1998, pp. 77–103.
63 Paul Waldau, "Speciesism in Christianity and Buddhism," unpublished thesis, University of Oxford, 1998, p. 62.
64 James Gustafson, *Ethics from a Theocentric Perspective*, Vol. 1, Chicago: The University of Chicago Press, 1981. Summarized in Lovin and Reynolds. Robin W. Lovin and Frank E. Reynolds, (eds) "In the Beginning," *Cosmogony and Ethical Order*, Chicago: University of Chicago Press, 1985, p. 2.
65 Yrjo Haila and Richard Levins, *Humanity and Nature*, London: Pluto Press, 1992, pp. 10–12.
66 Allan Greenbaum, "Environmental Thought as Cosmological Intervention," *Environmental Values*, 8, 1999, p. 493.
67 Tibor R. Machan, "Do Animals Have Rights?" in James E. White (ed.) *Contemporary Moral Problems*, Sixth Edn; Belmont, CA: Wadsworth Publishing Company, 2000, p. 512. In his last analysis, Machan does not give humans freedom to do with non-humans as they please.
68 Eugene Hargrove, "Weak Anthropocentric Intrinsic Value," in Andrew Light and Holmes Rolston III (eds) *Environmental Ethics: An Anthology*, Oxford: Blackwell Publishing, 2003, p. 175.
69 Tim Hayward, "Anthropocentrism: A Misunderstood Problem," in *Environmental Values 6*, 1997, 49.
70 Val Plumwood, "Paths Beyond Human-Centeredness: Lessons From Liberation Struggles," in Anthony Weston (ed.) *An Invitation to Environmental Philosophy*, New York and Oxford: Oxford University Press, 1999, p. 75.
71 For example Hargrove, "Weak Anthropocentric Intrinsic Value," and Bryan G.

Norton, "Environmental Ethics and Weak Anthropocentrism," in Andrew Light and Holmes Rolston III (eds) *Environmental Ethics: An Anthology*, Oxford: Blackwell Publishing, 2003.

72 Hargrove, "Weak Anthropocentric Intrinsic Value," p. 175.

73 Norton, "Environmental Ethics and Weak Anthropocentrism," pp. 164–5. This entire paragraph, is in fact, based on Norton's argument but differs in detail.

74 John O'Neill, "The Varieties of Intrinsic Value," in Andrew Light and Holmes Rolston III (eds) *Environmental Ethics: An Anthology*, Oxford: Blackwell Publishers Ltd, 2003, p. 139.

75 W. H. Murdy, "Anthropocentrism: A Modern Version," in Donald Scherer and Thomas Attig (eds) *Ethics and the Environment*, New Jersey: Prentice-Hall, 1983, p. 20.

76 The use of these virtues is deliberate as these are the four *Brahma-vihāras* or sublime attitudes of early Buddhism. I will elaborate further on these in the next chapter.

77 One of the major proponents of biocentrism, Paul Taylor, suggested some rules for making such decisions. But these rules face crucial limitations that have often been challenged. See Paul Taylor, *Respect for Nature*, Princeton: Princeton University Press, 1986.

78 The discussion in this paragraph is inspired by Tim Hayward's, "Anthropocentrism: A Misunderstood Problem," pp. 60–62. It also draws from Norton's analysis of weak anthropocentrism.

79 Certain aspects of Buddhism have been referred to as anthropocentric by Lambert Schmithausen (See Chapter 1).

80 Of course the argument need not be taken a step forward at all. But this is at the risk of being inconclusive particularly when the discussion insinuates such an outcome overwhelmingly.

81 Dp 166.

82 *Kathañca bhikkhave attānaṃ rakkhanto paraṃ rakkhati, āsevanāya bhāvanāya bahulīkammena . . . Kathañca bhikkhave paraṃ rakkhanto attānaṃ rakkhati, khantiyā avihiṃsāya mettatāya anudayatāya . . .* (S V 169)

83 Steven Collins, *Selfless Persons: Imagery and Thought in Theravāda Buddhism*, Cambridge: Cambridge University Press, 1982, p. 193.

84 M I 45.

85 Piyadassi Thera, *The Buddha's Ancient Path*, London: Rider and Company, 1964, p.179.

86 A II 95.

87 A IV 134–135. The word used for "advantage" in this case is *attha*, however I doubt it is being used in the economic sense. One meaning of *attha* in the *Pali-English Dictionary* is "(moral) good, blessing or welfare" and fits into this context. See Rhys Davids and Stede, *Pali-English Dictionary*, s.v. "attha," 23.

88 D II 45, S I 105 and many other places in the *Nikāyas.*

89 The reference here is to Mahākassapa, who lives secluded in a forest for a pleasant dwelling for himself and also because he has compassion for later generations who might learn from his example. (S II 202–203)

90 K. Jayatilleke, "The Ethical Theory of Buddhism," *The Mahābodhi* 78, 1970, p. 195; quoted in Damien Keown, *The Nature of Buddhist Ethics*, Basingstoke, Hampshire: Palgrave, 1992; reprinted (with minor alterations) 2001, p. 7.

91 I would be cautious here because there are problems with merging the interests of beings in an environmental setting. Interests may coincide sometimes but not at others.

92 Tim Hayward, "Anthropocentrism," from *Encyclopedia of Applied Ethics*, Vol. 1, 1998, p. 179. This paragraph is inspired by Hayward's very excellent description.
93 I will argue that this is not the case in the next chapter.
94 It has often been questioned whether Buddhism is a religion at all. I am in agreement with Damien Keown that it is. He adequately demonstrates how in his book *Buddhism: A Very Short Introduction*. See Damien Keown, *Buddhism: A Very Short Introduction*, Oxford: Oxford University Press, 1996, pp. 3–15.
95 Laura Westra, "Virtue Ethics as Foundational for a Global Ethic," in Ronald Sandler and Philip Cafaro (eds) *Environmental Virtue Ethics*, Lanham, Boulder: Rowman and Littlefield Publishers, Inc., 2005, p. 81.

4 ENVIRONMENTAL VIRTUE ETHICS IN EARLY BUDDHISM

1 For instance, the five precepts can be looked upon as instructive virtues; their nature will be discussed in the next chapter.
2 Alan Sponberg, "The Buddhist Conception of an Ecological Self," in Sallie B. King and Paul O. Ingram (eds) *The Sound of Liberating Truth: Buddhist-Christian Dialogues in Honour of Frederick J Streng*, Richmond, Surrey: Curzon Press, 1999, pp. 107–27; David J. Kalupahana, *Ethics in Early Buddhism*, Honolulu: University of Hawaii Press, 1975.
3 David E. Cooper and Simon P. James, *Buddhism, Virtue and the Environment*, U.K.: Ashgate, 2005.
4 Daniel Statman (ed.) *Virtue Ethics: A Critical Reader*, Edinburgh: Edinburgh University Press, 1977, p. 2. This section is in fact inspired by Statman's book.
5 David Solomon has mentioned this division impressively. The following example is mine. See David Solomon, "Internal Objections to Virtue Ethics," in Daniel Statman (ed.) *Virtue Ethics: A Critical Reader*, Edinburgh: Edinburgh University Press, 1997, p. 166.
6 Statman, *Virtue Ethics*, p. 7, emphasis in original. He mentions just the first two forms.
7 G. E. M. Anscombe, "Modern Moral Philosophy," *Philosophy* XXXIII, 1958, pp. 8–9. I also relied upon Phillip Montague's understanding of this view. See his "Virtue Ethics: A Qualified Success Story," in Daniel Statman (ed.) *Virtue Ethics: A Critical Reader*, Edinburgh: Edinburgh University Press, 1997, p. 194.
8 Michael Slote, *From Morality to Virtue*, New York, Oxford: Oxford University Press, 1992, p. 89. Emphasis in original.
9 James Rachels, "The Ethics of Virtue," in Christina Sommers and Fred Sommers (eds) *Vice and Virtue in Everyday Life*, Fort Worth: Harcourt College Publishers, 2001, pp. 352–3, emphasis in original.
10 Robert B. Louden, "On Some Vices of Virtue Ethics," in Daniel Statman (ed.) *Virtue Ethics: A Critical Reader*, Edinburgh: Edinburgh University Press, 1997, p. 191.
11 See a translation of Plato's *Meno* in *The Dialogues of Plato*, Vol. I, trans. with analysis R. E. Allen, New Haven and London: Yale University Press, 1984. The definition of "virtue" is an important feature of any virtue ethics. Various attempts have been made to define the concept. Among classical thinkers, B. Spinoza saw virtue as ". . . the very essence, or nature, of man, insofar as he has the power of bringing about certain things, which can be understood through the laws of his nature alone." See Benedict De Spinoza, *Ethics*, ed. and trans. by Edwin Curley, USA: Princeton University Press, 1994; Penguin Books, 1996, p. 117. Another is the view of modern day ethicist Andre Comte-Sponville who believes that a virtue, among other things "is a force that has or can have an effect." See Andre Comte-

Sponville, *A Short Treatise on the Great Virtues*, trans. Catherine Temerson, Great Britain: Vintage, 2003, p. 2. A more typically ethical definition is Steven Duncan's, who writes that "any trait that we see or discover to be a necessary condition for participation in the intrinsic good is a virtue. . . ." See Steven M. Duncan, *A Primer of Modern Virtue Ethics*, Lanham, New York: University Press of America, p. 78.

12 Intention plays an important role in early Buddhism as well, as will be pointed out later.

13 Both Philippa Foot and Rosalind Hursthouse have devoted considerable attention to the question of intention.

14 Philippa Foot, *Virtues and Vices*, Oxford: Basil Blackwell, 1978, p. 2.

15 Rosalind Hursthouse, *On Virtue Ethics*, Oxford: Oxford University Press, 1999, p. 123.

16 Aristotle, *The Ethics of Aristotle: The Nichomachean Ethics*, trans. J. A. K. Thompson. Revised by Hugh Tredennick. Intro and Bibliography by Jonathan Barnes, revised edition, London: Penguin Books, 1976, Book 1, p. 7.

17 Richard Norman, *The Moral Philosophers* Oxford: Clarendon Press, 1983, p. 42.

18 James Whitehill, "Buddhism and the Virtues," in Damien Keown (ed.) *Contemporary Buddhist Ethics*, Richmond, Surrey: Curzon Press, 2000, p. 17. This article first appeared in 1994.

19 Barbara Clayton, "Ethics in the Śikṣā-samuccaya: A Study in Mahāyāna Morality" unpublished thesis, McGill University, 2002, p. 181.

20 Ibid.

21 Damien Keown, *The Nature of Buddhist Ethics*, Basingstoke, Hampshire: Palgrave, 1992; reprinted (with minor alterations) 2001, pp. 177–9.

22 A I 249–250

23 Peter Harvey, *An Introduction to Buddhist Ethics*, Cambridge, UK: Cambridge University Press, 2000, p. 26.

24 *Cetanāhaṃ bhikkhave kammaṃ vadāmi; cetayitvā kammaṃ karoti kāyena vācāya manasā.* (A III 415)

25 . . . *ekacco sāpekho dānaṃ deti, paṭibaddha citto dānaṃ deti, sannidhipekho dānaṃ deti, 'imaṃ pecca paribhuñjissāmī' ti dānaṃ deti.*
. . . *ekacco na h'eva kho sāpekho dānaṃ deti, na paṭibaddhacitto dānaṃ deti, na sannidhipekho dānaṃ deti, na 'imaṃ pecca paribhuñjissāmi' ti dānaṃ deti, api ca kho 'sāhu dānan' ti dānaṃ deti* . . . (A IV 61)

26 *Dīgha Nikāya, Sutta* 31.

27 Peter Harvey, *An Introduction to Buddhist Ethics*, p. 51.

28 See Keown, *The Nature of Buddhist Ethics*, p. 58. More will be said on *Abhidhamma* and the virtues in the next section.

29 Padmasiri de Silva, "Buddhist Ethics," in Peter Singer (ed.) *A Companion to Ethics*, Oxford: Blackwell Publishers Ltd, 1991; reprinted in paperback (with corrections) 1993, p. 64.

30 Edward Conze, *Buddhist Thought in India*, London: George, Allen and Unwin Ltd, 1962, pp. 47–55. More will be said on wisdom as a virtue later.

31 See Keown, *The Nature of Buddhist Ethics*, pp. 57f; and Whitehill, "Buddhism and the Virtues," pp. 17–36.

32 I shall be using the words insight and wisdom synonymously to represent *paññā*.

33 Whitehill, "Buddhism and the Virtues," p. 23.

34 *Taṇhakkhayo hi Rādha nibbānan ti.* (S III 190)

35 Keown, *The Nature of Buddhist Ethics*, p. 202, emphasis in original.

36 Gary Watson, "On the Primacy of Character," in Daniel Statman (ed.) *Virtue Ethics: A Critical Reader*, Edinburgh: Edinburgh University Press, 1997, p. 57, emphasis in original.

37 Th 70.
38 Edward Conze, *Buddhist Thought in India*, p. 55.
39 Harvey, *An Introduction to Buddhist Ethics*, p. 41.
40 See next section on *Abhidhamma.*
41 This is essentially inspired by the methodology that Rosalind Hursthouse has adopted in her book *On Virtue Ethics*, where her argument is mostly defensive. She finds it unfair that certain criticisms are levied against virtue ethics that hold equally towards consequentialism and deontology. The example, however, is mine.
42 Th 614.
43 Harvey, *An Introduction to Buddhist Ethics*, p. 5.
44 Keown, *The Nature of Buddhist Ethics*, p. 59. Keown's entire analysis and insight are extremely important even though he has relied on *The Treasury of Metaphysics* (and therefore, the *Abhidharma*) rather than *Therāvadin Abhidhamma.*
45 Peter Harvey, *An Introduction to Buddhism*, Cambridge: Cambridge University Press, 1990, p. 83.
46 Narada Mahathera, "A Simple Introduction to Abhidhamma," [*Sambhasha* 56, 1948, pp. 97–8].
47 The synthesis and conditionality of the *dhammas* is shown in a later book (*Paṭṭhāna*, Book 7).
48 Keown, *The Nature of Buddhist Ethics*, p. 60.
49 Ibid. This reference is from *Visuddhimagga* I 17.
50 Ibid.
51 The *Dhammasangani* classifies the neutral category into two – results of action (*vipāka*) and the neutral functions of action (*kriyā*).
52 One example is Christmas Humphreys definition. See Christmas Humphreys, *A Popular Dictionary of Buddhism*, London: Curzon Press, 1984, p. 57.
53 Keown, *The Nature of Buddhist Ethics*, p. 62.
54 Herbert V. Guenther, *Philosophy and Psychology in the Abhidharma*, Delhi: Motilal Banarsidass Publishers Private Limited; Second Revised edition, 1974, p. 12.
55 Details of the *Dhammasangani* categories is from Nyanatiloka's book. See Nyanatiloka Mahathera, *Guide Through the Abhidhamma-Piṭaka*, Kandy, Ceylon: Buddhist Publication Society, 1971, pp. 12–19.
56 Nyanaponika, *Abhidhamma Studies: Researches in Buddhist Psychology*, Colombo: Frewin and Co. Ltd., 1949, p. 48.
57 Lama Anagarika Govinda, *The Psychological Attitude of Early Buddhist Philosophy*, Great Britain, 1961; reprinted, Delhi: Motilal Banarsidass Publishers Private Limited, 1991, p. 115.
58 Ibid.
59 Ibid.
60 Keown, *The Nature of Buddhist Ethics*, p. 63.
61 I have not mentioned these as they are not directly relevant for the ongoing discussion.
62 This format is the one followed by Lama Govinda. For more details see Lama Govinda, *Psychological Attitude of Early Buddhist Philosophy*, pp. 115–25. The translation of *hirī* and *ahirika* is mine.
63 Ibid. p. 122.
64 Harvey, *An Introduction to Buddhism*, p. 84.
65 For this and more details see Nina van Gorkom, *Cetasikas*, London: Zolag, 1999, pp. 4–6.
66 Lama Govinda, *Psychological Attitude of Early Buddhist Philosophy*, p. 99.
67 The *Abhidhamma* also seems centrally concerned with this question, as has become clear from the previous section.

68 Geoffrey B. Frasz, "Environmental Virtue Ethics," *Environmental Ethics* 15, no. 3 1993, pp. 259–60.
69 Thomas E. Hill Jr, "Ideals of Human Excellence and Preserving Natural Environments," in David Schmidtz and Elizabeth Willott (eds) *Environmental Ethics: What Really Matters, What Really Works*, New York, Oxford: Oxford University Press, 2002, p. 192, emphasis in original.
70 The term is translated as "a sense of shame" in T. W. Rhys Davids and William Stede's *Pali-English Dictionary*. However, Keown in his book *The Nature of Buddhist Ethics* understands it as "modesty." The dictionary also recognizes both "*hiri*" and "*hirī*" as valid transliterated terms. In this text I shall be using the latter.
71 S II 206.
72 *Hirīnisedhā tanuyā. Ye caranti sadā satā*
Antaṃ dukkhassa pappuyya. Caranti visame saman-ti. (S I 7)
73 *Pare ahirikā bhavissanti, mayam-ettha hirimanā bhavissāmāti. . . .* (M I 43)
74 Even though the texts do not treat *hirī* as the opposite of *ahaṃkāra* (as is made clear in M I 363, where it is said that with the support of non-arrogance, arrogance is to be abandoned, *Anatimānaṃ nissāya atimāno pahātabbo*) there is no doubt that the absence of the latter is conducive to the presence of the former.
75 Sn 4.
76 *Tesaṃ vaṇṇātimāna-paccayā mānātimāna-jātikānaṃ rasa-paṭhavī antaradhāyi.* (D III 86).
77 M I 185.
78 Walpole Rahula, *What the Buddha Taught*, 2nd enlarged edition London and Bedford: Gordan Fraser, 1967; reprinted as Gordan Fraser paperback, 1978, p. 51.
79 S III 44–45.
80 M I 47.
81 Hill, "Ideals of Human Excellence," p. 196.
82 Kathryn R.Blackstone, *Women in the Footsteps of the Buddha*, Richmond, Surrey: Curzon Press, 1998, p. 83.
83 Rahula, *What the Buddha Taught*, p. 68.
84 Frasz, "Environmental Virtue Ethics," p. 274.
85 The *Brahma-vihāras* can be treated as virtues. It is interesting to note that Roderick Hindery while speaking of Hindu ethics singled out *ahiṃsā, dāna, satya* (truth) and *niṣkāma-karma* (non-attached action) as four key Hindu virtues. He then goes on to say that *dāna* may be compared to the four compassionate virtues (*Brahma-vihāras*) of Buddhism. Thus, clearly, the *Brahma-vihāras* are virtues according to his analysis. However, I treat them as virtues simply because they fit in with the definition of "virtue" given earlier in this chapter. See Roderick Hindery, *Comparative Ethics in Hindu and Buddhist Traditions*, Delhi: Motilal Banarsidass, 1978, pp. 27–8.
86 M I 169.
87 A I 211.
88 Keown, *The Nature of Buddhist Ethics*, pp. 72–3.
89 Harvey Aronson, *Love and Sympathy in Theravāda Buddhism*, Delhi: Motilal Banarsidass, 1980, pp. 14–15.
90 Ibid. p. 16.
91 *Tasmā ti ha bhikkhave evaṃ sikkhitabbaṃ. Mettā no cetovimutti bhāvitā bhavissati. Bahulikatā yānikatā vatthukatā anuṭṭhitā paricitā susamāraddhāti.* (S II 264)
92 M I 351.
93 M I 424.
94 M I 127.

95 . . . *so mettāsahagatena cetasā ekaṃ disaṃ pharitvā viharāmi tathā dutiyaṃ tathā tatiyaṃ tathā catutthiṃ. Iti uddham adho tiriyaṃ sabbadhi sabbattatāya sabbāvantaṃ lokaṃ mettāsahagatena cetasā vipulena mahaggatena appamāṇena averena avyāpajjhena pharitvā viharāmi. Karuṇāsahagatena cetasā* . . . *muditāsahagatena cetasā* . . . *upekkhāsahagatena cetasā*. . . . (A I 183)

96 Katie McShane, "Anthropocentrism vs. Nonanthropocentrism: Why Should We Care?" Joint Conference Papers: 8, http://www.environmentalphilosophy.org/environmentalphilosophy/upcoming/katie_mcshane-anthropocentrism_vs._nonanthropocentrism.pdf (accessed 14 January 2006), Emphasis in original.

97 M I 123–124.

98 Sn 142–151.

99 . . . *sukhino vā khemino hontu, sabbe sattā bhavantu sukhitaṭṭā.* (Sn 144)

100 Harvey, *An Introduction to Buddhism*, p. 209.

5 THE ENVIRONMENTAL VIRTUES OF EARLY BUDDHISM

1 Ronald Sandler, "Introduction: Environmental Virtue Ethics," in Ronald Sandler and Philip Cafaro (eds) *Environmental Virtue Ethics*, Lanham, Boulder: Rowman and Littlefield Publishers, Inc., 2005, p. 3.

2 A III 53.

3 This refers to the range of precepts contained in the *Vinaya*.

4 *Dīgha Nikāya, Sutta* 1.

5 M I 181.

6 Many of the virtues and vices discussed in this section are found in the *Abhidhammic* discussion of *citta* and *cetasika*. For instance, insight or *paññā* is a *kusala* state or virtue and hatred or *dosa* is an *akusala* state or vice. For a detailed discussion see the section on *Abhidhamma* in the previous chapter.

7 *Pāṇātipātaṃ pahāya pāṇātipātā paṭivirato Samaṇo Gotamo nihita-daṇḍo nihita-sattho lajjī dayāpanno sabb- pāṇa-bhūta-hitānukampī viharatī ti.* (D I 4)

8 *sabbe tasanti daṇḍassa*
sabbesaṃ jīvita piyaṃ
Attānaṃ upamaṃ katvā
Na haneyya na ghātaye (Dp 130)

9 Th 602–03.

10 *Pañc'imā bhikkhave vaṇijjā upāsakena akaraṇīyā. Katamā pañca? Satthavaṇijjā, sattavaṇijjā, maṃsavaṇijjā, majjavaṇijjā, visavaṇijjā.* (A III 208)

11 M I 343. There is also a discussion on the unfortunate fate of cow-butchers in S II 255f.

12 The 242–43.

13 Th 143–44

14 See Chapter 1 (the section on Schmithausen) and Chapter 2 (the section on Plants) for more details.

15 Th 77.

16 *Appassādā kāmā vuttā mayā bahudukkhā bahupāyāsā, ādīnavo ettha bhiyyo* . . . (M I 132)

17 M I 132f.

18 The 58.

19 A II 27–29.

20 A II 205.

21 A V 181–82. For an interesting discussion on wealth see Frank E. Reynolds, "Ethics and Wealth in Theravāda Buddhism," in Russell F. Sizemore and Donald

K. Swearer (eds) *Ethics, Wealth and Salvation: A Study in Buddhist Social Ethics*, South Carolina: University of South Carolina Press, 1990, pp. 59–76.

22 A III 48.

23 A IV 61. For more on *dāna* see D III 258f, where the eight bases for giving and the eight rebirths that may follow for a moral person are clarified.

24 Sn 101.

25 *Ahaṃ kho pana Vaccha evaṃ vadāmi: ye pi te candanikāya vā oḷigalle vā pāṇā tatra pi yo thāli-dhovanaṃ vā sarāvadhovanaṃ vā chaḍḍeti- ye tattha pāṇā te yena yāpentū ti- tatonidānaṃ pāhaṃ Vaccha puññassa āgamaṃ vadāmi, kho pana vādo manussabhūte.* (A I 161)

26 For why Buddhism cannot be purely consequential see the previous chapter.

27 An examination of the nature of duty in relation to the environment in Buddhism also makes the Buddhist position as a form of moderate environmental virtue ethics more plausible.

28 *Dīgha Nikāya, Sutta* 31.

29 P. D. Ryan, *Buddhism and the Natural World*, Birmingham: Windhorse Publications, 1998, p. 100.

30 Hans Jonas, *The Imperative of Responsibility: In Search for an Ethics for the Technological Age*, trans. Hans Jonas with the collaboration of David Herr, Chicago and London: University of Chicago Press, 1984, p. 39.

31 Ibid. p. 90.

32 *Puna ca paraṃ brāhmaṇa etarahi manussā adhammarāgarattā visamalobhābhibhūtā micchādhammaparetā. Tesaṃ adhammarāgarattānaṃ visamalobhābhibhūtānaṃ micchādhammaparetānaṃ devo na sammā dhāraṃ anuppavecchati. Tena dubbhikkhaṃ hoti dussassaṃ setaṭṭhikaṃ salākāvuttaṃ tena bahū manussā kālaṃ karonti.* (A I 159–160)

33 . . . *visamaṃ candamasuriyā parivattanti* . . . *visamaṃ nakkhattāni tārakarūpāni parivattanti* . . . *visamaṃ rattindivā parivattanti* . . . *māsaddhmāsā parivattanti* . . . *visamaṃ utusaṃvaccharā parivattanti* . . . *visamaṃ vātā vāyanti visamaṃ apañjasā, visamaṃ vātesu vāyantesu visamesu apañjasesu devatā parikupitā bhavanti, devatāsu parikupitāsu devo na sammādhāraṃ anupanecchati, deve na sammādhāraṃ anuparecchante visamapākīni sassāni bhavanti, visamapākīni bhikkhave sassāni manussā paribhuñjantā appāyukā ca honti dubbaṇṇā ca dubbalā ca bavhābādhā ca.* (A II 74)

34 Another instance where this passage has been cited is in a discussion on morality by Lily de Silva, "The Hills Wherein My Soul Delights," in Martine Batchelor and Kerry Brown (eds) *Buddhism and Ecology*, London, UK: Cassell Publishers Limited, 1992, p. 20.

35 See James Paul McDermott, "Is there Group Karma in Theravada Buddhism?" *Numen* XXIII, Fasc. 1, 1976, p. 80.

36 Sue Hamilton, *Early Buddhism: A New Approach: The I of the Beholder*, Richmond, Surrey: Curzon Press, 2000, p. 214, emphasis in original.

37 John Passmore, "Attitudes to Nature," in Robert Elliot (ed.) *Environmental Ethics*, Oxford: Oxford University Press, 1995, p. 137.

38 A II 211–212.

39 Sn 1033.

40 Dp 15.

41 M III 163–65.

42 Th 494.

43 *Aṭṭhani bhikkhave asaddhamehi abhibhūto pariyādinna citto Devadatto āpāyiko nerayiko kappaṭṭho atekiccho.* (A IV 158) This however is quite a mild description.

44 *Taṇhaṃ paṭicca pariyesanā, pariyesanaṃ paṭicca lābho, lābhaṃ paṭicca vinicchayo, vinicchayaṃ paṭicca chandarāgo* . . . (A IV 400–401)
45 S I 117.
46 G. P. Malalasekera, "The Status of the Individual in Theravada Buddhism." *Philosophy East and West* XIV, no. 2, 1964, 152.
47 M I 51.
48 A IV 88–89.
49 Sn 164.
50 *Tīhi kho ahaṃ Jīvaka ṭhānehi maṃsaṃ aparibhogan- ti vadāmi: diṭṭhaṃ sutaṃ parisaṅkitaṃ*. (M I 369)
51 *Yam-pi so evamāha: gacchatha amukaṃ nāma pāṇaṃ ānethāti, iminā paṭhamena ṭhānena bahuṃ apuññaṃ pasavati; yam-pi so pāṇo galappavedhakena ānīyamāno dukkhaṃ domanassaṃ paṭisaṃvedeti, iminā dutiyena . . .; yam-pi so evam- āha: gacchatha imaṃ pāṇaṃ ārabhathāti, iminā tatiyena . . .; yam-pi so pāṇo ārabhiyamāno dukkhaṃ domanassaṃ paṭisaṃvedeti, iminā catutthena . . .; yam-pi so Tathāgataṃ vā Tathāgatasāvakaṃ vā akappiyena āsādeti, iminā pañcamena* . . . (M I 371)
52 Vin IV 87.
53 Rupert Gethin, *The Foundations of Buddhism*, Oxford: Oxford University Press, 1998, p. 173.
54 *Yad-eva tvaṃ Rāhula kāyena kammaṃ kattukāmo hosi tad-eva te kāyakammaṃ paccavekkhitabbaṃ: Yaṃ nu kho ahaṃ idaṃ kāyena kammaṃ kattukāmo idam-me kāyakammaṃ attabyābādhāya pi saṃvatteyya parabyābādhāya pi saṃvatteyya ubhayabyābādhāya pi saṃvatteyya, akusalaṃ idaṃ kāyakammaṃ dukkhadrayaṃ dukkhavipākan-ti.* (M I 415)
55 This instance and the next are reminiscent of consequentialism. For detailed discussion of consequentialism and other theories see Chapter 4.
56 Dp 290.
57 This question was tackled in the previous chapter with reference to virtue theory as well.
58 Louke van Wensveen, "The Emergence of Ecological Virtue language," in Ronald Sandler and Philip Cafaro (eds) *Environmental Virtue Ethics*, Lanham, Boulder: Rowman and Littlefield Publishers, Inc., 2005, p. 27.
59 David Schmidtz and Matt Zwolinski, "Virtue Ethics and Repugnant Conclusions," in Ronald Sandler and Philip Cafaro (eds) *Environmental Virtue Ethics*, Lanham, Boulder: Rowman and Littlefield Publishers, Inc., 2005, p. 114.
60 Alan Sponberg, "The Buddhist Conception of an Ecological Self," in Sallie B. King and Paul O. Ingram (eds) *The Sound of Liberating Truth: Buddhist-Christian Dialogues in Honour of Frederick J Streng*, Richmond, Surrey: Curzon Press, 1999, p. 125, emphasis in original.
61 Philip Cafaro, "Thoreau, Leopold and Carson: Towards an Environmental Virtue Ethics," *Environmental Ethics* 23, no. 1, 2001, p. 4.

6 ENVIRONMENTAL VIRTUE ETHICS IN THE *JĀTAKAS*

1 T. W. Rhys Davids, *Buddhist India*, London: 1903; reprint, Delhi: Motilal Banarsidass Publishers Private Limited, 197, pp. 207–8.
2 James Whitehill, "Buddhism and the Virtues," in Damien Keown (ed.) *Contemporary Buddhist Ethics*, Richmond, Surrey: Curzon Press, 2000, p. 27.
3 K. R. Norman, *Pali Literature*, Wiesbaden: Otto Harrassowitz, 1983, p. 81.
4 The *Jātakatthavaṇṇanā* includes the commentary on the *Jātaka* book.
5 Nirmala Salgado, "The Structure of Evil and Ethical Action," 310–311.

6 See Alan Sponberg, "The Buddhist Conception of an Ecological Self," in Sallie B. King and Paul O. Ingram (eds) *The Sound of Liberating Truth: Buddhist-Christian Dialogues in Honour of Frederick J. Streng*, Richmond, Surrey: Curzon Press, 1999, pp. 121–2.
7 Lambert Schmithausen, *Buddhism and Nature*, Studia Philologica Buddhica Occasional Paper Series VII, Tokyo: The International Institute for Buddhist Studies, 1991, pp. 20–21
8 Lambert Schmithausen, *The Problem of Sentience in Earliest Buddhism*, Studio Philologica Buddhica Monograph Series, VI, Tokyo: The International Institute for Buddhist Studies, 1991.
9 Lambert Schmithausen, "The Early Buddhist Tradition and Ecological Ethics," *Journal of Buddhist Ethics* 4, 1997, p. 31, http://jbe.gold.ac.uk (accessed 7 October 1999). The hermit strand was mentioned in Chapter 1.
10 Christopher Key Chapple, "Animals and Environment in the Buddhist Birth Stories," in Mary Evelyn Tucker and Duncan Ryūken Williams (eds) *Buddhism and Ecology: The Interconnection of Dharma and Deeds*, Cambridge, Massachusetts: Cambridge University Press, 1997, pp. 131–48.
11 Rafe Martin, "Thoughts on the Jatakas," in Stephanie Kaza and Kenneth Kraft (eds) *Dharma Rain*, Boston, London: Shambhala Press, 2000, p. 106.
12 Ananda K. Coomaraswamy, *Buddha and the Gospel of Buddhism*, London: George G. Harrap and Company, 1916; reprint, rev. New York: Harper and Row Publishers, 1964, p. 267.
13 According to K. R. Norman it is hard to establish the exact number of stories even though Fausboll's Pali edition contains 547 tales. See Norman, *Pali Literature*, p. 79.
14 The *bodhisatta* is generally understood as a being striving to attain *nibbāna* over countless births.
15 I also refer variously to the *Jātakas* as folklore, stories, tales and parables as I find it is not inconsistent to address them by any of these titles. It would be hard to classify them specifically as one type or other.
16 Rhys Davids, *Buddhist India*, p. 207.
17 J I 441–3. This story has been discussed for its positive environmental value alone by Chapple.
18 Chapple, "Buddhist Birth Stories," p. 141.
19 J III 33–5.
20 J III 208–10.
21 J I 198–206.
22 . . . *musalena pāsāṇe ubbattetvā pavaṭṭenti, yānānaṃ akkhapaṭighātarukkhe haranti, visamaṃ samaṃ karonti, setuṃ attharanti, pokkharaṇiyo khaṇanti, sālaṃ karonti, dānāni denti, sīlaṃ rakkhanti.* . . . (J I 199)
23 J I 322–7.
24 J IV 236
25 J III 375. It is stated "*amaccā dārūnaṃ sakaṭasatamattena citakaṃ kariṃsu.*"
26 J II 60–63.
27 J IV 236–42.
28 Holmes Rolston III, "Environmental Virtue Ethics: Half the Truth but Dangerous as a Whole," in Ronald Sandler and Philip Cafaro (eds) *Environmental Virtue Ethics*, Lanham, Boulder: Rowman and Littlefield Publishers, Inc., 2005, p. 72. Italics in original.
29 J I 145–53.
30 J III 369–75.

31 *taṃ maṃ na tapate bandho, vadho me na tapessati*
sukham āharitaṃ tesaṃ yesaṃ rajjam akārayiṃ. (J III 373)

32 A similar duty is assigned to kings in the *Nikāyas*. An example is D III 61. These examples appear to contradict the notion of anthropocentrism (weak or otherwise), as was supported in other parts of the Canon, where looking after your own self interest is primary. However it must be remembered that these tales signify exemplary personalities whose own identity and self-interest get inextricably tangled with that of whom they are responsible for. Thus here the sense of responsibility runs deeper than self-interest, but in a way it does not overrule the latter. Rather it is inclusive of it. More will be said on the anthropocentric nature of these tales later.

33 The *samodhāna* of the *littajātaka* (J I 379–80) contains the warning from the Buddha ".... the thoughtless use of things is like the thoughtless taking of deadly poison" (... *bhikkhave apaccavekkhitaparibhogo nāma apaccavekkhitvā katavisaparibhogosadiso hotī ti*, J I 380).

34 J IV 288–97.

35 J III 106–9.

36 J I 106–10.

37 J I 126–33.

38 J III 84–6.

39 The *Vātamigajātaka* tells the story of a deer, who in order to satisfy his craving for honey, was captured by the royal gardener. *Rasataṇhā* is seen as one of the basest cravings. (J I 156–9)

40 J V 67–74. This *Mahākapijātaka* is different from the one mentioned earlier. Occasionally *Jātaka* stories share common names.

41 J I 272–5.

42 J II 262–3.

43 *puttadāram pi ce hantvā deti dānaṃ asaññato*
bhuñjamāno pi sappañño na pāpena upalippatīti (J II 263).

44 The debate on meat-eating based on the *Nikāyas* is included in Chapter 5.

45 J II 251–60.

46 J II 121–5.

47 *sace hi rājā adhammiko hoti devo akāle vassati kāle na vassati, chātakabhayaṃ rogabhayaṃ satthabhayan ti imāni tīṇi bhayāni upagatān* ... (J II 124)

48 Chapple, "Buddhist Birth Stories," pp. 145–6. Chapple has listed the different types of animals exhaustively.

49 The *Mātiposatajātaka* (J IV 90–95) speaks of the kindness and loyalty of an elephant whereas the *Indasāmanagottajātaka* (J II 41–3) describes the destructive nature of an elephant.

50 J I 166–8.

51 *Dummedhajātaka*, J I 259–61.

52 This is the meaning that is implicit in the *Nikāyas*. See the section on animals in Chapter 2 and the environmental virtues in Chapter 4.

53 See the *Āyācitabhattajātaka* (J I 169) as an exemplification.

54 J II 196–9.

55 J II 356–8.

56 Two examples are Chapple, "Buddhist Birth Stories," and Florin Deleanu, "Buddhist 'Ethology' in the Pali Canon: Between Symbol and Observation," *The Eastern Buddhist* XXXII, no. 2, 2000. Schmithausen also makes a reference to this story.

57 Deleanu, "Buddhist Ethology," p. 115.

58 Chapple, "Buddhist Birth Stories," p. 143.

59 Paul Waldau, "Buddhism and Animal Rights," in Damien Keown (ed.) *Contemporary Buddhist Ethics*, Richmond, Surrey: Curzon Press, 2000, pp. 81–112.
60 Ibid. p. 99.
61 J I 414–6.
62 Waldau, "Buddhism and Animal Rights," p. 104.
63 Paul Waldau, "Speciesism in Christianity and Buddhism" unpublished thesis, University of Oxford, 1998, pp. 174–5.
64 Deleanu, "Buddhist Ethology," p. 115. The *Jātaka* being referred to is number 452. For more detailed conceptions and misconceptions regarding animals see the same article, pp. 91–116.
65 Ian Harris, "Buddhism and Ecology," in Damien Keown (ed.) *Contemporary Buddhist Ethics*, Richmond, Surrey: Curzon Press, 2000, p. 121.
66 J III 490–94.
67 J II 79–81.
68 *Yamhi jīve tamhi gacche. . . .* Go wherever there is life. (J II 80)
69 *The Jātakas or the Stories of the Buddha's Former Births*, Vol. I, trans. E. B. Cowell, Cambridge: Cambridge University Press, 1890; Indian edn Delhi: Motilal Banarsidass, 1990, p. xxii.
70 J I 212–15.
71 *mayhaṃ cāpi ekaṃ saccaṃ atthi, saṃvijjamāno eko sabhāvadhammo paññāyati . . .* (J I 214)
72 It may be said that a person may be non-ecological unintentionally. However, the point is that on Buddhist principles, virtue cannot beget evil consequences. Thus under most circumstances a virtuous character would ensure a healthy environment.
73 J III 267–70.
74 J III 375.
75 J II 318–21.

CONCLUSION

1 Sn 560. Buddha is often called a physician or healer (*Sallakatta* or one who works on the poisoned arrow) in the *Theragāthā*. One example is Th 830.

BIBLIOGRAPHY

Pali sources and their translations

Aṅguttara Nikāya, Richard Morris and E. Hardy (eds). 6 Vols, London: PTS, 1885–1910; translated by F. L. Woodard and E. M. Hare as *The Book of Gradual Sayings*. 5 Vols, London: PTS, 1932–6.

Dīgha Nikāya, T. W. Rhys Davids and Estlin Carpenter (eds). 3 Vols, London: PTS, 1890–1911; translated by T. W. Rhys Davids as *Dialogues of the Buddha*. 3 Vols, London: PTS, 1899–1921; translated by Maurice Walshe as *The Long Discourses of the Buddha*. Boston: Wisdom Publications, 1987.

Dhammapada, Pali Text and Translation (with stories in brief and notes), Narada Thera. Taiwan: The Corporate Body of the Buddha Educational Foundation, 4th edition, 1993.

Jātaka (together with its Commentary), V. Fausboll (ed.). 6 Vols, London: Trübner & Co, 1877–96; translated by various hands under the editorship of E. B. Cowell as *The Jātaka or Stories of the Buddha's Former Births*. Cambridge: Cambridge University Press, 1890; Indian edition Delhi: Motilal Banarsidass, 1990.

Majjhima Nikāya, V. Trenckner and Robert Chalmers (eds). 4 Vols, London: PTS, 1888–1925; translated by I. B. Horner as *The Middle Length Sayings*. 3 Vols, London: PTS, 1954–9; translated by Ñāṇamoli as *The Middle Length Discourses of the Buddha*. Edited and revised by Bhikkhu Bodhi. Boston: Wisdom Publications, 1995.

Saṃyutta Nikāya, Leon M. Freer (ed.). 6 Vols, London: PTS, 1884–1904; translated by C. A. F. Rhys Davids and F. L. Woodard as *The Book of Gradual Sayings*. 5 Vols, London: PTS, 1917–30; translated by Bhikkhu Bodhi as *The Connected Discourses of the Buddha*. 2 Vols, Boston: Wisdom Publications, 1987.

Theragāthā/Therīgāthā, H. Oldenberg and R. Pischel (eds). London: PTS, 1966. Also available as online from Sri Lanka Tripitaka Project, Pali_Tipitaka_utf8_html.zip (from www.jbe.gold.ac.uk) (accessed on 1 February 2006); translated by Mrs. Rhys Davids as *Psalms of the Early Buddhists:* Part I, *Psalms of the sisters*, Part II, *Psalms of the Brethren*, London: PTS, 1909–13.

Sutta-Nipāta, D. Anderson and H. Smith (eds). London: PTS, 1913. Also available online from Sri Lanka Tripitaka Project, Pali_Tipitaka_utf8_html.zip (from www.jbe.gold.ac.uk) (accessed on 1 February 2006); translated by V. Fausboll as *The Sutta-Nipata: A Collection of Discourses*, in Sacred Books of the East, Vol. X, ed. F. Max Muller, Oxford: Oxford University Press, 1881.

Vinaya Piṭaka, Hermann Oldenberg (ed.). 5 Vols, London: PTS, 1879–83; translated by I. B. Horner as *The Book of Discipline*. 6 Vols, London: PTS, 1938–66; translated as *The Buddhist Monastic Code*. Text Online: 16 May 2001, http://www.accesstoinsight.org/lib/modern/bmc.html (accessed 13 July 2001).

Other sources

Atharva Veda Vol. V, translated by Muir (original Sanskrit texts). Quoted in Radhakrishnan. 1940. *Indian Philosophy* Vol. 1. London: George, Allen and Unwin Ltd.

Adams, Madonna R. 1997. "Environmental Ethics in Plato's *Timaeus*." In Laura Westra and Thomas M. Robinson (eds) *The Greeks and the Environment*, pp. 55–72. Lanham: Rowman and Littlefield Publishers.

Anscombe, G. E. M. 1958. "Modern Moral Philosophy." *Philosophy* XXXIII, pp. 1–19.

Aristotle. 1976. *The Ethics of Aristotle: The Nichomachean Ethics*; translated by J. A. K. Thompson, revised by Hugh Tredennick, and introduction and Bibliography by Jonathan Barnes. Revised edn, London: Penguin Books.

Aronson, Harvey B. 1980. *Love and Sympathy in Theravāda Buddhism*. Delhi: Motilal Banarsidass.

Attfield, Robin. 1994. *Environmental Philosophy: Principles and Prospects*. Avebury: Aldershot.

Badiner, Allan Hunt (ed.). 1990. *Dharma Gaia*. California: Parallax Press.

Basham, A. L. 1989. *The Origins and Development of Classical Hinduism*. Kenneth Zysk (ed. and annotated.) Boston: Beacon Press.

Batchelor, Martine. 1992. "Even the Stones Smile." In Martine Batchelor and Kerry Brown (eds) *Buddhism and Ecology*, pp. 2–17. London, UK: Cassell Publishers Limited.

Batchelor, Martine and Kerry Brown (eds). 1992. *Buddhism and Ecology*. London, UK: Cassell Publishers Limited.

Batchelor, Stephen. 1990. "Buddhist Economics Reconsidered." In Allan Hunt Badiner (ed.) *Dharma Gaia*, pp. 178–82. California: Parallax Press.

——. 1992. "The Sands of the Ganges." In Martine Batchelor and Kerry Brown (eds) *Buddhism and Ecology*, pp. 31–9. London, UK: Cassell Publishers Limited.

Blackstone, Kathryn R. 1998. *Women in the Footsteps of the Buddha*. Richmond, Surrey: Curzon Press.

Boyd, James. 1980. "The Theravāda View of Saṃsāra." In Somaratna Balasooriya, Andre Bareau, Richard Gombrich, Siri Gunasingha, Udaye Mallawarachchi and Edmund Perry (eds) *Buddhist Studies in Honour of Walpola Rahula*, pp. 29–43. London: Gordan Fraser.

Brown, Kerry. 1992. "In the Water There Were Fish and the Fields Were Full of Rice." In Martine Batchelor and Kerry Brown (eds) *Buddhism and Ecology*, pp. 87–99. London, UK: Cassell Publishers Limited.

Burnet, John. 1914. *Greek Philosophy*. London and Basingstoke: The Macmillan Press Ltd, reprint and reset 1964.

Cafaro, Philip. 2001. "Thoreau, Leopold and Carson: Towards an Environmental Virtue Ethics." *Environmental Ethics* 23, no. 1, pp. 3–17.

Callicott, J. Baird and Roger T. Ames. 1989. "Introduction: The Asian Traditions as a Conceptual Resource for Environmental Philosophy." In *Nature in Asian Traditions of Thought: Essays in Environmental Philosophy*, pp. 1–21. New York: State University of New York Press. Reprinted as Indian edition Delhi: Sri Satguru Publications, 1991.

Carone, Gabriela Roxana. 1988. "Plato and the Environment." *Environmental Ethics* 20, no. 2, pp. 115–33.

Carrithers, Michael. 1992. *Why Humans Have Cultures: Explaining Anthropology and Social Diversity*. Oxford: Oxford University Press.

Carter, John Ross. 1978. *Dhamma: Western Academic and Sinhalese Buddhist Interpretations: A Study of a Religious Concept*. Tokyo: The Hokuseido Press.

Chapple, Christopher Key. 1997. "Animals and Environment in the Buddhist Birth Stories." In Mary Evelyn Tucker and Duncan Ryūken Williams (eds) *Buddhism and Ecology: The Interconnection of Dharma and Deeds*, pp. 131–48. Cambridge, Massachusetts: Harvard University Press.

Clayton, Barbara. 2002. "Ethics in the Śikṣā-samuccaya: A Study in Mahāyāna Morality." Unpublished thesis, McGill University.

Collins, Steven. 1982. *Selfless Persons: Imagery and Thought in Theravāda Buddhism*. Cambridge: Cambridge University Press.

Comte-Sponville, Andre. 2003. *A Short Treatise on the Great Virtues*; translated by Catherine Temerson. Great Britain: Vintage.

Conze, Edward. 1962. *Buddhist Thought in India*. London: George, Allen and Unwin Ltd.

Coomaraswamy, Ananda K. 1916. *Buddha and the Gospel of Buddhism*. London: George G. Harrap and Company. Reprinted and revised New York: Harper and Row Publishers, 1964.

Cooper, David E. 1998. "Aestheticism and Environmentalism." In David E. Cooper and Joy A. Palmer (eds) *Spirit of the Environment*, pp. 100–12. London and New York: Routledge.

Cooper, David E. and Simon P. James. 2005. *Buddhism, Virtue and the Environment* U.K.: Ashgate.

Cornford, Francis M. 1935. *Plato's Cosmology: The Timaeus of Plato*. Routledge. Reprinted Indianapolis, Cambridge: Hackett Publishing Company, 1997.

Cottingham, John. 1986. *Descartes*. Oxford, New York: Basil Blackwell.

Darlington, Susan. 2000. "Tree ordination in Thailand." In Stephanie Kaza and Kenneth Kraft (eds) *Dharma Rain*, pp. 198–205. Boston and London: Shambhala.

Deleanu, Florin. 2000 "Buddhist 'Ethology' in the Pāli Canon: Between Symbol and Observation." *The Eastern Buddhist XXXII*, no. 2, pp. 79–127.

de Silva, Lily. 1992. "The Hills Wherein My Soul Delights." In Martine Batchelor and Kerry Brown (eds) *Buddhism and Ecology*, pp. 18–30. London, UK: Cassell Publishers Limited.

de Silva, Padmasiri. 1990. "Buddhist Environmental Ethics." In Allan Hunt Badiner (ed.) *Dharma Gaia*, pp. 14–19. California: Parallax Press.

——. 1991. "Buddhist Ethics." In Peter Singer (ed.) *A Companion to Ethics*, pp. 58–68. Oxford: Blackwell Publishers Ltd. Reprinted in paperback (with corrections) 1993.

——. 1998. *Environmental Philosophy and Ethics in Buddhism*. Basingstoke, Hampshire: Macmillan Press Ltd.

Descartes, R. 1997. *Key Philosophical Writings*. Enrique Chàvez-Arvizo (ed.); translated by Elizabeth S. Haldane and G. R. T. Ross. Hertfordshire: Wordsworth Editions Limited.

De-Shalit, Avner. 1995. *Why Posterity Matters*. London and New York: Routledge.

Duncan, Steven M. 1995. *A Primer of Modern Virtue Ethics*. Lanham, New York: University Press of America.

Eckel, Malcolm David. 1997. "Is There a Buddhist Philosophy of Nature?" In Mary Evelyn Tucker and Duncan Ryūken Williams (eds) *Buddhism and Ecology: The Interconnection of Dharma and Deeds*, pp. 327–49. Cambridge, Massachusetts: Harvard University Press.

Edwards, Colin. 2000. "Response to Letter: The Buddha: Friendship and Beauty." *Buddhist Studies Review* 17, no. 1, pp. 49–64.

Embree, A. T. (ed.) 1972. *The Hindu Tradition*. New York: Vintage Books.

Fabel, Arthur. 1994. "Environmental Ethics and the Question of Cosmic Purpose." *Environmental Ethics* 1, no. 3, pp. 303–14.

Fawcett, Thomas. 1970. *The Symbolic Language of Religion: An Introductory Study*. London: SCM Press.

Foot, Philippa. 1978. *Virtues and Vices*. Oxford: Basil Blackwell.

Frasz, Geoffrey B. 1993. "Environmental Virtue Ethics." *Environmental Ethics* 15, no. 3 pp. 259–74.

Gethin, Rupert. 1998. *The Foundations of Buddhism*. Oxford: Oxford University Press.

Gokhale, Balkrishna Govind. 1994. *New Light on Early Buddhism*. Mumbai, India: Bombay Popular Prakashan.

Gombrich, Richard. 1992. "The Buddha's Book of Genesis?", *Indo-Iranian Journal* 35, pp. 159–78.

——. 1996. *How Buddhism Began: The Conditioned Genesis of the Early Buddhist Teaching*. N.J.: Athlone.

Govinda, Lama Anagarika. 1961. *The Psychological Attitude of Early Buddhist Philosophy*. Great Britain. Reprinted Delhi: Motilal Banarsidass Publishers Private Limited, 1991.

Greenbaum, Alan. 1999. "Environmental Thought as Cosmological Intervention." *Environmental Values* 8, pp. 485–97.

Gross, Rita M. 1997. "Buddhist Resources for Issues of Population, Consumption and the Environment." In Mary Evelyn Tucker and Duncan Ryūken Williams (eds) *Buddhism and Ecology: The Interconnections of Dharma and Deeds*, pp. 291–312. Cambridge, Massachusetts: Harvard University Press.

Guenther, Herbert V. 1974. *Philosophy and Psychology in the Abhidharma*. Delhi: Motilal Banarsidass Publishers Private Limited; Second Revised Edition.

Gustafson, James. 1981. *Ethics from a Theocentric Perspective*, Vol. 1. Chicago: University of Chicago Press. Summarized in Robin W. Lovin and Frank E. Reynolds. "In the Beginning." *Cosmogony and Ethical Order*, pp. 1–35. Chicago: The University of Chicago Press, 1985.

Gutherie W. K. C. 1987. *A History of Greek Philosophy: The Later Plato and the Academy*, Vol. V. Cambridge and London: Cambridge University Press.

Haila, Yrjo and Richard Levins. 1992. *Humanity and Nature*. London: Pluto Press.

Hakamaya, Noriaki. 1990. "Shizen-hihen to-shite no Bukkyō" (Buddhism as a Criticism of "*Physis/Natura*"). *Komazawa-daiguku Bukkyōgakubu Ronshū* 21, pp. 380–403.

——. 1992. "Nihon-jin to animizmu." *Komazawa-daiguku Bukkyōgakubu Ronshū* 23, pp. 351–78.

Hamilton, Sue. 2000. *Early Buddhism: A New Approach: The I of the Beholder*. Richmond, Surrey: Curzon Press.

Harris, Ian. 1991. "How Environmentalist is Buddhism?" *Religion* 21, pp. 101–14.

——. 1994. "Buddhism." In Jean Holm with John Bowker (eds) *Attitudes to Nature*, pp. 8–27. London, New York: Printer Publishers.

——. 1994. "Causation and 'Telos': The Problem of Buddhist Environmental Ethics." *Journal of Buddhist Ethics* 1, pp. 45–56, http://jbe.gold.ac.uk (accessed 7 October 1999).

——. 1995. "Buddhist Environmental Ethics and Detraditionalization: The Case of Eco-Buddhism." *Religion* 25, pp. 199–211.

——. 1995. "Getting to Grips with Buddhist Environmentalism: A Provisional Typology." *Journal of Buddhist Ethics* 2, pp. 173–90, http://jbe.gold.ac.uk (accessed 7 October 1999).

——. 1997. "Buddhism and the Discourse of Environmental Concern: Some Methodological Problems Considered." In Mary Evelyn Tucker and Duncan Ryūken Williams (eds) *Buddhism and Ecology: The Interconnection of Dharma and Deeds*, pp. 377–402. Cambridge, Massachusetts: Harvard University Press.

——. 2000. "Buddhism and Ecology." In Damien Keown (ed.) *Contemporary Buddhist Ethics*, pp. 113–35. Richmond, Surrey: Curzon Press.

Hargrove Eugene. 2003. "Weak Anthropocentric Intrinsic Value." In Andrew Light and Holmes Rolston III (eds) *Environmental Ethics: An Anthology*, pp. 175–90. Oxford: Blackwell Publishing.

Harvey, Peter. 1990. *An Introduction to Buddhism*. Cambridge: Cambridge University Press.

——. 2000. *An Introduction to Buddhist Ethics*. Cambridge, UK: Cambridge University Press.

Hayward, Jeremy. 1990. "Ecology and the Experience of Sacredness." In Alan Hunt Badiner (ed.) *Dharma Gaia*, pp. 64–74. California: Parallax Press.

Hayward, Tim. 1997. "Anthropocentrism: A Misunderstood Problem." In *Environmental Values* 6, pp. 49–63.

——. 1998. "Anthropocentrism." In *Encyclopedia of Applied Ethics*, Vol. 1, pp. 173–81.

Head, Suzzane. 1990. "Creating Space for Nature." In Alan Hunt Badiner (ed.) *Dharma Gaia*, pp. 112–28. California: Parallax Press.

Hill Jr, Thomas E. 2002. "Ideals of Human Excellence and Preserving Natural Environments." In David Schmidtz and Elizabeth Willott (eds) *Environmental Ethics: What Really Matters, What Really Works*, pp. 189–99. New York, Oxford: Oxford University Press.

Hindery, Roderick. 1978. *Comparative Ethics in Hindu and Buddhist Traditions*. Delhi: Motilal Banarsidass.

Hiriyanna, M. 1949. *The Essentials of Indian Philosophy*. London: George, Allen and Unwin Ltd.

Horner, I. B. 1954. "Introduction," *Middle Length Sayings: A Translation of the Majjhima Nikaya*. London: Pali Text Society.

Humphreys, Christmas. 1984. *A Popular Dictionary of Buddhism*. London: Curzon Press.

Hursthouse, Rosalind. 1999. *On Virtue Ethics*. Oxford: Oxford University Press.

Jayatilleke, K. 1970. "The Ethical Theory of Buddhism," *The Mahābodhi* 78, pp. 192–97. Quoted in Damien Keown. 1992. *The Nature of Buddhist Ethics*. Basingstoke, Hampshire: Palgrave, reprinted (with minor alterations) 2001.

Jonas, Hans. 1984. *The Imperative of Responsibility: In Search for an Ethics for the Technological Age*; translated by Hans Jonas with the collaboration of David Herr. Chicago and London: University of Chicago Press.

Jones, Ken. 1990. "Getting Out of Our Own Light." In Allan Hunt Badiner (ed.) *Dharma Gaia*, pp. 183–90. California: Parallax Press.

Kalupahana, David J. 1975. *Causality: The Central Philosophy of Buddhism*. Honolulu: The University Press of Hawaii.

——. 1991. "Toward a Middle Path of Survival." In J. Baird Callicott and Roger T. Ames (eds) *Nature in Asian Traditions of Thought: Essays in Environmental Philosophy*, 247–56. New York: State University of New York Press, 1989; reprinted as Indian edition Delhi: Sri Satguru Publications.

——. 1995. *Ethics in Early Buddhism*. Honolulu: University of Hawaii Press.

Kaza, Stephanie and Kenneth Kraft (eds). 2000. *Dharma Rain*. Boston and London: Shambhala.

Keith, A. Berriedale. 1963. *Buddhist Philosophy in India and Ceylon*. India: Chowkhamba Sanskrit Series Office.

Keown, Damien. 1992. *The Nature of Buddhist Ethics*. Basingstoke, Hampshire: Palgrave, 1992; reprinted (with minor alterations) 2001.

——. 1996. *Buddhism: A Very Short Introduction*. Oxford: Oxford University Press.

——. 2003. *A Dictionary of Buddhism*. Oxford: Oxford University Press.

King, Winston. 1964. *In the Hope of Nibbāna*. La Salle: Open Court.

Krebs, Angelica. 1999. *Ethics of Nature*. Berlin, New York: Walter de Gruyter.

Lafleur, William. 1989. "Saigyō and the Buddhist Value of Nature." In J. Baird Callicott and Roger T. Ames (eds) *Nature in Asian Traditions of Thought: Essays in Environmental Philosophy*, pp. 183–209. New York: State University of New York Press. Reprinted as Indian edition Delhi: Sri Satguru Publications, 1991.

Little, David. 1981. "The Present State of the Study of Comparative Religious Ethics." *Journal of Religious Ethics* 9, pp. 186–98. Quoted in Robin W. Lovin and Frank E. Reynolds. 1985. "In the Beginning." *Cosmogony and Ethical Order*, pp. 1–35. Chicago: The University of Chicago Press.

Louden, Robert B. 1997. "On Some Vices of Virtue Ethics." In Daniel Statman (ed.) *Virtue Ethics: A Critical Reader*, pp. 180–93. Edinburgh: Edinburgh University Press.

Lovin, Robin W. and Frank E. Reynolds. 1985. "In the Beginning." *Cosmogony and Ethical Order*, pp. 1–35. Chicago: The University of Chicago Press.

McDermott, James Paul. 1976. "Is There Group Karma in Theravada Buddhism?" *Numen* XXIII, Fasc. 1, pp. 67–80.

Machan, Tibor R. 2000. "Do Animals Have Rights?" In James E. White (ed.) *Contemporary Moral Problems*, pp. 509–15. Sixth Edn; Belmont, CA: Wadsworth Publishing Company.

McShane, Katie. "Anthropocentrism vs. Nonanthropocentrism: Why Should We Care?" Joint Conference Papers: 8, http://www.environmentalphilosophy.org/environmentalphilosophy/upcoming/katie_mcshane-anthropocentrism_vs._nonanthropocentrism.pdf (accessed 14 January 2006).

Macy, Joanna. 1991. *World as Lover, World as Self*. Berkeley, California: Parallax Press.

——. 1991. *Mutual Causality in Buddhism and General Systems Theory: The Dharma of Natural Systems*. Albany: State University of New York Press. Reprint, India: Manohar, 1992.

Mahoney, Timothy A. 1997. "Platonic Ecology, Deep Ecology." In Laura Westra and Thomas M. Robinson (eds) *The Greeks and the Environment*, pp. 45–54. Lanham: Rowman and Littlefield Publishers.

Malalasekera, G. P. 1964. "The Status of the Individual in Theravada Buddhism." *Philosophy East and West* XIV, no. 2, pp. 145–56.

Martin, Rafe. 2000. "Thoughts on the Jatakas." In Stephanie Kaza and Kenneth Kraft (eds) *Dharma Rain*, pp. 104–8. Boston and London: Shambhala Press.

Montague, Phillip. 1997. "Virtue Ethics: A Qualified Success Story." In Daniel Statman (ed) *Virtue Ethics: A Critical Reader*, pp. 194–204. Edinburgh: Edinburgh University Press.

Murdy, W H. 1983. "Anthropocentrism: A Modern Version." In Donald Scherer and Thomas Attig (eds) *Ethics and the Environment*, pp. 12–21. New Jersey: Prentice-Hall.

Narada Mahathera. 1948. "A Simple Introduction to Abhidhamma." In *Sambhasha* 56, pp. 10–23.

Norman, K. R. 1983. *Pali Literature*. Wiesbaden: Otto Harrassowitz.

Norman, Richard. 1983. *The Moral Philosophers*. Oxford: Clarendon Press.

Norton, Bryan G. 2003. "Environmental Ethics and Weak Anthropocentrism." In Andrew Light and Holmes Rolston III (eds) *Environmental Ethics: An Anthology*, pp. 163–74, Oxford: Blackwell Publishing.

Nyanaponika. 1949. *Abhidhamma Studies: Researches in Buddhist Psychology*. Colombo: Frewin and Co. Ltd.

Nyanatiloka Mahathera. 1971. *Guide Through the Abhidhamma-Piṭaka*. Kandy, Ceylon: Buddhist Publication Society.

O'Neill, John. 2003. "The Varieties of Intrinsic Value." In Andrew Light and Holmes Rolston III (eds) *Environmental Ethics: An Anthology*, pp. 131–42. Oxford: Blackwell Publisher Ltd.

Page, Tony. 1999. *Buddhism and Animals*. London: UKAVIS Publications.

Passmore, John. 1995. "Attitudes to Nature." In Robert Elliot (ed.) *Environmental Ethics*, pp. 129–41. Oxford: Oxford University Press.

Pitt, Martin. 1990. "The Pebble and the Tide." In Alan Hunt Badiner (ed.) *Dharma Gaia*, pp. 102–5. California: Parallax Press.

Piyadassi Thera. 1964. *The Buddha's Ancient Path*. London: Rider and Company.

Plato. 1984. *The Dialogues of Plato*. Vol. I. Translated with analysis R. E. Allen. New Haven and London: Yale University Press.

Plumwood, Val. 1999. "Paths Beyond Human-Centeredness: Lessons from Liberation Struggles." In Anthony Weston (ed.) *An Invitation to Environmental Philosophy*, pp. 69–105. New York and Oxford: Oxford University Press.

Puligandla, Ramakrishna. 1996. "What is the Status of the Doctrine of Dependent Origination?" In Frank Hoffman and Deegalle Mahinda (eds) *Pali Buddhism*, pp. 175–83. Richmond, Surrey: Curzon Press.

Rachels, James. 2001. "The Ethics of Virtue." In Christina Sommers and Fred Sommers (eds) *Vice and Virtue in Everyday Life*, pp. 335–54. Fort Worth: Harcourt College Publishers.

Rahula, Walpole. 1967. *What the Buddha Taught*. 2nd enlarged edition London and Bedford: Gordan Fraser; reprinted as Gordan Fraser paperback, 1978.

Regan, Tom. 1988. *The Case for Animal Rights*. new edition London: Routledge.
Reynolds, Frank E. 1985. "Multiple Cosmogonies and Ethics: The Case of Theravada Buddhism." In Robin W. Lovin and Frank E. Reynolds (eds) *Cosmogony and Ethical Order*, pp. 203–24. Chicago: The University of Chicago Press.
——. 1990. "Ethics and Wealth in Theravāda Buddhism." In Russell F. Sizemore and Donald K. Swearer (eds) *Ethics, Wealth and Salvation: A Study in Buddhist Social Ethics*, pp. 59–76. South Carolina: University of South Carolina Press.
Rhys Davids, Mrs. 1912. *Buddhism: A Study of a Buddhist Norm*. London: Williams and Norgate.
Rhys Davids, T. W. 1903. *Buddhist India*. London, 1903; reprinted Delhi: Motilal Banarsidass Publishers Private Limited 1971.
Rhys Davids, T. W. and William Stede. 1921–25. *Pali-English Dictionary*. London. Indian edition Delhi: Motilal Banarsidass 1993.
Rist, John. 1997. "Why Greek Philosophers Might Have Been Concerned About the Environment." In Laura Westra and Thomas M. Robinson (eds) *The Greeks and the Environment*, pp. 19–32. Lanham: Rowman and Littlefield Publishers.
Rolston III, Holmes. 2005. "Environmental Virtue Ethics: Half the Truth but Dangerous as a Whole." In Ronald Sandler and Philip Cafaro (eds) *Environmental Virtue Ethics*, pp. 61–78. Lanham, Boulder: Rowman and Littlefield Publishers, Inc.
Ryan, P. D. 1998. *Buddhism and the Natural World*. Birmingham: Windhorse Publications.
Salgado, Nirmala. 1992. "The Structure of Evil and Ethical Action in the 'Jātakatthavaṇṇanā'." Unpublished thesis. Northwestern University.
Sandler, Ronald. 2005. "Introduction: Environmental Virtue Ethics." In Ronald Sandler and Philip Cafaro (eds) *Environmental Virtue Ethics*, pp. 1–12. Lanham, Boulder: Rowman and Littlefield Publishers, Inc.
Schmidtz, David and Matt Zwolinski. 2005. "Virtue Ethics and Repugnant Conclusions." In Ronald Sandler and Philip Cafaro (eds) *Environmental Virtue Ethics*, pp. 107–17. Lanham, Boulder: Rowman and Littlefield Publishers, Inc.
Schmithausen, Lambert. 1991. *Buddhism and Nature*. Studia Philologica Buddhica Occasional Paper Series VII. Tokyo: The International Institute for Buddhist Studies.
——. 1991. *The Problem of Sentience of Plants in Earliest Buddhism*. Studia Philologica Buddhica Monograph Series, VI. Tokyo: The International Institute for Buddhist Studies.
——. 2000. "Buddhism and the Ethics of Nature – Some Remarks." *The Eastern Buddhist New Series* XXXII, no. 2, pp. 26–78.
——. 1997. "The Early Buddhist Tradition and Ecological Ethics." *Journal of Buddhist Ethics* 4, pp. 1–74, http://jbe.gold.ac.uk (accessed 7 October 1999).
Slote, Michael. 1992. *From Morality to Virtue*. New York, Oxford: Oxford University Press.
Solomon, David. 1997. "Internal Objections to Virtue Ethics." In Daniel Statman (ed.) *Virtue Ethics: A Critical Reader*, pp. 165–79. Edinburgh: Edinburgh University Press.
Spinoza, Benedict De. 1994. *Ethics*. Edited and translated by Edwin Curley. USA: Princeton University Press, Penguin Books 1996.
Spiro, Melford E. 1982. *Buddhism and Society: A Great Tradition and Its Burmese Vicissitudes*. Berkeley: University of California Press.

Sponberg, Alan. 1997. "Green Buddhism and the Hierarchy of Compassion." In Mary Evelyn Tucker and Duncan Ryūken Williams (eds) *Buddhism and Ecology: The Interconnection of Dharma and Deeds*, pp. 351–76. Cambridge, Massachusetts: Harvard University Press.

——. 1999. "The Buddhist Conception of an Ecological Self." In Sallie B. King and Paul O. Ingram (eds) *The Sound of Liberating Truth: Buddhist-Christian Dialogues in Honour of Frederick J Streng*, pp. 107–27. Richmond, Surrey: Curzon Press.

Statman, Daniel (ed.) 1997. *Virtue Ethics: A Critical Reader*. Edinburgh: Edinburgh University Press.

Swearer, Donald K. 1997. "The Hermeneutics of Buddhist Ecology in Contemporary Thailand: Buddhadāsa and Dhammapiṭaka." In Mary Evelyn Tucker and Duncan Ryūken Williams (eds) *Buddhism and Ecology: The Interconnection of Dharma and Deeds*, pp. 21–44. Cambridge, Massachusetts: Harvard University Press.

Tachibana, S. 1926. *The Ethics of Buddhism*. Oxford: Clarendon Press; reprint, London: Curzon Press, 1975.

Taylor, Paul. 1986. *Respect for Nature*. Princeton: Princeton University Press.

Tucker, Mary Evelyn and Duncan Ryūken Williams (eds) 1997. *Buddhism and Ecology: The Interconnection of Dharma and Deeds*. Cambridge, Massachusetts: Harvard University Press.

Van Gorkom, Nina. 1999. *Cetasikas*. London: Zolag.

Vlastos, Gregory. 1975. *Plato's Universe*. Oxford: Clarendon Press.

Waldau, Paul. 2000. "Buddhism and Animal Rights." In Damien Keown (ed.) *Contemporary Buddhist Ethics*, pp. 81–112. Richmond, Surrey: Curzon Press.

——. 1998. "Speciesism in Christianity and Buddhism." Unpublished thesis, University of Oxford.

Walshe, Maurice. 1995. *The Long Discourses of the Buddha: A Translation of the Dīgha Nikāya*, Boston: Wisdom Publications.

Warder, A. K. 1970. *Indian Buddhism*. Delhi: Motilal Banarsidass.

Watson, Gary. 1997. "On the Primacy of Character." In Daniel Statman (ed.) *Virtue Ethics: A Critical Reader*, pp. 56–81. Edinburgh: Edinburgh University Press.

Wensveen, Louke van. 2005. "The Emergence of Ecological Virtue language." In Ronald Sandler and Philip Cafaro (eds) *Environmental Virtue Ethics*, pp. 13–30. Lanham, Boulder: Rowman and Littlefield Publishers, Inc.

Westra, Laura. 2005. "Virtue Ethics as Foundational for a Global Ethic." In Ronald Sandler and Philip Cafaro (eds) *Environmental Virtue Ethics*, pp. 79–91. Lanham, Boulder: Rowman and Littlefield Publishers, Inc.

Whitehill, James. 2000. "Buddhism and the Virtues." In Damien Keown (ed.) *Contemporary Buddhist Ethics*, pp. 17–36. Richmond, Surrey: Curzon Press.

Williams, Paul (with Anthony Tribe). 2000. *Buddhist Thought*. London and New York: Routledge.

INDEX

Abhidhamma/ic/ikas/lists (*abhidharna*) 7, 8, 17, 64, 103–104, 106–109, 111–113, 125
Abhidharma see Abhidhamma
Abhijjhā 134
Abhilepana 134
Adams, Madonna 41
Adosa (hatelessness) 110–111
Aesthetic: appreciation 56–58, 62; descriptions 45, 56; experiences 58
Āghāto 135
Aggañña Sutta 10, 73–79, 90, 115
Ahaṃkāra/o (*māna*) 115, 135
Ahiṃsā 21–22, 24–25, 28–29, 104, 125–126, 138, 140, 152–153, 162
Ahirika 111–112
air 39, 54–56, 75, 77
Ajahn Pongsak 15
Akataññutaṃ 153
Akusala 109–113; *kamma* 104; *mūla* 111
Ālasa see lazy/laziness
Alobha (greedlessness) 110–112
altruism/tic 9, 81, 84, 86–89, 153, 155, 158
Ambalaṭṭhikārāhulovāda Sutta 141
Amoha 110
Anabhijjhā (non-covetousness) 104
Anasaṇa 48
Anātman see Anattā
Anattā (*anātman*) 14–15, 18, 20, 55; *vāda* 116
Aṅguttara Nikāya 7, 46, 58, 68, 87, 129, 132, 154
Aniccā 55
animal/s 1, 10–11, 21–26, 28–29, 35, 38, 40–41, 45–50, 52, 54, 57, 59–62, 68, 71, 77–78, 80, 82, 85, 95, 114, 134, 137–141, 146–149, 151–153, 155–162
rights 10; sacrifice 47–48, 155; domestic 48, 59
Anscombe, G. E. M. 96
anthropocentrism/tric 22–26, 31–33, 52, 79–86, 88–90, 157–158; angle 25; weak 81–84, 86, 89, 90, 158; strong 81–85, 88–89, 158
anthropomorphism 156–158
Anudāya 86
Anukampā 104, 120
Āpo 54
Arāga 125, 127
Arakajātaka 151
Arête 98
Aristotle 98–99, 105–106
Ariyapariyesanā Sutta 119
Arnauld, Antoine 37
Aronson, Harvey 72–73, 120
arrogance/ant 75, 77, 115–116, 118–119, 134
Artefacts 35, 36
Arthaśāstra 28
artificial/ity 23, 27, 35, 52–53, 117, 128, 150–151
Āsavas 125, 136
Asurās 71
Atharva veda 65
Atitavatthu 148
Attha 179n
Aṭṭhangasīla 124
avarice *see Macchariya*
aversion 116, 120, 140
Avīci 53
Avihiṃsā 86
Avijjā 66–67, 70
Āvudhamuttama 107
Avyākata 109–110

Bālapaṇḍita Sutta 135
Barth, Karl 27–28
Basham, A. L. 65
Batchelor, Martine 13
Batchelor, Stephen 14
Bhāvanā 117–118
Bhūta 23, 49; *Mahā* 54
biocentrism 83
birds 23, 28, 40, 59, 159, 161
Bodhisatta 22, 148–156, 159, 162
Boyd, James 73
Brahma-vihāras (sublime attitudes) 30, 119–121, 151
Brahmajāla Sutta 50, 124
Bṛhad-āraṇyaka Upaniṣad 76
Brown, Kerry 15
Buddha 4, 6–7, 9, 13–15, 17, 19, 27, 29–30, 46–52, 56, 58–61, 64, 66, 69, 73–74, 84–87, 93, 99, 101–103, 105, 116–117, 119–120, 126–129, 133–134, 136–139, 141, 144, 146–148, 153–155, 158, 160, 162, 165–166
Buddhadāsa Bhikkhu 15
Buddhaghosa 109, 148
Burnet, John 40
butcher/s 49, 60, 126, 138

Cāga see Dāna
Cakkavatisīhanāda Sutta 13, 28, 53
Carone, Gabriela 39–42
Carrithers, Michael 76
Carter, John Ross 64
categorical imperative 102
causation/causality 5, 17, 18, 20, 28, 30, 68, 69, 70, 88, 90, 118, 164: law of 17; *see also Paṭiccasamupāda*
Cetanā 101, 110
Cetasikas 109–112
Chapple, Christopher Key 147, 149, 156
charity 111, 126, 128, 150, 151; *see also Dāna*
Citta 109–112
Clayton, Barbara 100
Collins, Stevens 87
compassion/ate 9–10, 14, 22, 46, 48, 60, 73, 83, 87, 90, 95, 103–104, 107, 112, 119–121, 123, 126, 138–141, 147, 155, 157–158, 162; *see also Karunā*
consequential/ism/ist 92, 94–95, 98, 102, 105, 106, 129, 142
conservation/ist 3, 16, 25, 27, 35–36, 39, 43–59, 61–63, 78, 83, 90, 127, 161; approach 45, 50, 55, 63; ethics 54; view 43, 45, 62, 90
considered preference 82–84, 86, 88
contentment 5, 125, 127–128, 136, 142
Conze, Edward 104, 106
Coomaraswamy, Ananda K. 147
Cooper, David E. 93
cosmic law 64–66; *see also Paṭiccasamupāda*
cosmogony 73–78, 90
cosmological 39–45, 62–64, 70–72, 74, 77, 79, 88, 90–92, 121, 164; approach 62–64, 70–72, 77–79, 90; outlook 71; perspective 44; value 43
cosmos 35, 40–42, 44, 63, 70
courage 98, 99, 153
covetousness 135
Cowell, E. B. 160
craving (*taṇhā*) 14, 55, 67–68, 74–75, 104–106, 116, 125–126, 134–136, 153
Crosby, Kate 174n

Dalai Lama 15
Dāna (*cāga*) 104, 125, 128, 151–152
Darlington, Susan 16
Dasasīla 124
De Silva, Lily 13
De Silva, Padmasiri 11, 14, 103
decorum 24, 56; and hygiene 24
Deep ecology 27
deer 50, 57, 60, 138, 152
deity/ies 23, 48, 51, 149–150, 156–157; tree 149–150, 156–157
Deleanu, Florin 10, 11, 50, 62, 156–157
delusion (*moha*) 14, 54, 61, 68, 73, 104, 110–112, 125, 136, 140, 165
demiurge 40–42
deontology/logical 94–96, 98, 100, 102, 106–107
dependent co-arising/ origination 3, 11, 17–19, 66, 69; *see also Paṭiccasamupāda*
Descartes, René 34, 36–39, 43–44
De-Shalit, Avner 72
Devadhammajātaka 153
Devadutta Sutta 135
Dhamma (*dharma*) 14, 15, 17, 49, 55, 61, 63–66, 69, 74, 76, 79, 103, 108–109, 154; *Paramaṭṭha* 109
Dhammaddhajajātaka 162
Dhammapada 7, 61, 126, 141
Dhammasangani 109–110

Dharma see Dhamma
Dharmatā 27, 69
Dhātu 54
Dīgha Nikāya 7, 13, 47, 50, 75, 124
Diṭṭhi 141
Dosa 73, 104, 110, 111, 125, 136, 165
Dubbalakaṭṭhajātaka 157
dukkha 1, 5, 20, 49, 66, 68, 70–71, 85, 103, 126, 136, 166
Dūtajātaka 162
duty/duties 14, 95, 97, 102, 106–107, 112–113, 122, 130, 152

earth element 54
Eckel, Malcolm David 10, 26
eco-self 19–20
ecology, concept of 33
eco-systems 21–22, 26, 161
Edwards, Colin 58
ego 14, 105, 116
egoism/centrism/istic/tism 71, 80, 83, 84–89, 102, 111, 116, 118, 125, 135, 158
Eightfold Path 5, 60, 71, 85, 104, 117, 126
Eka indrīya jīva 50
elements 30, 40, 54–56, 60, 77–78, 83, 95, 103, 109, 110, 116
Elephant 29, 50, 61–62, 124, 127, 155–157
Embree, A.T. 65
enlightenment 2, 4–5, 15, 21, 52, 56, 69, 70, 85, 86, 102, 105, 107, 118–120, 137, 165
environment, idea of 34
Equanimity 83, 119–120, 128, 151
Eudaemonia 99, 105

Fabel, Arthur 74, 76
felt preference 82, 86
fire 54, 77, 160
Foot, Philippa 97
Forms, theory of 39–41
Frasz, Geoffrey 114, 118
friendliness/ship 29, 47, 58, 62, 120, 150, 152, 160
future generations 1, 32, 72

Gāma 23
Gāthās 148
Gati see Realms
generosity 100, 103–104, 125, 128–129, 135, 151–153
Gethin, Rupert 140
Giddhilobha 135
God/s 4, 37, 65, 71, 85, 106, 132, 154; Varuna 65
Godhajātaka 153
Gokhale, B. G. 57
Govinda, Lama 110, 112–113
gratitude 15, 51, 82, 103, 151–153, 159, 160
greed 75, 77, 104, 110–112, 125, 135–136, 140, 153–154, 165; *see also lobha, lola, giddhilobha, rāga*
greedlessness *see Alobha*
Greenbaum, Allan 46, 79
Gross, Rita 14
Guenther, Herbert 110

Haeckel, Ernst 33
Haila, Yrjo 33, 78–79
Hakamaya, Noriaki 168n
Hamilton, Sue 133
Hargrove, Eugene 81–82
Harris, Ian 10–12, 20–21, 26–30, 36, 53, 93, 158, 164
Harvey, Peter 9–10, 53, 101–102, 106, 108–109, 112
hatelessness see *Adosa*
hatred 104, 110–111, 116, 118, 125, 126, 136, 165; *see also Dosa*
Hayward, Jeremy 14–15
Hayward, Tim 81
Head, Suzzane 15
heaven 4–5, 52, 71, 102, 136, 151
hell 4, 53, 71, 76, 101
hermit strand 23, 26, 52, 56, 147
Hill Jr, Thomas E. 114–118
Hirī 104, 111–112, 115, 152–153
Hiriyanna, M. 65
Horner, I. B 64
Hume, David 27
humility 98, 114–116, 118, 124, 135, 152–153
hunter/s/ing 21, 49, 126, 138, 149, 152–153
Hursthouse, Rosalind 98, 101–102

Icchā 48
insight (*paññā*) 104, 106, 112, 125
intentional actions 4, 101, 103, 126, 131; *see also Cetanā*
interconnectedness 17, 27
interdependence 10, 19, 20, 129

Jala 59
James, Simon 93
Jarā 48
Jātakas 7–8, 31, 144–163
Jayatilleke, K. 88
Jīvaka Sutta 138–139
Jonas, Hans 131
Jones, Ken 14

Kacchapajātaka 159
Kāliṅgabodhijātaka 151
Kalupahana, David 9, 27, 69, 93
Kamma/ic (*karma*) 4, 14, 17–19, 25, 48, 67, 70, 72–73, 76, 85, 99–101, 104, 125, 128–129, 131–133, 135, 154–155, 157
Kammatic Buddhism 72
Kandaraka Sutta 49
Kant 102
Karma *see Kamma*
Karunā 73, 104, 112, 119
Kāsāvajātaka 155–156
Kataññutaṃ 152–153
Keown, Damien 64, 100–101, 103–106, 108–109, 111, 119
Kesi Sutta 59
Khandha/s 54–55, 67, 84, 108, 116
Khanti 86
Khuddaka Nikāya 7–8, 144
kindness 46–48, 60, 62, 83, 86, 119, 126, 138, 151, 153
King, Winston 72
Krebs, Angelica 34–36, 44–45
Kriyā 110
Kurudhammajātaka 154
Kusala 106, 109–112, 184n; *mula* 110–111
Kusanāḷijātaka 149
Kūṭadanta Sutta 47, 50, 52
Kulāvakajātaka 150

lay persons, ethical instructions for 146
lazy/laziness (*ālasa*) 75, 135, 153
Levins, Richard 33, 78–79
liberation 1, 4, 21, 51, 60, 66, 69, 70–74, 85–86, 88–89, 113, 115, 120, 127, 129, 136, 146
Little, David 3
Lobha/Lola 77, 110–112, 153
Louden, Robert 97
Loving Kindness 83, 86; *see also Mettā*
loyalty 149, 159–160

Machan, Tibor R 80
Macy, Joanna 11, 17–21
Macchariya (avarice) 111, 135
Maddava 104
Mahāgosiṅga Sutta 52
Mahākapijātaka 151–153, 162
Mahāparinibbāna Sutta/ Mahaparinirvāṇasūtra 22, 139
Mahāsudassana Sutta 52
Mahāsukajātaka 159
Mahāukkusajātaka 152
Mahāyāna 9, 17, 22
Majjhima Nikāya 7, 49, 56, 60, 120, 135
Malalasekera, G. P. 136
Māna see Ahaṃkāra and *Arrogance*
Manda 135
Manicorajātaka 154
Māra 51, 59–60
marginal-ism/ist 39, 44, 90
marginalization/izing/lizes 38, 39, 43–45, 63, 72–73, 89–90; of nature 38
Martin, Rafe 147
Matakabhattajātaka 155, 157
material elements/entities 40, 54–56, 59, 77–78, 116
McDermott, James 132
meat eating 95, 138, 140
meditation 15, 16, 20, 25, 52, 56, 61–62, 86, 104, 106, 117–118, 120, 127, 137
Meno 97
metaphor/s 7, 45, 59–62, 127, 141
Mettā 29, 46–47, 73, 86, 104, 119–121, 140, 152
Mettā Sutta 121
mindfulness 10, 60, 86, 104, 111, 118
modesty 5, 104, 107, 111–112, 115, 118, 152–153
Moha see Delusion
monkey 50, 152, 155, 157
moral concern, sentiment of 119
motivation, moral 98
mountains 28, 35, 37, 45, 53–55, 62, 136, 161
Muditā 112, 119
Mūlapariyāya Sutta 55
Murdy, W. H. 83

Naess, Arne 20
Narada Mahathera 108
nature, description of 31; definition of 27, 34, 36, 63
Nibbāna 1, 5, 56, 63, 70–73, 85, 89, 100–101, 104–106, 109, 117, 142–143

Nibbāna-centric 89
Nibbanic Buddhism 72
Nichomachean Ethics 98
Nigrodhamigajātaka 152
Niṣkāma-karma 183n
Noble Truth/s 4, 66–67, 136
no-self 9, 20, 116
non-injury/non-violence 2, 5, 24, 50–51, 60, 86, 104, 126, 127, 138–140, 149, 152–154; *see also Ahiṃsā*
non-covetousness *see Anabhijjhā*
Norman, K. R. 145
Norman, Richard 99
Norton, Bryan 82, 84, 88
nun's 23, 128
Nyanaponika 110

Oikos 33, 35
open systems 18–20
openness 118–119, 121, 124, 135
ordination of trees 15

Pabbajja 16
Paccuppannavatthu 148
Page, Toni 11
Palāsajātaka 150, 161
Pali Canon 6–7, 10, 17, 28, 50, 103, 113, 127, 138, 144, 146, 149
Pañcasīla 124
Pañcāvudhajātaka 153
Paññā 104, 106, 112, 125, 140, 142
Paññindrīya 106, 112
Passmore, John 34, 38
Pātavyatā 23
Paṭhavī 54; *Rasa* 75
Paṭiccasamuppāda (*tyasamutpāda*) 14, 17–18, 20, 27, 63–64, 66–70, 74, 77–79, 88, 90, 108
Pātimokkha/sutta 23, 50, 124
perception, Buddhist theory of 18
perseverance *see viriya*
Petals 71
Phassa 54, 67, 110
Phra Prayudh 15
Pitt, Martin 15
Piyadassi Thera 87
plants 9, 21–24, 26–27, 29, 40–41, 45, 47–48, 50, 52–54, 59, 62, 68, 74, 78, 82, 127, 134, 146–147, 150, 161
Plato/platonic 34, 39–44, 63, 70, 97
Plumwood, Val 81
Pratītyasamutpāda see Paṭiccasamuppāda
precept/s 21–22, 50–52, 102, 124–128, 131, 135, 137–138, 140, 150, 154–155, 160, 162
pride 61, 115–116
pro-civilization strand 22, 26
Pucimandajātaka 150
Puligandla, Ramakrishna 68

Rachel, James 97
Rāga 73, 104, 125, 136, 165
Rahula, Walpole 117
Ramanīya 58
Rasataṇhā 153
realms (*gati*) 4, 70–71
rebirth 4, 5, 28–29, 50, 66, 68, 71, 73, 76, 129, 135, 157
Regan, Tom 38
respect for life 125–127, 135, 138, 153, 155
responsibility, virtue of 125, 131, 154
Reynolds, Frank E. 74
Rhys Davids, Mrs 57, 64,
Rhys Davids, T. W. 145, 148
river/s 28, 45, 54–55, 61–62, 65, 70, 101, 159, 161
Rolston III, Holmes 151
Ṛta 65, 176n
Rūpa 67, 109, 116
Ryan, P. D. 10, 62, 77, 130
Ryle, Gilbert 37

Saccaṃkirajātaka 151
sacrifices 47–48, 51, 152, 155
Salgado, Nirmala 145
Sallekha Sutta 87
Samādhi 104, 106, 117, 140, 142
Samodhāna 148
Saṃsāra 4–5, 28, 63, 67, 70–74, 78–79, 85, 88, 90, 102
Saṃyutta Nikāya 7, 64, 68, 86, 105
Sangha/s 15–16, 64, 100, 129
Saṅkappa 104, 141
Santuṭṭhi /Santuṭṭha 125, 127, 142
Sati 104, 111, 118; *see also mindfulness*
Sattā 49, 59, 75, 77, 78
Schmithausen, Lambert 9, 21–26, 47, 52, 56, 93, 146–147
seas 35, 54, 65
Sedaka Sutta 86
seeds 23–24, 50–51, 61, 68, 125, 127

self, greening of the 11, 19–20
self acceptance 114, 116, 118, 124
self control 153
self sacrifice 151
sentience 9, 23–24, 26, 51, 146
Sigālaka Sutta 102, 130
Sīla 104–105, 106, 109, 140, 142
simple living 125, 127–128, 136
Slote, Michael 96
sloth 111, 135, 153
Soracca 104
Spiro, Melford 72
Sponberg, Alan 9, 11, 21, 93, 143, 146
Statman, Daniel 94, 96
Subha nimitta 58
sublime attitudes *see Brahma-vihāras*
suffering 1, 18, 20, 25, 28–29, 56, 63, 66–67, 71, 76, 81, 84–85, 95, 115, 119, 121, 136, 147, 153
Sutta-Nipāta 7, 115, 121
Sutta Piṭaka (*Sūtra Piṭaka*) 7–8, 23–24, 144
Swearer, K. Donald 15
sympathetic joy 83, 112, 119, 120–121; *see also Muditā*
sympathy 11, 81, 86, 98, 104, 107, 119– 120, 138, 140, 151; *see also Anukampā*
systems theory 18–20

Tandī 135
Taṇhā see craving
Taylor, Paul 179n
Tejo 54
Telos 105, 164
Telovādajātaka 154
Theragāthā 7, 52, 57–58, 126
Theravāda 73–74, 100, 132
Therīgāthā 7, 56, 126, 128
Timaeus 39, 40, 42–43
Titans 71
tree/s 1, 6, 15–16, 22–25, 47, 50–53, 55–57, 59, 61, 68, 148–151, 155–157, 159–162

Udaka 59
universal love 29, 46, 50, 73, 86, 104, 119–120, 152; *see also Mettā*
Upekkhā 119, 121; *see also Equanimity*
utilitarianism/ utilitarian 100–102, 107

Van Gorkom, Nina 112
value, instrumental 78–80, 82; intrinsic 25, 29, 78–79, 143
Vaṇṇupathajātaka 153
Vaṭṭakajātaka 160
Vāyo 54
Vedanā 67, 110
vegetarianism 11, 77, 139, 140
vices 5, 31, 77, 103–104, 111–113, 125–126, 134–136, 153, 156, 165
Vinaya/*Piṭaka* 7–8, 17, 22, 29, 50–52, 56, 139, 154
Viriya (perseverance) 152, 153
virtue ethics, nature of 94; moderate 96, 103; radical 96, 97
virtue, definition of 97, 103, 111
vivisection 11, 140
Vlastos, Gregory 41
volition 101, 110; *see also Cetanā*
Vyagghajātaka 156

Waldau, Paul 10–11, 49–50, 77, 156–157
Warder, A. K. 7
water 6, 22, 24, 39, 49, 54–56, 59, 75, 77, 82, 101, 127, 153
Watson, Gary 105
Wensveen, Louke Van 142
Whitehill, James 100, 104–105, 145
wilderness 10, 15, 29, 52–53, 62, 117, 151, 160
wisdom 20, 38, 55, 73, 97–99, 104, 106, 107, 118–119, 123, 125, 134, 136, 138, 140–141, 157, 160, 162–163; *see also Paññā*